My Road

My Road

PETER DE POLNAY

An Autobiography

W. H. ALLEN · London
A HOWARD & WYNDHAM COMPANY
1978

PHOTOSET, PRINTED AND BOUND IN GREAT BRITAIN BY
REDWOOD BURN LIMITED
TROWBRIDGE & ESHER

FOR THE PUBLISHERS
W. H. ALLEN & CO. LTD., 44 HILL STREET, LONDON W1X 8LB

ISBN 0 491 02492 4

To Igor and Julian Vinogradoff

After the Requiem Mass for my wife Margaret, Mrs Eileen Garrett, my then American publisher, invited me and anybody I wished to take along to luncheon in her suite at Claridge's. My wife had died a week before on 21 June 1950 at the age of thirty-six. There would be no summer for me, I said on that day. As a matter of fact, there were no summers for the next four years.

It isn't a long way from Farm Street to Claridge's. My nostrils still filled with incense, my ears still ringing with the Dies Irae I walked beside Cyril Connolly who observed, 'This is the worst thing that could happen to you except your own death.' I shook my head because at that moment death would have been my only relief. On my other side trotted Robert Tredinnick who said in the pause that followed Connolly's words, 'You're such a staunch believer. I fear you might enter a monastery.'

'I can't go to God empty handed,' I said.

Out of that phrase was born my novel *No Empty Hands* which I wrote ten years later. The novelist is never asleep.

We were about ten at the post-requiem lunch, the noisiest of the ten being Francis Newhorne who saw himself as a latter day Bulldog Drummond, and who liked behaving as if he were a cad straight out of a Victorian melodrama, enjoying every minute of it. He had an excellent war record, dressed ostentatiously well, wore a bowler hat, and married only rich women. He loved catching people out, also annoying them. His first conversational gambit was to ask Connolly whether châteauneuf du pape was a burgundy or a claret. Connolly didn't deign to answer. As the guest of honour (an honour I could have done without) I sat on the right of Mrs Garrett. On her left was Roger Senhouse, my closest friend for many years, and my first publisher. Through him I had met Margaret.

Our first meeting took place in April 1942 in Roger's book-filled flat in Great Ormond Street. I was at the time a private in 270 Company Pioneer Corps, stationed at Burnham Beeches. The company was made up of British-born Italians who rightly considered the company as the richest in the British Army since nearly all of them owned fish and chip shops or icecream shops or both. There were two ways of going to London. You could take the train from Burnham Beeches to Paddington, but you risked being picked up by the Red Caps (Military Police) at Paddington if you had no sleeping out pass. Or you could go by bus to Uxbridge, then proceed by the Piccadilly Line – longer but without fear of the Red Caps. Some of my brothers in arms bought a twopenny ticket at Uxbridge which they conveniently dropped in the train. On reaching their destination they declared they had lost their ticket and came from a twopenny distance. Thus with fourpence they made the journey from one end of the Line to the other. It wasn't lack of pennies: it was the fun of cheating. As I manage to find my fun in other compartments so to speak, I didn't follow their example, though I wouldn't have remonstrated with them. Scrounging is the soldier's lot would have been their answer. I travelled by train from Burnham Beeches on that April day in 1942, since I was on honest-to-God privilege leave.

I took tea with Cyril Connolly in the office of *Horizon*, where Roger Senhouse came to pick me up and take me out to dinner. His other guest should have been Nancy Mitford. As we left *Horizon* Roger said that Nancy couldn't come for some reason or other, so we would dine alone. 'Can't you,' I asked him, 'find another woman? I'm sick and tired of constant male company. And there's nothing else in the camp and outside it.' He promised he would ring an awfully nice young woman who didn't live far from him. He telephoned her from his flat, and when his doorbell rang he said, 'That's Margaret Mitchell-Banks who's dining with us,' and went downstairs to open the door for her. Much later, she told me that he had said on the doorstep, 'I've one of my authors with me. He talks about himself all the time.'

I saw a fairly tall woman with blue eyes and long black hair entering the flat, wearing a checked grey coat and skirt. It is difficult to remember first impressions, so I won't try to conjure them up. Roger left us alone to go to the next room to fetch drinks. 'Are you soldiering?' she asked. I answered that was the only reason I wore uniform. Silence ensued till Roger came back with the glasses. After that there was no more silence. We dined at the White Tower, and were joined by Elisabeth Bowen whom I much admired as a person and writer, and, to be candid, because she used to give my books flattering reviews.

Margaret's father, who died two years before our meeting, had been a KC and the Conservative MP for Swindon for some time. She had inherited from him a number of forensic jokes, some of which she related during dinner. She told them well. We returned to Roger's flat, and when the party broke up I offered to see her home in the blackout. They both laughed, I left with her, and as we came out into the darkness she wished me good night. She lived in the house next to his. However, she gave me her telephone number before we parted.

I continued my privilege leave in Little Somerford in Wiltshire, where my brother farmed. On the fourth or fifth day the urge of writing to the stranger I had met but once grabbed me like an iron hand, and I wrote to her. One sentence in that letter sticks out. 'In your presence I had my finger on the pulse of life again.'

Looking at Roger Senhouse from Mrs Garrett's right I said to myself that my finger was no longer on the pulse of life. It had dropped off it the day Margaret died. As a matter of fact, it had dropped off on the day a doctor had told me she wouldn't live another month. Robert Tredinnick, who had been a disc-jockey at the BBC before the war, told us with tears in his kind blue eyes that as Margaret's coffin was lowered into the grave in Kensall Green Cemetery on the bank of the tube line two trains had passed each other in contrary directions. 'Very symbolic,' Tredinnick added.

'Symbolic of what?' I grunted.

'You met and you parted,' he said.

I exchanged a look with Senhouse. You're in for a lot of this well intentioned nonsense, signalled his eyes.

Francis said there was nothing finer than being on one's own. Then he went on to say he was waiting for the next world war which was bound to come in a year or two. In the meantime one should keep oneself fit. 'Keep yourself fit, and the war will make you forget her.' The last thing I wanted was to forget her. I wanted my pain to remain as burning as it was on that day, though I knew that was humanly impossible. I feared Time the proverbial healer because he would bring balm to my wound.

Before my privilege leave ended I returned to London. I had telephoned Margaret from the country, and she was willing to dine with me. When she came to open the door of her flat we were both so confused that neither of us spoke; and when we spoke we had little to say to each other. Again we dined at the White Tower, and were married six weeks later.

At last the luncheon party broke up. I went down the stairs with Cyril Connolly who asked whether I would marry again. 'I can't stand loneliness,' I said. 'I used not to mind it. The idea of spending my nights and days with a woman hadn't appealed to me before I met her. After her I fear loneliness, and the thought of becoming a lonely old man petrifies me.'

'Will it help you when you are eighty to have an old woman of seventy limping round you?' said Connolly.

Francis Newhorne came galloping down the stairs. Connolly saw him, and swiftly left, promising to ring me on Sunday as Sunday was a lonely day in London. I left Claridge's with Francis who took me to an afternoon drinking club in Albermarle Street which was one of his haunts. He said in his loud and harsh voice for all and sundry to overhear him, 'We've been kind and patient with you, but a whole week of it is too much. From now on you'd better fend for yourself because everybody is sick of widowers who are harbingers of death, lepers too because in their presence one is continuously reminded of death, especially if the dead wife is younger than the lot of us put together.'

I saw myself as one of the clocheteurs des trépassés, the bellringers of the dead, dressed in white, their coats embroidered with black skull and crossbones, they would run through the streets of sixteenth and seventeenth century Paris at night, ringing their handbells until they were sure that all the inhabitants had been wakened. Then they shouted:

> Réveillez-vous, gens qui dormez,
> Priez Dieu pour les trépassés.

I felt Francis was right in as much as widowers aren't a cheerful crowd, and if they are or try to be they are stigmatised as cold and hard. The widower is forced to fall between two stools. And in my case the fact that Margaret had been a gay, smart, remarkably goodlooking woman must have given those who now saw me alone a sense of dismay, a memento mori no one particularly cares for. I would carry death in my wake for a considerable time.

'I ought to hide my wet widower's weeds,' I said.

Later I ran into Dylan Thomas of whom both Margaret and I had been fond, and whose company we enjoyed. She had said to him once that he looked like a Welsh pit pony blinded by daylight. Dylan was fascinated by death, a fascination I share, and which dates from my childhood. I had to give him every detail of her illness (generalised cancer), her death and the funeral, also of my feelings during the agony. He nodded approvingly when I said a wall rises between the living and the dying, and as you can't shout across that wall you become a bad insincere actor in fear of giving yourself away, that is to say make the dying see that you know they are dying. 'And when the coffin was lowered into the grave?' Dylan asked, his round face almost touching me.

'I felt terribly small,' I said, 'looking at the plaque. Margaret de Polnay. She was going under my name into eternity.'

'And you knew,' shouted Dylan, 'that your responsibility is eternal.'

When he died three and half years later his words came back to me.

John Davenport looked at Margaret's death from another angle. 'How can an intelligent man become a widower?' he asked. He was to find out, poor John.

I had telegraphed Nancy Mitford who was already living in Paris and who had seen Margaret only a few weeks before her death. 'I cried,' she wired back.

On the Saturday after the funeral I travelled down to Bedford to see an old friend who was the Catholic priest there. We went for a walk beside the Ouse, and I asked (it sounded like blurting it out), 'Father, will I see her again?' I needed him to say I would.

'We have it on Authority that you will,' he said.

I was given four days' compassionate leave to get married. The sergeant-major in best sergeant-major tradition observed that I wanted to get married so as to be given some extra leave. The other ranks saw it differently. 'Aren't you lucky,' said several of them. 'Now you'll have a woman whenever you want without having to run after her.' I travelled up to London. The train like all wartime trains was filled with men in uniform, and the barrage balloons were silver in the sky. The next day my wife and I travelled down on the same line on our way to Henley of all places to spend our honeymoon in some sort of country club, recommended by a friend of hers. The country club was full of uniforms too as an RAF airfield was nearby. During one of our long walks I said to Margaret, 'I can see the years ahead of us, and they are numberless, and

5

they'll never end.'

On my return to London from Bedford I lunched with a friend who had recently lost his wife. Perhaps, I thought, I could learn from him. He was in excellent form, told me he had just come from his hairdresser who had tinged his hair because he wanted no grey streaks to accompany him in his new life. He had, he explained, made out a list of his female acquaintances, giving each a number. 'What for?' I inquired. He would start with number one, and if he didn't find her satisfactory he would move on to number two. 'What for?' I asked again.

'To choose my next wife,' he said. 'What else did you think? When I married ten years ago I was too young and too inexperienced to know what I really wanted. Now I know.'

He died still a widower twenty years later.

Leaving him after the meal I couldn't help reflecting that it would be mighty difficult for me to find another wife since Margaret had been the logical conclusion of my life, my road to her starting from the beginning of my time. All that happened to me had pushed me in her direction.

Every year I receive the proofs of my entry in *Who's Who,* the titles of my books taking up more space than my biographical details, yet those few, short sentences are the story of my life. 'Educated privately in England, Switzerland and Italy.' That stands for a lot, for there must be very few people who are educated privately nowadays. Not only is it too expensive, but private education is suspect in this age of certificates and diplomas. In my childhood tutors were cheap and easily found, especially on the Continent, where there were lots of young and even middle-aged Englishmen without careers or a desire to work, always eager to earn some money at the effortless task of imparting the little they knew to boys who knew less.

Anyway, the tutors came later. I was born in Hungary in 1906, but before my memory could start working I was taken to Devonshire which left only three impressions: a golden retriever, a monkey puzzle tree and the suicide of a footman. My mother died when I was three, and though for years I maintained that I remembered her it was just a pious wish, the fact being that I didn't. If in my novels I write about mother's love and child's devotion they are the fruit of observation and hearsay only. What one hasn't experienced one doesn't miss, consequently I can't cry over myself as a motherless orphan. My sister, brother and I weren't encouraged to talk or ask questions about her. Paternal authority was rarely in evidence, though when it was we were mercilessly beaten. Our so-called father, years later informed me that I wasn't his son, but I knew that already from servants' gossip. He was a frightening dark shadow that still appears in my nightmares half a century later. I thought I put him into *Children, My Children,* my second novel written on the eve of the Second World War, but rereading it the other day I found him a comic character. There was nothing comical in our relations while I was at the beck and call of his cane, so it wasn't he. Anyway, I never set eyes on him or was in touch with him after I reached the age of seventeen, a relief for both of us.

We were ruled and run by two governesses, one English and grim, the other Swiss-French and gentle. Miss Rosy, the English governess had a stronger personality than Swiss Mlle Barbey, hence when I started to write I instinctively chose to write in English.

My first lasting impression was the suicide of the footman who was called Denis. He had, so the nursery maid told me in confidence, filled a jug of water with aspirins, and taken his life when they dissolved. Three hundred and fifty aspirins, she said. I was seven years old at the time. Shortly after his death we left for Switzerland, first staying in Zurich, then in Montreux, and four years later moving to Cernobbio near Como. My childhood was one lake after another. It was early in Switzerland that I broached the subject of Denis's suicide to the governesses. 'Denis,' they declared in unison, 'had never existed, so he couldn't have committed suicide.' Grown-ups were liars, I decided, and haven't changed my opinion since. If the governesses had said, yes, the poor misguided fellow had committed the worst possible sin by taking his life, I would have left the matter and Denis there. However, the blatant lie started my imagination working. First I recognised him in every second man I saw in Zurich, then I told myself long stories at night about him before falling asleep. They were so vivid that I believed they were true. They were more a serial than stories.

In the Dolder Hotel, where we were living above the town of Zurich, my brother and I had adjacent rooms. When Miss Rosy had switched off the light I rose and put on a grown-up's suit since it stood to reason that if people saw a boy of eight travelling in the night they might want to stop him, even take him back to bed. I buckled on my sword, and went into my brother's room. 'We're off,' I said, 'to unearth Denis. He was buried alive.' (Isn't it better not to lie to children?)

Unknown to him since it all took place in my imagination my brother rose, dressed at once (he was wearing his sailor suit as I couldn't be bothered to think up a grown-up's suit for him) and we set out. The hotel's nightwatchman had two large mastiffs, the shorter one I specially fancied, so I called him and he came with us. We took two caparisoned horses from the livery stable adjoining the hotel intending to gallop that night as far as unknown France, cross France the next night, and on the following night our horses would swim the Channel so as to reach Maud, the nursery maid who stayed behind in England, before dawn broke. If she knew that Denis took three hundred and fifty aspirins she must also know where he was buried. We would have to make haste, for if we reached the grave too late, that is if Denis had died in his coffin, he would be gone to Hell before we could unearth him, hence save him.

I took much trouble over the roads we would choose and the landscapes. Already I was a voracious reader, and kept in my mind every description I read and every illustration I looked at. On the road we saw Gessler and his men who made off when they caught sight of us. Then out of a bush came William Tell with his mealy-mouthed son squinting at the apple. Tell declared we had saved his life, so he would do us a good turn by taking us to a tunnel, and if we rode fast enough we could reach Compiègne the next night. We entered the tunnel, and I fell asleep. The next day I waited feverishly for the night to continue our journey.

It was pitch-dark in Compiègne, the stars were covered with bombazine, (a material Mlle Barbey was fond of), and huge black cats jumped from rooftops. My brother and I careered through the forest of Compiègne. Suddenly my horse shied. The darkness vanished, and I saw we were in a clearing. There was a hut at the end of the clearing, a big fire burned before the hut, and a dwarf stood in front of it, a charcoal-burner as I immediately guessed. He spoke with the mannerism of Ivanhoe and other Walter Scott figures. Miss Rosy used to read us Walter Scott novels during supper. The dwarf put his dog at our disposal. He called me Sir Knight and 'methinks' was every second word he uttered. Mention of the little dog reminded me of the nightwatchman's mastiff, which meant that I would have to start all over again or leave him in the tunnel. I chose the latter course. The little dog was a French bulldog, the spit of one I had seen on some of my mother's photographs, and the charcoal burner said the bulldog's name was Rémy. The dog spoke only Swiss-German, with which I was acquainted at the time only to forget it after we moved to Montreux.

Rémy said we should hurry because dawn was coming and the boat must sail on dark waters. The dwarf wished us Godspeed, and we galloped with Rémy running at our side, chatting incessantly. He spoke of frogs, toadstools and a girl who was killed in an avalanche and found years later still beautiful, her frozen smile showing her lovely teeth. (I had overheard two chambermaids in the Dolder talking about a girl killed in an avalanche.) Rémy turned out to be a chatterbox, talking nineteen to the dozen about snakes and dragons and polar bears. He took us to a dark river at the edge of a thick forest. The boat was white, there were four oarsmen, all four resembling toadstools, and Rémy whispered, this time in English, that we mustn't speak in the boat, otherwise the whales would come and swallow us. He, on the other hand, saluted the oarsmen, and asked them as we pushed off whether they knew me and my brother. The oarsmen didn't answer, for what else could you expect from four toadstools?

I wanted to get to Maud at once. Moreover, I was tired of Rémy, the black river and the oarsmen. 'We are in Devonshire,' I declared. 'There's Maud's house.' It looked like a Swiss chalet.

'Miss Rosy has specially asked me to accompany you,' said Rémy's voice behind me. I had thought I was rid of him.

I fell asleep, and the next night we found Maud, roasting chestnuts in a huge fire, I beckoned to her and she took us to Denis' unmarked grave. However, she knew he was buried there because she herself had put stones on it. 'I was certain,' she said, 'that you would come.' We dug as hard as we could with Maud helping us, and suddenly our shovels fell from our hands and dropped into the grave. It was huge, dark and empty, and as I looked into it in sheer despair a screeching voice spoke from behind. I thought it was Miss Rosy's, then saw it was Rémy who had slunk up from behind. 'Now you can see for yourself,' he said, 'there never was a footman called Denis.'

I told myself that story many times, now and then changing the end with Denis climbing out of the grave and telling me he wouldn't sin again but wait for me to grow up and take me into his service. I tired of the story after a time. The stories that followed were on a larger scale, for I was the king of all the boys, my sister the queen of all the girls, we declared war on each other, and after many sieges and battles I defeated her, brought her in chains back to my kingdom, and then I married her. As I grew older my stories became more elaborate. Maria Mancini, with whom I fell in love after seeing a copy of her portrait, declared after many adventures in which she and I shared that she preferred me to the Sun King. So we got married, only to start unmarried on our adventures again on the following night, such as my wounding one of Louis XIV's musketeers or vice versa, but invariably ending in marriage. I was the most married male between the age of eight and fourteen.

However, my main preoccupation during those years was my fervent wish to run away. We were kept from other children and the world around us. To run away, seemed simple to me, since I had no idea what I would do or what would happen to me subsequently. To run away meant putting a distance between me and the rod; once that was achieved nothing and nobody could hurt or harm me any more. I am not a rebel by temperament. A traditionalist like myself would have risen in the Forty-Five and fought with the Catholic and Royal Army of the Vendée during the French Revolution. I would have preferred to die like Lord Balmerino or Georges Cadoudal to living like Cumberland or Hoche. I wanted to run away because fundamentally I was a justice seeker, and even my child's mind appreciated that justice didn't reign in our closed existence. The governesses said if I told the truth I wouldn't be punished: I told the truth and was punished. Running away was the only answer. My first effort was at the age of ten.

Our first tutor was a Mr Dickson whom my brother and I walked off his feet during our strolls in the countryside. I think he was fairly young though he looked to me as old as all the other grown-ups. One day he witnessed a beating I received, and made some mildly disapproving sounds. He was dismissed on the spot. Before leaving he said to me, 'If I were you I'd run away, even if it meant working in a coalmine.' I was ready and willing to work in a coalmine.

On the following day Mlle Barbey took my brother and me for our morning walk, on the Dolderberg, which meant that she sat down on a bench in the park, and left us to our own devices. My mind was made up, but I had decided to tell my seven year old brother nothing till we were too far gone to turn back. I said we would run and it would be interesting to see how far he could run. He assured me he could run as far as I, which was precisely what I wanted. At the end of the park was a gate: I ran through it, my brother followed, and there was the road leading to liberty and, incidentally, to Zurich in a roundabout way. I stopped, explained to him we were running away, and when he asked why I told him it was none of his business, which was Mr Dickson's favourite expression.

We walked along the road; there were the snowcapped mountains in the distance, and I wondered whether they contained coalmines. We walked about three miles, by which time we were tired and hungry, yet on we went. We were somewhere on the outskirts of the town, for I saw trams. We sat down eventually on a bench, and because he was exhausted my brother fell asleep. A frightening man appeared, waving a stick and singing lustily. I heard a passer-by observe that he was drunk. He staggered on, stopped abruptly, turned round and came to a halt before the bench. My brother slept with his head against my shoulder. The sight of the two little boys visibly moved the drunk who had a large rosy face, wore no collar and his suit was dusty. 'You look tired,' he said at last, 'especially the little one.' He spoke in Swiss-German at which we were adepts by then. I said we had come a long way, and that was why my brother was asleep.

He meditated on that. 'Where's your mother?' he asked. I didn't answer. 'Where's your mother?' he repeated.

'In Heaven,' I said, looking down at my shoes.

'Poor little boys,' he said, and I thought he would burst into tears. Instead he lifted his stick, and for a second I was petrified, but all he did was to ask with whom we lived. 'With an aunt,' I said, which was safe enough since I had none.

'You don't seem to care for her,' said the drunk, adding it was very difficult to live with an aunt. 'And you little one?' he asked, turning to my brother who had woken up, and was staring at him. I explained my brother was only a few months old when our mother died, so he knew nothing. The drunk shook his head, saying 'Poor boys.' He scratched his chin, then asked why we sat on the bench. Because we were tired and hungry. 'Hungry? Doesn't she give you enough to eat?'

'Only once a day, and that in the evening.'

The drunk was shocked. Children of our age should eat a lot of food because children of our age were still growing. 'Poor boys, you'll eat with me. Come my children.'

He took my brother by the hand, I trotted at his side, and he lead us into an inn, the first place of its kind I had ever seen. It was cool and smelt of beer. Nobody was about except for a fat, fair woman who received him with scant respect. They spoke in such fast Swiss-German that I hardly understood a word they said. The woman beamed on us, especially on my brother. We sat down at a long table, the drunk immediately calling for wine, but the woman said beer would do him more good. He said he would sing a song, started to sing, the woman silenced him, then he poured us out beer. It was my first glass of beer, and I found it delicious. We were given Landjaeger sausage which, what with its, for us, silly name (land-hunter) and strong flavour made us devour slice after slice as though we hadn't eaten for a week. The drunk was jubilant, repeating, 'At last you have a decent meal.'

My brother suddenly rose, and went out to be sick. The woman followed him. I drained my glass of beer, and the effect was instantaneous: I fell asleep. It was deep and dark and as warm as a quilt. Then the quilt was lifted by Miss Rosy's voice penetrating into the warmth and darkness. 'Wake up,' she said in a gruff voice. I awoke at once. The drunk and my brother were nowhere, the fat woman stood obsequiously at Miss Rosy's side.

'We are going,' said Miss Rosy in a friendlier tone than I expected. 'We've a cab outside. Now say goodbye to this lady.'

'Where is he?' I asked the Swiss woman.

'I sent him home,' she said. 'It was time too. At least you have seen, young gentleman, the harm drink can do some people. Don't forget him. Let him be an example to you.'

'He's the best man I ever met,' I said to Miss Rosy, feeling bitterly ashamed of myself, for if I hadn't succumbed to sleep because of the beer and the sausage with the ridiculous name, the best of all men would surely have taken me to the nearest coalmine.

In the cab drawn by a grey horse Miss Rosy explained what had happened. My brother had confessed everything to the Swiss woman, in fact had begged her to take him back, the galley slave wanting to be back in chains in the galley. She sent him back with her grown-up son; the rest needed no explanation. I sighed because I had a traitor as a brother, but Miss Rosy's friendly behaviour surprised me most. She didn't say a word about punishment and retribution, she sat amiably at my side in the cab, the horse was walking since the road had become steep. Authority was away, so I had no fear of being beaten within an inch of my life (one of his expressions), yet Miss Rosy could be pretty hard too. In my gratitude I told her that Mr Dickson had counselled me to run away. She nodded, smiling grimly, but as she had no other smile I wasn't perturbed. We alighted at the hotel, went upstairs, she accompanied me to my room, boxed my ears which I didn't mind too much, then fetched a book I knew since she had read bits of it to my sister and me, *Shakespeare's Plays*. She opened it and said, 'This is *Julius Caesar,* and you're not allowed to leave your room and speak to anybody till you have learned Mark Antony's part by heart.'

My next attempt took place three years later, in Italy. A deep change had come over me as Italy burst into my life with its sky, colours, air and smells. No more Denis, no more Rémy, no more empty graves, only an immense longing caused by Canova's Amor and Psyche in Cadenabia on Lake Como not far from Cernobbio, where we lived. That change was greatly helped by the Italian tutor my brother and I were given. I remember him as Adolfino because one day his mother called and asked whether Adolfino had left. His was a pragmatic mind assailed by no questions and no doubts. The five greatest poets were Homer, Horace, Dante, Shakespeare and Goethe, and it would be a silly waste of time and thought to think of other names, though he hoped as an Italian that a sixth was in the making: he was thinking of d'Annunzio.

'But Virgil?' I asked. 'Isn't he as great as Horace?'

'No,' he would say, astonished by my question, 'he isn't.'

Adolfino had a brother who was a priest and a sister who had taken the veil. He told me more than once that if he didn't find the ideal wife he would end his life in a monastery. After our roads parted we corresponded for a few years, then letters ceased, thus I never found out whether he became a monk or the husband of the ideal wife. Anyhow, both vocations lead to Paradise.

In the Villa d'Este, where we stayed, an American marchesa lived on the same floor. No marchese was ever in evidence. She was a tall, good-looking woman, and now and then she spoke to me. Miss Rosy once saw me walking at her side in the gardens, and called out sharply to me, saying I should go straight up to my room and do sums. The marchesa was astonished. The next day Authority arrived from Rome, and gave me a memorable thrashing. I found out afterwards that the marchesa had spoken to him in the American bar, and in the course of their chat told him what she thought about the way I was brought up. He naturally imagined that I had dared to complain to her. I felt I had reached the end of my tether. Probably it was Adolfino's fault for having opened my eyes, as he would have put it, to beauty and everything that flowed from it. The day being Sunday there would be no Adolfino as he spent his Sundays with his mother who lived in the town of Como. My mind was made up. I wouldn't wait till I grew older: I would run away that same afternoon.

It was easy to leave the hotel. Moreover, I who was never given pocket money, had a few lire on me which I took from Mlle Barbey, my pretext being that as Miss Rosy's birthday was approaching I wanted to buy her a present. I went to the small pier, where I waited for the next ship to take me to Como. I was in great physical pain owing to the thrashing, the pain aiding my grim determination. *Unione,* the gay little paddle steamer, always looking a busybody as she paddled along belching smoke, took me and many others to the town. I arrived in Como and asked for the street where Adolfino's mother lived. It was suggested I should board a tram, but ignorant of the sum you needed for the fare (I had ten times more on me) I chose to walk, turning round from time to time to see whether I was being followed. Afraid of being intercepted I took to my heels, and arrived panting at the house in which Adolfino's mother lived. It was a high building and there were no bells. I knocked on the heavy front door, and windows on every floor opened. Craning their necks, the inhabitants looked at me. None of those faces belonged to Adolfino. I became frightened since all my plans, or rather lack of them, were built on him. 'Whom do you want to see?' they chorused. I said I wanted to see the Signora Giola, Adolfino's mother.

'But that's me,' called a grey haired woman. 'You're the boy whom he teaches. Come upstairs.'

In my excitement I hadn't recognised her.

She was dressed in black, and had the same mild brown eyes as her son. She said he was out, but if I came back towards the evening I was sure to find him. The idea of roaming the streets of Como and perhaps being picked up by Miss Rosy or an emmissary sent by her far from appealed to me, so I asked her whether I could wait for him in her flat.

'It's not the Villa d'Este,' she said.

'Thank God,' I said.

She led me upstairs, made me sit in a wicker chair while she sat in a rocking chair, and many of the Saints of God looked down on us from dark frames. She chatted about Adolfino, his priest brother and nun sister. Once or twice I interrupted her, asking her how long it took to get to Genoa. She had no idea. 'I've never been so far,' she said, and went on talking about her sons and daughter. I explained I wanted to go to South America. She said there were lots of Italians in South America, in fact one of her neighbours had a son in the Argentine. Then she asked me whether I admired Adolfino as much as she. At half-past seven or there-abouts Adolfino entered the room, caught sight of me, stopped and stared and I stood up, hoping he would guess at once how badly I needed him.

'What are you doing here?' he exclaimed. 'You ought to be at the Villa d'Este, dining.' His mother said I had come to see him, and she had asked me to wait for him as he was sure to come back in the evening. 'What are you doing here?' asked Adolfino again.

'I've run away, and you must help me.'

'He wants to go to Genoa,' said the mother.

'One moment, mamma,' said Adolfino, and took me to his room which you reached through the kitchen. I saw a Crucifix, a narrow bed, a large writing table littered with books, and in a frame a coloured view of Vesuvius. 'In the name of God tell me, boy, what you are up to.'

I told him I had run away, spoke of the beating I'd had the night before, said it had been like that ever since I could remember, in short felt bitterly sorry for myself, but that went as I outlined my plan. He should give me enough money for the railway fare to Genoa, where I was bound to find a ship, and could work my passage to South America or Australia or similar places. Mr Drew, the tutor, who had followed Mr Dickson in Switzerland and was eventually taken away by the police for housebreaking and stealing silver, had been a steward on a liner and had jumped his ship in Genoa. Of course that was discovered only after his arrest. If Mr Drew had no difficulty in his time to find work on ships I saw no reason why I shouldn't fare as well as he.

'Come to your senses,' said Adolfino.

'Signore professore, my mind is made up. I'll scrub decks, I don't mind how hard I'll have to work, I must get away.'

'My poor boy,' said Adolfino. 'It isn't that. The carabinieri would catch you and bring you back, and then you'd get an even bigger beating.' I said I looked older than my age. 'And you'd be caught too when going on board ship. You have no papers.' I said, but people do run away to sea, I've read about it in books, and there was no mention about papers. 'Those books were written before our time. Nowadays it just can't be done, besides however much I feel sorry for you I'm not entitled to help you to run away.'

The upshot of it was that he took me back to Cernobbio, and apologised to Miss Rosy for having forgotten to tell her that I would spend the Sunday with him and his mother.

The third time I was lucky.

About a month after Margaret's death I was taken to dine at the Étoile

Restaurant in Charlotte Street by a woman with strong literary pretentions. She told me I had become a sort of ghost, living only in the past, hovering over my years with Margaret instead of glancing at the future. I answered that ghosts aren't interested in the future, for they are preoccupied only with the past. She brushed that aside, saying I should go to some country where I hadn't been with Margaret, and look at landscapes and meet people she hadn't known. As if to prove her point M. Rossi, the then proprietor of the Étoile, came to the table, and after condoling with me said he would never forget Mrs de Polnay. When in 1944 a German fire bomb had dropped into the restaurant, she had been the person who saved it from being burned down. My companion asked how that happened.

Margaret and I had been dining with Cyril Connolly and Lys Lubbock in the Étoile during an air raid. It was the end of February. With a fearful noise the fire bomb dropped into the cocktail bar at the back of the restaurant. The Italian waiters lost their heads and ran round the place, even lifting wine glasses from the tables to throw their contents on the leaping flames. Immediately Margaret saw that the only way of putting out the flames was through the window of the lavatory halfway up the stairs. Coolly and firmly she organised the waiters, and I can still see her standing on the lavatory seat pouring water on the fire from buckets passed up in a chain. 'Without her we would never have put it out.'

'You see?' said the literary lady. 'Take my advice, and go away.'

I did go away, that is went to Paris, where Margaret and I had lived on and off for two years. On the evening of my arrival I looked into a bar we had often frequented. 'Alone?' asked the proprietor. He looked pleased with himself, and his smile betrayed he hadn't a worry in the world. Why spoil it? I said, yes I was alone.

'So you left madame behind to enjoy yourself alone in Paris,' he laughed, leering at me.

2

During my summerless summer in 1950 I saw a lot of Dylan Thomas. I knew few people with whom it was as easy to get on as with him. He never jockeyed for position, and I never heard a human being boasting less than he. I had a woolly friend who one day told Dylan in front of me that he had read one of his poems, but couldn't understand it. A few weeks later Dylan said to me, 'Tell your friend that I'm writing a new poem for him not to understand.' The woolly friend sagely nodded when I repeated this. As the summer was ending I told him and Tommy Earp (T. W. Earp) that I was going to Paris. 'Paris is tolerable only à deux,' said Tommy whose fame was based on two words he had uttered in a magistrate's court in his young days. He was arrested on Boat Race Night for biffing a policeman. 'Why did you hit the policeman?' the magistrate asked.

'For purely valetudinarian reasons,' Tommy answered in his unforgettable drawl.

'You speak as if you were the president of the Oxford Union,' said the magistrate.

'I am,' said Tommy.

A novel of mine was published by Michael Sadleir who was at the time the head of Constable & Co, the publishers. Aware of my being on friendly terms with Tommy Earp he asked me one day to remind Tommy of the life of Stendhal he had commissioned him to write over a decade before, and find out when the life would be ready for delivery. I repeated Sadleir's words to Tommy. 'Tell him,' he said, 'that Stendhal is growing up. He's nearly six by now.'

To revert to my meeting Tommy and Dylan which took place as usual in the Back Bar of the Café Royal (it doesn't exist any more) where one day an enthusiastic American publisher exclaimed, 'There is more talent here than in a whole town,' and Augustus John, who overheard him, said to me there was nothing more bloody boring than enthusiasm. Dylan said going to Paris would have the same effect on me as staying on in London. I mentioned that I had written to a French woman friend about Margaret's death, easier in a letter than hearing one's voice saying it. I had started the letter, 'Ma femme, si belle, si brave, si bonne . . .'

'That's not French,' said Dylan. 'That's Elisabethan.'

Tommy and Dylan were right in that Paris is made for two to share it, and I missed Margaret as much as in London. Nancy Mitford, who then lived in the rue Monsieur, amidst a world of convents not far from the Invalides, was the centre of my Paris life, and without her friendship and sympathy my days would have been unbearable. In London the centre of my life were Igor and Julian Vinogradoff, still the best friends I have. Nancy wasn't like the lady at the Étoile: she gave no advice, only her deep understanding.

Suddenly I decided I would feel better in Souillac, where only six months before I had been with Margaret. So I took a train to Souillac in the Department of the Lot beside the Dordogne, a town of three thousand inhabitants still uninfested by tourists. The three cupolas of its church, which are Romanesque of Aquitania and not Byzantine as many think, are the outstanding sight next to the river and its banks. Margaret and I had discovered Souillac only eighteen months before, and we both fell in love with it. After our first stay the hotelkeeper's wife died, so now he and I had a lot in common. Eventually he remarried, his second wife being the owner of another three star hotel. His reason, he explained was that their overheads would be reduced thanks to the marriage. Undoubtedly, he was a man with a strong business sense.

I fell into the old routine, that is to say I followed the timetable of my happier existence, breakfast on the hotel terrace, then a long walk beside the river which, owing to several weeks of rain, was flowing fast, bringing down branches, tree trunks, and, I was told, a drowned mule one afternoon. The weeping willows and the poplars seemed to cheer it along. Towards noon I returned to the square because at twelve sharp the siren went. The dogs of the town assembled in the square, waiting for the siren so as to howl with it. Some of the dogs tried out their voices a few minutes before twelve to see whether they were up to the task. Then the siren went, and raising their heads the dogs howled lustily. When the siren ceased each dog returned to his homestead, the next gathering tomorrow, same time, same place.

After the dogs' performance I went to the Café de Paris, above which lived Pierre Betz, an Alsatian man of letters who had come to Souillac at the outbreak of the second world war when by order of the French government most of Alsace was evacuated. During the war Betz went into hiding because the Germans rounded up the Alsatians in order to take them back to Alsace to become good German citizens and soldiers. A peasant up in the hills was willing to give Betz the hospitality he needed, naturally at a stiff price. The Germans seldom went to the hills, and if they did one was warned in time.

The peasant's house had two rooms and a kitchen. In one room the peasant and his wife slept, the other had one bed in it, and used to be the bedroom of the son, now a prisoner of war in Germany. To Betz's surprise he was told to sleep in the same room as the peasant and his wife. A bed was rigged up for him, and for three long years he slept a few feet from the couple, witnessing their copulations. The peasant, Betz said, was as randy as a billy goat. At the end of the third year a new refugee appeared, a young woman connected with the Resistance. The Germans were looking for her. The peasant took her in, then told Betz he should move to the son's room as the newcomer would sleep with them. Betz asked why he was moving him.

'Because we've known you for three years, and know we can trust you. The girl we don't know at all, so we want to keep an eye on her.'

'I don't understand,' said Betz.

'The gold is hidden under the floorboards in the son's room,' whispered the peasant.

When the war ended Betz decided to remain in Souillac which was lucky for me since he was an excellent companion, to whom I could pour my heart out. After our chat in the Café de Paris I returned to the hotel; in the afternoon I went to the river again, trailing my memories along. She had said of those three birches, 'They'll dance away any minute now.' She had been fascinated by the idea of meeting a wild boar, but we never came upon one, though there are plenty in the Lot. In the evening I was back in the Café de Paris, and when dinner was over there was only one thing left to do, namely go to bed, for the cafés were closed, and the whole town settled down to sleep. Then the fun began, consisting of thinking of Margaret and listening to the church clock striking the hours.

It was no good, so I decided to go to Collioure beside the Mediterranean not far from the Spanish frontier. I hadn't been there before, so it had no memories for me. Betz thought it was a good idea. I travelled to Toulouse, still in Margaret's orbit as we had been there together the year before, though saw little of the town because of the bitter wind blowing from the Pyrénées. This time I just changed trains. When the auto-rail, in which I travelled, stopped in Collioure station I saw a tall, reed-like man approaching, an exaggerated stage smile showing his yellow teeth. 'Sir,' he addressed me in excellent English, 'are you looking for a hotel?'

'I am,' I said. 'Where did you learn such good English?'

'I used to be theatrical wigmaker in Drury Lane before the first world war.'

He was a native of Collioure, and his fellow natives called him la Baronne because of his homosexual inclinations, but he did find me a decent hotel. I arrived on All Saint's Day, the season was long over, the sun had departed with the tourists, leaving only some strange creatures like the Dutchman and his wife, who lived in a caravan on the beach next to boats pulled ashore for the winter. The natives thought they were spies, I found them extremely dull. In the hotel resided an out of work documentary film director, whom I had vaguely known in London. He was with a darkhaired girl who doped and drank, and he carried her upstairs every night. Not for me, I said to myself on the fifth day. The sea lapping the pebbles, the famous lighthouse straight out of a picture postcard, the empty streets and gloomy Catalans didn't add to the gaiety of the nations. No answer here for me, I thought, so I took leave of la Baronne, and entrained for Toulouse, where I would spend the night, then return straight to London. My dog Jamie, who had been Margaret's and my companion for seven years, was coming out of quarantine in a month's time.

In Toulouse I dined in a restaurant in the centre of the town. The cassoulet toulousain wasn't exceptional, and walking back to the hotel I entered a bar to have a drink. There were only a few customers, I stood at the counter, and a fairhaired woman on a barstool gave me encouraging smiles. I wasn't in the mood to return them. She asked me to offer her a drink. Her accent was faintly familiar, and her cow-like expression moved distant memories, a dim light in the dark night. I said she could have whatever she fancied. She thanked me, and I couldn't resist asking her where she came from. 'You're not from these parts,' I added.

'I'm Swiss,' she said. 'I come from Montreux.'

Memory is a strange instrument. I left the bar ten minutes later, thus our acquaintannce lasted only that time, yet she remains stuck in my memory because she hailed from Montreux and for a brief instant brought back my childhood.

*   *   *

My mother had had a friend, an eccentric woman who lived in Geneva. She came to see us children in Montreux, and took me out for a walk. I was twelve and already aware that my lot wasn't enviable. I must have talked a great deal because on parting she told me if I ever needed help all I had to do was to write to her. Despite the web of lies spun round me I believed her, and when I finally decided to go for good (I was nearly nineteen by then) I wrote to her, asking her to pay my own and my brother's fare to South America. Not for a moment did I think of leaving my brother behind to receive the wrath intended for me. In the letter I told a lie, namely that we had jobs waiting for us. However, it didn't seem a lie to me as I was convinced that the Argentine was waiting for us with open arms, that is jobs galore. She sent us the money, and without saying a word even to Miss Rosy I set out from Southampton on a one-class German liner, the *Madrid*, which took sixteen days to reach Buenos Aires. My brother had left on an Italian ship a few weeks earlier.

I had no qualifications whatever. The governesses and the tutors, with the exception of Adolfino, had given me little to prepare me for the life I was to enter. Anyway, they couldn't imagine it. Adolfino had made me love literature, history, painting and architecture, taught me Latin and Greek but nothing beyond them. Mathematics, geometry and science were left untouched. I had no idea about the meaning of money. In our enclosed artificial life it wasn't ever discussed. I sailed to South America to get away from fear and servitude and find freedom. I appreciated that I would have to work, but in my ignorance I was convinced that that would be the easiest thing in the world. 'We'll make good,' I said to my brother, so we sailed in order to make good. Already I could look at myself from the outside, that is to say I was both the actor and the spectator. The actor believed he played superbly the part God had given him; the critical spectator wasn't of the same opinion, and as befits a spectator he whistled and hooted at times. There was to be plenty of whistling and hooting in South America.

On the *Madrid* four Brazilian gentlemen first taught me to play poker, then won most of the cash I had. That should have been a warning: warnings are not for the young. I shared a cabin with an old German planter from somewhere near the Amazon who used to lie on his bunk most of the day, singing Schubert's Lieder. He got off in Rio de Janeiro. There was another German with whom I became friendly. He said he was an explorer, which impressed me, and said he was going to Bolivia to discover unknown Red Indian tribes. That impressed me even more. I

21

saw him several times in Buenos Aires, where he gave an interview to one of the daily papers, announcing his departure to meet dangerous savages. He took leave of me, saying the Indians might kill him. About a fortnight later I caught sight of him in the Avenida de Mayo. I was tactful enough not to approach him. From a fellow passenger with whom I kept in touch I learnt later that having been unable to sell German fire engines to Argentine municipalities he had sailed back to Germany.

'And the savages?' I asked disappointed.

'He invented all that to sound important.'

I was slowly learning.

My brother waited for me at the Darsena Norte when the ship docked in Buenos Aires. It was September with winter still in the air. The sky was grey, the town looked grey, and it remained grey for me even in the heat of January. From the mast of an Argentine destroyer floated a lot of washing.

My brother had a job. He had travelled out with an Italian engineer who was employed by an agricultural college outside the town. He had found my brother his job in the college, not teaching since he knew no more about agriculture than I, but a kind of supervisor's job in the grounds, where several peones worked. A good sign, I thought.

Where to stay with the very little cash the Brazilians left me was the first question. My brother suggested I go along the Calle Lavallol, a street of boarding houses, and take a room in the cheapest of them. I followed his advice, and took a room in the second boarding house I saw, in my simplicity not realising that it was no better than a brothel, though I did notice as I brought in my luggage several fat women wandering about the corridor, onto which all the bedrooms opened. Most of them shouted to each other in French. I dined with my brother, eating the eternal puchero, then we went to the Richmond Bar, where I asked the waiter who served the eternal San Martin for an ashtray. 'Isn't the floor good enough for you?' he grunted. On the ship I had studied Spanish, and as I pick up languages quickly I appreciated what he meant. I didn't ask for an ashtray in South America again.

My brother had to go back to the college, so I returned alone to the boarding-house. A woman all dolled up, one of the boarding-house inmates, stood in the doorway, smiling at the passersby. I received a smile too, I said sorry, and went past her up the stairs. I still didn't twig. There was a lot of coming and going in the corridor. The women, who had been wearing dressing-gowns in the afternoon, were dressed like the one downstairs, and were either going out alone or coming in accompanied by men. I lay down, and when I woke up in the night I heard bidets running and saw shadows passing on the other side of the glass door that gave on the corridor.

Next day I telephoned the Argentine millionaire I had known in my Villa d'Este days. He remembered me, asked whether my sister was with me. I said she wasn't, then after a long silence he invited me to lunch. That man, I felt certain, would give me a job. He had estancias, owned race horses, so he couldn't get out of helping me to make good. He lived near the Palermo in his own mansion, with a liveried porter. Outside the door was a Renault with a uniformed chauffeur inside it. I was let in by a butler, and two footmen hovered in the wide hall. I hadn't a doubt left. The millionaire was larger than I remembered. He warmly shook my hand, congratulated me on coming to the gran país, the great country as the Argentines call Argentina. I was young, Argentina had an enormous future, and as the future belonged to the young I was wise to bring my youth to the great country on account of its future. He would be only too pleased to show me round, and make me see and feel the great future. 'You come from the past to the future,' he said shaking my hand again. It looked easy, incredibly so.

We lunched in a vast dining room, the butler and the footmen talking to each other as if their master and his guest weren't in the room. 'This is a great democratic country,' said the millionaire. Towards the end of the unsavoury meal I said I wanted to find work in the Argentine. Had he any suggestions?

'Breed polo ponies,' he said. 'Lot of money in that.'

I observed that was a good and sound idea, alas my financial position would not permit me to embark on breeding polo ponies or any other ponies. 'I don't want to be indiscreet,' he said. 'What is your financial position?'

'I've a little over sixteen pounds in the world.'

The millionaire gasped for air, then recovered enough to look at his Cartier wristwatch. 'I've an important meeting at the other end of the town,' he said. 'So excuse me for not offering you pudding and coffee.' Already he was halfway to the door. 'The butler will see you to the door.' The butler practically rushed me to the front door.

'Perhaps he did have an important meeting,' said my brother when I told him about the luncheon. He was as naive as I. Following his advice I telephoned the millionaire next day. The butler asked who was speaking, I gave my name, he asked me to wait, then came back to say that his master had gone to one of his estancias, and wouldn't be back for months.

In the late twenties you could still starve in Buenos Aires. Everybody seemed to be chasing the same small loaf. One of my fellow passengers from the *Madrid* sent me to a German insurance company that was looking for someone who knew English and French. There were about thirty people in the waiting room, and I was received with hostile glances, one more to fight for the small loaf. I didn't have to wait long, for a man with a Hindenburg moustache came out of an office to tell us to hop it as he was suited. We went out into the grey street like a defeated army.

I saw in the *Buenos Aires Herald* an advertisement of The National Bank of Boston, asking for young clerks, previous banking experience not needed. The right job for me, I thought, and saw myself as the president of the bank, riding in a Locomobile. I was received by the staff manager, an Englishman called Little, and I was engaged in the cypher and cable department as a beginner. I could start on Monday. See how easy it is, I said to myself.

On the Sunday afternoon I sat in my room in the boarding-house with the glass door open. If I closed it there was hardly any light in the room. I was trying to sew on a button, quite a struggle as I wasn't clever at it. A fat, fairhaired woman in a blue dressing-gown stopped outside the door. 'Do you understand French?' she asked. I assured her I did. 'That's not the way to sew on a button,' she said. 'Come to my room, I'll sew it on for you.'

I thanked her, went to her room, and sat on her large bed while sitting beside me she attended to the button. She told me the story of her life in a quiet matter of fact voice. She had worked for some years in a brothel in Lille, where a client suggested sending her to Buenos Aires as Frenchwomen were much appreciated by Argentines, especially if they had plenty of curves. 'They can't complain about my figure,' she said, patting her belly. I thought I knew all about prostitutes having recently read Edmond de Goncourt's *La fille Elisa*, but the motherly woman beside me looked so different from my idea about vice that I stared at her openmouthed. 'Ten years here,' she said, 'and I'll have enough put aside to go back to France. My name is Madeleine, but everybody calls me Mado. Now we'll go to your room and see if you need any other button sewed on. Men need women to look after them.'

She wore glasses while she sewed, and it was like being in the presence

24

of a benevolent aunt. Looking back Mado appears as one of the answers to the timeless question of why some women become prostitutes. In her case as in so many others it was a choice of working on a farm or on her back. I am sure she entered the brothel with the same lack of enthusiasm as she would have shown picking cabbages. She was a well meaning, ordinary woman without vice or nastiness, plying her task conscientiously, taking no pleasure in it, and accepting unwashed, repugnant male bodies as she would driving cows into a field. When not at work she didn't think for a moment about her profession.

On that Monday morning, I started on my banking career. The cypher and cable department was a busy office in as much as most of the bank's clients and a number of its better paid staff gambled on the New York Stock Exchange. There were plenty of cables, and my task was to enter each cable into a ledger, putting beside the entry its cost. The clients accounts were charged with the cable fees and the staff paid cash which I had to put inside a tin box. On Saturday morning I had to take it with the ledger to one of the accountants. I worked slowly, finding the cables fascinating. During that week a bank in New Orleans got into trouble, and I followed its fate as if I were reading an exciting story. Alas, I left the bank before its fate was settled.

The staff was cosmopolitan. The head was a Dutchman, my own chief was a sallow faced German girl who disliked me from the start, and the other three men in the department were Italians. 'Why is there no American here?' I asked one of them.

'They wouldn't work for such low wages,' was the answer.

On the Wednesday evening Mado came to my room, still in her dressing-gown as she began work only towards ten. She said she had an idea that would surely appeal to me. To begin with she liked me a lot, since I was so superior to the Argentines she met, and far more polite than they. I wasn't flattered by that since I haven't met in my life people with worse manners than the Porteños as the inhabitants of Buenos Aires are called. Mado went on to say she hated the boarding-house, and the other Frenchwomen in it were vulgar and illbred. She wanted to take a small flat, furnish it with her savings, but in Buenos Aires it wasn't safe for a woman to be alone in a flat, men being beasts and dangerous. 'I should like you,' she said, 'to move in with me. Naturally, I'll pay, so you won't have to bother about the rent, and if a man tries to be nasty or just follows me without any intention of paying I can say I've my man waiting for me at home. We would get on very well. I'm sure of that.'

I laughed. What would they say at the bank if I told them I was living with a prostitute? I saw the face of the Dutchman and the German girl, so laughed louder. 'I'm serious,' said Mado.

'I'm too young to live with a woman,' I said to show myself how tactful I could be. 'I'm not yet ripe for it.'

Had I said, you can't expect a decent fellow like me to live with you and accept your immoral earnings, she wouldn't have grasped what I was speaking about for didn't she earn her living honestly, never taking a peso more than her price? She sighed, said it was a pity, and asked me to think it over. She assured me she wouldn't ever bring a client to the flat, ours would be a normal, quiet life, and when she came home towards dawn she wouldn't wake me. 'Think it over,' she repeated.

I promised to, and related it to my brother, laughing a lot. The austere outlook that was to grip him after our South American adventure showed itself as he said, 'It's too disgusting to laugh about.'

Came Saturday, the bank closed at twelve, and I had a date at one o'clock in Belgrano with a girl I had met on the ship. Twelve o'clock was perilously near as I grappled with the entries in the ledger, and the contents of the cash box. However hard I tried two pesos remained missing in the cash box. When the others got ready to leave I took the ledger and the cash box to the accountant who was an Argentine.

'There's a discrepancy of two pesos,' I said. 'Here are two pesos from my own pocket.'

The accountant looked at me with dismay. I bowed, rushed from the bank, and took the electric train to Belgrano. When I arrived at the bank on Monday morning the Dutchman told me that Mr Little, the staff manager, wanted to see me. Promotion, I said to myself.

'Mr de Polnay,' said Mr Little as I entered his room, 'I'm sure you'll go a long way in life, but you'll never make a banker.'

'But why not?'

'Hasn't it occurred to you that those two pesos you gave the accountant will mean a lot of work for us?'

'I don't see why. There were two pesos missing, but as I gave two pesos to the accountant they aren't missing any more.'

'Quite,' said Mr Little. 'Don't think I don't see your point. You'll go now to the staff cashier who'll give you a week's salary. Good luck.'

I left feeling that an immense injustice had been done to me. After all, I had paid the two pesos, not the bank. Then I cheered up because I wouldn't have to see the German girl again.

That same night I made the acquaintance of the Vicomte de Saint-Sauveur. I sat in a café in the Calle Florida, and a birdlike little man with a yellow complexion and a beaky nose stopped at my table, asking whether I wanted him to draw my profile. I said no because I hadn't any money. He said he found me simpático, so would draw my profile without charging me for it. He sat down, drew, and we chatted. He gave me his card on which was printed Le Vicomte de Saint-Sauveur. 'So you're French,' I said.

'I'm Mexican. I don't speak French.'

'Then why have you a French title?'

'Because it's my name.'

I didn't insist. He finished the drawing which could have been the profile of anybody in the café or anywhere else. A waiter called him to draw the profile of some customer at the other end of the room. The Vicomte asked me to wait for him, and when he had finished the drawing he proudly showed it me. It strikingly resembled the profile he had drawn for me. When he was paid he sat down with me, and I spoke about my lost job and the urgent need of a new one. The Vicomte said I should accompany him to a café in Callao (the Argentines don't put calle before their streets), where he would introduce me to several young men who, he was certain, might help me. During our progress to Callao I thought I saw Mado at a street corner. The café he took me to was large with glaring lights. At a table sat several young men who waved to the Vicomte. We went up, he introduced me, and explained I was in urgent need of a job. We sat down, and I examined my new acquaintances, most of whom were university students, and of course hadn't the foggiest idea about jobs and where to find them. One of the young men's face was covered with ugly pimples that looked like sores. The student next to me whispered that he was a medical student and had syphilis of the third degree. The lot of them were broke, could hardly pay for their coffees, and the Vicomte rubbed his hands sure that I was in the right company to find a job.

An enormous man appeared at the table, his hair coal black, his eyes ditto, and his hands those of a strangler. He was the elder brother of one of the students who wasn't too pleased to see him. Their name was Achaval. Big Achaval addressed me in American: 'What are you doing here?' he asked. I explained I had come to the Argentine to make good, and at the present moment I needed a job. He frowned as he stared at me, his eyes almost popping out. 'I might take you with me,' he said.

'Where?'

'To Patagonia. Boy, that's a real man's world. Snow, silence, sheep, the Cordilleras, and fortunes to be picked up. But it's a tough life.'

'I'd love a tough life,' I said enchanted by the prospect.

'I bummed in the States,' said Achaval. Bumming and being a bum were his favourite expressions. 'It's far tougher in Patagonia.'

'Know it?'

'Of course I know it. I've a chacra there.' A chacra is a small farm. 'I want to work it, and take a lot more land. You could work for me.'

I said there was nothing I wanted more.

'But it's tough, very tough.'

Then he changed the subject in that he spoke about smuggling goods from the Argentine to Chile. In a convoy of laden mules you crossed the icy peaks, looked down precipices, were up to the belly in the snow, and frontier guards fired at you. 'Boy, you make a fortune in one journey.' I saw myself crossing the Cordilleras and working on the chacra simultaneously. We agreed to meet the next night in the café. Achaval intended to leave at the end of the week. I hardly dared to believe in my luck.

The Vicomte accompanied me to Lavallol filled with the sounds of tangos, *Valencia* and *Cà c'est Paris* bursting from the night clubs. Achaval, related the Vicomte, was the son of an Argentine senator. He had quarrelled with him, gone off to the States and came back only recently. We parted outside the boarding-house. I rushed up the stairs, heard a noisy altercation between a female French voice and a male Argentine voice, locked myself into my room, and threw myself on the bed. It had been an excellent day, for I wasn't made to be a bank clerk, a fate from which the two pesos had saved me, cheap at the price. I was made for high seas, high mountains like the Andes and the high adventure in store for me.

Next night Achaval and I met again, and he agreed to take me to his chacra in Patagonia. In my gratitude I paid for his whisky, whisky being his favourite drink. Had I, he inquired, enough money for my railway fare to Zapala, where the railway line stopped, a journey of about eighteen hundred kilometres? I said I had enough as the bank had paid the day before. The following day we met in the morning. He told me he had had a brainwave, namely to get me an immigrant's railway permit. Any newcomer to the Argentine who wanted to work in the interior was entitled to such a permit. He took me to some dim building near the port, where he filled in a form which I signed, and a special railway warrant was given me to Zapala.

'As you saved plenty of money buy me a whisky,' said Achaval.

Over the third whisky, for which I paid too, he told me he had been Jack Dempsey's sparring partner while he bummed in the States.

We entrained for Bahía Blanca on the Saturday night, the Vicomte accompanying us to take a tearful farewell from me. As a goodbye present he gave me a brand new profile which he drew in the railway bar. The reason for our stopping in Bahía Blanca where his father was senator was because Achaval wanted to collect some money due to him. He left me alone in the third class compartment after the train pulled out of Plaza Constitución, but came back with the ticket puncher, explaining he had arranged for us to sleep in the sleeping car, a whole night's journey would be far too tiring on third class wooden benches. All we had to do was to let me pay for the sleeping car. As I had saved the fare that was the least I could do. We moved to the sleeping car, I a little disappointed because I had wanted to start my tough life right in the train.

There was trouble when we got off in Bahía Blanca. The station master was called by the man who took our tickets, and he and Achaval had a noisy row, mala fe (dishonesty) being slung at him several times. I slowly gathered that I hadn't been entitled to buy myself a sleeping birth with my immigrant's travel warrant. After a lot of shouting Achaval won the battle, and we were allowed to go. 'I told them you don't understand a word of Castilian, and you're a poor dumb kid.'

He went to collect the money he said he was owed, leaving me to my own devices till the evening. The sky, the streets and the houses were dull, the port smelt of wool and corned beef. I heard Mass in a half empty church, praying fervently for the success of my Patagonian venture. Achaval met me in a café near the station, looking despondent, and complaining about his married sister who had refused to let him have money.

'What about the man who owes you money?'

'That's in Buenos Aires, not here. You don't want me to go back there.'

In my childhood I had bitterly learned not to remind people of having said something different last time. Anyhow, we would travel in the morning to Neuquen, spend the night there, and take the train to Zapala at dawn next day. After several whiskies Achaval left me to find myself a hotel. I slept in a room above a café, and was at the station at the crack of dawn. Unshaven Achaval arrived a few minutes before the train left. He immediately took me to the dining car.

In that dining car travelled a fattish, greyhaired man, the owner of *La Crítica*, the top radical newspaper of Buenos Aires. He was in the company of two journalists, and his black bodyguard sat alone at the next table, glaring threateningly at any one who dared approach the great man. Achaval gazed for hours at the newspaper boss, saying that with a flick of a finger he could get us both out of our troubles, and he for one wouldn't mind taking the black man's job. Loyally I refused to compare his words with those he had uttered only the day before. However, I got my first fright in the afternoon when he said there would surely be a job or two going in Zapala. 'What about your chacra?' I asked.

'Chacra? I haven't a chacra. Who told you that nonsense?'

I grinned, then looked out through the window, and all I saw was sand and sand, which appeared more desolately sand as darkness approached. The railway stations were milestones. They just had numbers, the numbers signifying the distance from Buenos Aires. We were over fourteen hundred kilometres when night fell. We had a bottle of whisky in front of us, which Achaval slowly emptied, observing that at the newspaper boss's table they had reached the third bottle. The boss and his party got off at one of the milestones. Achaval sighed and said we had missed our chance.

We reached Neuquen in the night, and went straight to the nearest inn, where we took a room. I had noticed a lot of Indians in the taproom, small sickly men, not a patch on the Redskins of my childhood reading. Achaval lay down, complaining about the whisky he had drunk in the dining car. I went out to have a look round.

The southern sky was studied with fewer stars than I used to gaze at in England, Switzerland and Italy. It was bitterly cold which gave the stars an extra glow. Neuquen consisted of a few streets only, beyond them spread the flat back o' beyond. Electric street lights were everywhere, the lamp posts leading into the wilderness. It would be the same in Zapala, as electricity was dirt cheap in the shadow of the Cordilleras. Suddenly a man, wearing a gaucho hat and a poncho, burst from the inn, jumped on his horse, and galloped past me, singing loudly. He raised his pistol, and fired a shot at the stars. As if one shot weren't enough he fired a second, then a third, and by the time he had fired the fourth he was out of my ken. The stars remained unmoved, their silver light stronger than before. And that moment I knew. I knew as one knows when one rises above oneself. I don't know what I knew, but I knew it completely. Then I remembered I hadn't taken leave of Mado, which wasn't kind of me.

That meant I was back in myself, thus knew no longer. I found Achaval snoring on his back; the Indians in the taproom were silent and drunk.

At dawn I had to shake Achaval to wake him, then he didn't want to get out of bed, moaning that a day or two in Neuquen wouldn't hurt him or me. For once I was adamant, and cursing loudly he followed me to the station. The twice weekly train to Zapala had only a few coaches, and fewer travellers.

Already it was an established fact that Achaval had no chacra, no money and no connections in Patagonia, and we were a couple of bums looking for work. Towards noon we reached Zapala where the railway line ended. As we got out of the train we saw the end of the rails a hundred yards away. There was something frighteningly final about it. I hate and fear finality as I believe in and look for compromise. I well understand Mme Du Barry who pleaded with the executioner to give her another little minute. I always want another little minute. There were no little minutes where the rails ended. The Cordilleras dark below and covered in perpetual snow above closed the view.

'How will we find jobs?' I asked Achaval, disappointed by the town, which consisted of a dozen or so low houses.

'Stop worrying,' he said. 'We'll go to the fonda, and have a drink. Then we'll see.'

The fonda (inn) was near the station. On the wall were posters of a Singer sewing machine and Bayer's aspirin. The customers were a noisy and shabby lot, drinking caña, shouting at the top of their voices, stopping only when the gramophone played a record of jokes told by a nasal voice laughing a lot. The most successful joke was: how many are there in a matrimonial bed? Fourteen. Why fourteen? Alfonso XIII and his queen make fourteen. Achaval thought it a very good joke too. He got into conversation with the customers who suggested we see the mayor of Zapala who might find jobs for us. 'First we eat and drink,' said Achaval.

After the meal we went under a leaden sky to the mayor's house which wasn't any larger than the other houses. Martin Etcheluz, the mayor (I am glad I haven't forgotten his name), received us in his whitewashed parlour. He had blue eyes and red hair. The snow having thawed, he said, pipes would be laid to give the township sanitation. We could join the four workmen he employed. When could we start? I wanted to start right away, but Achaval said we were tired after our long journey, so would start next morning. The mayor nodded, we left and stopped to look at the four workmen digging to lay down the pipes. 'Looks too tough,' commented Achaval. He took me back to the fonda where he sat at the long table, drinking caña, and speaking to whoever entered the room. Through the window I saw a string of mules, all heavily laden, entering the township. 'Smugglers?' I asked the landlord.

'The regular mule train from Chile,' he said.

I went out, watched the mules being discharged, then walked for a while, my eyes on the Cordilleras, the end of the known world beyond which one wasn't allowed to carry one's imagination. Yet I broke the rule, imagining a blue sky, a hot sun, palms, parrots, camels and pineapples.

Next morning we reported to the mayor, were given shovels, and joined the workmen. Achaval was right in that it was tough. The earth was hard, and digging the narrow trenches made our arms and backs ache. Achaval said I wouldn't stick it; after the midday break I barely managed to persuade him to go back to work.

From Toulouse I returned to London. Winter was setting in, the Korean war was raging, and Jamie, my Dandy Dimont, was released from quarantine. The last time we were together Margaret was still with us. When Jamie saw a skirt in the street he hopefully pulled on the lead.

The previous year I had been commissioned to write a life of Prince Charles Edward Stuart, the Young Chevalier, known to posterity as Bonny Prince Charlie. I had started my research in the files of the Quai d'Orsay while Margaret and I lived in Paris. After her death Lord Amulree, an expert on the Stuarts, told me to go to Windsor, where I would find the complete Stuart Papers in the Royal Archives. The publishers obtained the gracious permission for me to consult and make use of material in the Royal Archives in Windsor Castle. I was given a room in the Round Tower, where I could examine the Stuart Papers at leisure. As Charles Edward was a profuse letter writer I was kept busy, but then came the disappointment because after the Forty-Five the Prince became a poor, drunken sot who sank from glory practically to nothingness. Still, it was good occupational therapy.

In the austere quiet of the Round Tower my work was agreeable in that I was greatly helped by Miss Mary Mackenzie, the Registrar of the Royal Archives. With her parchment-like skin, her grey hair worn in a bun she was always dressed in black and hers was a forbidding presence, yet I seldom have met a woman with so much wit, knowledge and kindness. Our friendship began with my going to her office at the other end of the passage, convinced that she would refuse my request.

'May I smoke here?' I asked.

She gave me an ashtray, not bothering to point out that the Stuart Papers were priceless, and I should be careful not to burn them.

For five months I went five days a week to the Round Tower, and when the book was written I brought the proofs to her, to ask for her advice. That was shortly after the death of King George VI.

'Was it very gloomy here after the King's death?' I asked.

'It is always very gloomy here,' Miss Mackenzie said.

3

One grasps at any straw when carried along by the fast flowing stream of misery. Thus I accepted from a publisher, whom I didn't particularly like as a person, a commission to write a short travel book, anything to get out of my routine of moaning for the past. He thought of Jamaica, I said South-Western France and Auvergne, and South-Western France and Auvergne it was. I knew South-Western France, that is Souillac, Gourdon and Cahors, but not Auvergne.

I set out from London in May 1951, my first stop being, of course, Paris, where I asked Nancy Mitford whether she knew anything about Auvergne. It is a little country as much on its own as Scotland, its emmigrants the café and bistrotkeepers of Paris; it is mainly unexplored by the non-Auvergnats, who call them the Scots of France. Nancy asked a knowledgeable French friend of hers what Auvergne was like. He told her that he himself had put the same question to Laval before the war when Laval with his radical views was still considered the good Laval, becoming the bad Laval only after the fall of France. Laval was an Auvergnat, and his mother kept a small hotel in Auvergne. Laval thought for a while, then said, 'Don't go to my mother's hotel. Too many flies there.' Armed with that piece of information I set out for Auvergne, starting my journey in Souillac, in short I was back in the past from which I had tried to escape.

Pierre Betz and all the others I knew there were surprised to see me, saying they had been convinced I wouldn't return. When they had heard of Margaret's death they said to each other, 'We won't see him again.' I explained I was like the criminal who goes back to the place of his crime, the sole difference that I went back to the place of my happiness. And to prove it I walked alone beside the Dordogne, looking at the birches that would dance away no longer.

Betz said that in Auvergne I should look out for the black Madonnas, there being no real explanation why they were black. Some held it was the smoke of tapers that had blackened the Madonnas through the centuries; others that they were painted black so as the English Routiers, who roamed and pillaged South-Western and Central France after the Hundred Years' War, shouldn't steal them. The fact that most of them were of solid gold strengthens that theory. However, many were not. Besides, there are black Madonnas outside South-Western France and Auvergne, such as Our Lady of Montserrat and Our Lady of Loretto. I saw most of the Auvergne black Madonnas during my journey, all of them wonderful, starting with Notre-Dame de Rocamadour, but I brought no fresh light on the problem, and why shouldn't it remain a mystery? Too few are left in any case.

I had imagined Auvergne as an arid land of burnt-out volcanoes, their yawning craters full of reproach. Lord, why did you give me fire to leave me in the cold? There is an old Auvergnat story about the beginning of the world. Since the Auvergnat is (in Auvergnat eyes) the finest of God's creation He, naturally, turned to the Auvergnat, offering him the shores of the Ganges or the Alps, in short any spot he wanted to live in. 'I want to live in Auvergne,' said the Auvergnat. 'But it's burning,' said God the Father. 'I can wait,' said the Auvergnat who then probably danced the bourrée, and ate a bit of tripoux and Cantal cheese to show the Father in Heaven that patience was one of his many qualities.

I found Auvergne a lush country with deep green pastures, only some of the peaks are barren as befits burnt-out volcanoes. Of fine Romanesque churches there are plenty, and rivers flow fast. The dams with their quiet artificial lakes alone deserve a visit to Auvergne. I stayed beside one at Saint-Etienne-Cantalès for a few days. The hotel and the few houses of the engineers of the Électricité de France were the only buildings; the rest was silence, grass, trees, the motionless lake and the cuckoo ticking the minutes. It was not a spot for one who was alone. The chief engineer, an Alsatian, showed me round the dam. I admired the turbines in order to please him, but at night the foam of the leaping water picked out by the lights of the power house filled me with joy, and made me think of Shelley's *Arethusa*, one of Adolfino's favourite poems.

The chief engineer said he had a high opinion of the Royal Navy. 'Did you fight alongside it in the first world war?' I asked.

'Against it,' he said. 'Being an Alsatian I was in the Kaiser's Navy.'

From Saint-Etienne-Cantalès I went to Salers, a town of dark stones that turn light in summer. On its ramparts I walked with the local schoolmaster, an Alsatian too, who had come to Salers, that most

Auvergnat of Auvergnat towns, shortly after the first world war, and stayed because of the stones. 'They grow on you like a mistress,' he said. Beyond the town there still lay snow though we were in June. He took me into the church to admire the painted Burgundian stone figures and the marble Christ of the Entombment, all life-like figures, the marble Christ truly dead and the stricken mourners dressed like well-to-do Burgundians of the fourteenth century. 'God in His mercy hides the future from us,' said the schoolmaster. And I couldn't help speculating what my behaviour and thoughts would be like if I knew the date of my death.

The most impressive, that is out of the ordinary, feature in Auvergne is the Auvergnat himself. In that almost wild country with pastures and cattle I would enter a village, go into the inn, smelling of tripoux and local wine, only to be asked whether I knew the cousin in Paris who kept a bistrot in the rue du Dragon, or the uncle who sold coal and wine in Montparnasse. I spoke to a little boy in a field who kept an eye on some sheep. 'You come from Paris?' he asked. I said I came from Paris.

'My father has a café in the rue Saint-Antoine. I'll join him when I'm eight.'

'What for?'

'To start learning the café trade while I go to school.'

An Auvergnat never becomes a Parisian, his constantly watered roots being too strong for that.

They are a canny lot those Scots of France. As I had many times heard and read about writers getting reductions in hotels if they tell the owners that they are writing about their district, I decided to try that out and see what happened. I tried it out in Vic-sur-Cère in the best hotel of that poor man's watering place. It was run by an old lady who faintly resembled Queen Victoria. I told her on arrival that I was writing a book about Auvergne, so would she charge me a little less. That was in the afternoon. She said she would give me her answer in the evening. I went out, was shown the cave where the inhabitants used to hide their possessions when the English Routiers advanced on Vic. Then I saw a signboard of the Touring-Club-de-France, saying the climb to the hilltop took fifty minutes. I, who have no taste for climbing, started to climb like one demented, and panting, with my heart near to bursting I reached the top in forty-one minutes. Why and what for? I have no answer.

Came the evening, and the proprietress asked me to enter her parlour, where her lawyer was waiting for me. 'Your lawyer?' She grimly nodded. The lawyer bowed, shook hands, then bade me sit down.

Madame, he said, was a widow, and it was he who looked after her interests. I had made a request which she had passed on to him. I wanted to bleat that it was just a stupid joke, I don't really need ten per cent off my bill, and, please, let us forget it. The lawyer didn't let me interrupt him. Madame, he said, had several times been let down by dishonest people who pretended they represented guide books. She had paid for space, and never heard from them again. How could I prove to them that my guidebook would really appear? I explained in a guilty voice that I wasn't writing a guidebook but a travel book, and if I mentioned her hotel in it that would have nothing to do with advertising. How many lines would I give her hotel? I said I had no idea, and wished the interview were over. 'In that case,' said the lawyer, 'Madame can't give you a reduction. I thought of five per cent if you guarantee a page of praise.' I said I didn't work that way, and rose to smile my way out.

'As I don't want monsieur to leave with a bad impression,' said the old woman of Auvergne, 'I won't charge him the bath he had this afternoon.'

'That's very handsome of you, madame,' said the lawyer, bowing to her.

Never again did I try that on. A few years later while I was in Andalucia a writer friend of mine appeared, hotels, restaurants, even the Renfe (Spanish State Railways) giving him enormous reductions. Verily, I don't know how to sell myself.

From Vic-sur-Cère I travelled to the Puy-de-Dôme, saw Romanesque churches, forests, sites of the Wars of Religion and mountains galore, but friendly mountains, not like the long prison wall the Cordilleras had seemed to me in Zapala.

On the third day of our work with the pipes Achaval walked off in the middle of the morning, declaring his back ached too much to go on working. 'He's no good,' said the other workmen. When I returned to the fonda during the lunch break I found him seated with the landlord, drinking caña, a potent Argentinian eau de vie. He whispered to the landlord who looked at me and laughed. 'You ought to come back to work this afternoon,' I said. 'The mayor isn't at all pleased.' He translated that to the landlord, they had another laugh, then Achaval said in English, 'I won't be told by a foreigner what to do or not to do in my own country.' That he translated into Spanish too. The landlord approved. When we sat down to lunch Achaval was friendly again, even asking me to massage his back after the meal. It hurt because of the bending and digging that laying down the pipes entailed. There followed the ridiculous sight of Jack Dempsey's sparring partner lying on his belly on the bed with the reedlike youth, who hadn't done any physical work in his life, massaging his back, he groaning, the young man panting, then returning to work, that is to bending and digging.

Don Martin, the mayor, visited the site in the afternoon. The pipes would be down by Saturday, and what did I intend to do afterwards since he had nothing else to offer me? I said I came to Patagonia with Achaval to find work and make good. I was ashamed to mention the chacra and the initial promises. 'He's a rotter,' said Don Martin. 'The quicker you part from him the better for you.' I nodded, and we left it at that. Later in the afternoon Achaval paid us a visit, smoking and smiling while we bent and dug. After we had knocked off he said he and I would walk to a nearby estancia owned by a Scotswoman and see whether we could find work on her vast estate. She had, he assured me, thousands of sheep.

We arrived at the gate, and clapped, which in the campo, the countryside, means we were strangers but without bad intentions. An Indian peon appeared, Achaval said he wanted to see the landowner, and a few minutes later a hardlooking middleaged Scotswoman came to the gate, followed by a collie, a sight which cheered me up as my sister had two. I thought I was in clover.

'Lady,' said Achaval, 'we're two bums looking for work.'

'I've no work to give you,' she said in a cold voice, turning her back on us, and the collie growled as though wanting to express his mistress's thoughts.

'You should have let me speak,' I said.

'Want me to knock you down?'

I didn't answer.

Later in the fonda I met the capataz, the foreman, of the mule convoy that would start out at dawn that Sunday to cross the Cordilleras into Chile. As Achaval was at the other end of the taproom I asked the capataz, a fairhaired bearded man with a friendly expression, whether there was any chance of finding work in Chile. 'More there than here,' he said. How much would he charge to take me along? He needed an extra hand, so he wouldn't charge me anything. In fact, if I knew how to load and unload and how to handle mules he would give me a little sum at the end of the crossing. I hastened to assure him that I was as good with loading and unloading as with handling mules, but not a word to Achaval about it. The capataz said he didn't think much of him, and even if he wanted to he wouldn't take the lazy bastard along. Things are brightening up, I said to myself.

That night, and for the next two days Achaval taunted me in vain, for nothing would interfere with the grand future awaiting me in Chile. Came Saturday and Don Martin added fifty pesos to the wage he had offered on the first day. 'You worked hard,' he said. When I went back to the fonda I found Achaval in a pleasant mood, and over dinner I warmed to him again, and with the stupidity or inexperience of youth I blurted out that I had received fifty pesos as a bonus. However, I did keep back that I was leaving him at dawn. He had complained at every meal that he wasn't given enough meat. In my excitement at the prospect of crossing the mountain range on muleback I wasn't hungry, so I said, 'Eat my meat.' He jumped up, and before I could rise or move he knocked me down. When I came round I found myself lying on the hard, cold ground outside the fonda, the stars veiled by the clotted blood on my eyes, nose and chin. I was almost reminded of the beatings I got in my childhood, except that this one was basically more terrible. But why was I outside the fonda? It took me some time to get on my feet. I touched my pockets: not a peso was left. I staggered to the door, and started to bang on it. The door burst open, revealing the landlord, pointing his gun at me.

'If you don't vanish at once, you dirty thief, I'll shoot you like a dog.'

'My money has been taken from me,' I said with no conviction in my voice. The beating up had taken the wind out of my sails.

'You damned foreigner, how dare you accuse an Argentine of stealing? Go or I shoot you.'

'I want my luggage.'

'I'm keeping it because you haven't the money to pay me.'

He banged the door in my bruised face, then locked it. Turning away I saw that the day was rising. I ran as fast as my pain let me, apprehension giving me the strength, and sure enough, the convoy had already left. No loading, no unloading, no handling of mules and no Chile. I felt finally crushed.

It was that state of mind that must have stopped me from following the obvious course, that is waiting till Don Martin awoke and telling him what Achaval and the landlord had done. It didn't even occur to me to go near that good man. I had been knocked down before I could defend myself, I had been robbed and my luggage held back under false pretences. My first window was broken, and I saw the edifice I had built for myself crumbling because of that broken window. I staggered with half-closed eyes to the railway station as if a train were waiting to give me a free ride back to Buenos Aires. All I found were railway trucks being shunted. I leaned against the wall of a shed while the trucks slowly turned into a train like words into a sentence. The trucks were empty, every one of them. The small shunting engine entered the shed, and out came a big engine that would pull the train away. When I saw that nobody was in sight I climbed into a truck, making myself as small as I could in a corner. I fell asleep at once, my indignation following me into the nightmares in which Achaval turned into parental authority. A banging chain woke me up, the truck was shaking, and I nearly shouted for joy. Achaval and Zapala, also the Cordilleras were behind me. I was thirsty, my body ached, yet I felt like one who had turned defeat into victory. I fell asleep again.

When I opened my eyes many hours later I saw I wasn't alone in the truck. Using his poncho as a blanket a short, slim man lay in the other corner. He wore a moustache that accentuated the pallor of his skin. He lifted his head, smiled at me, and waited for me to speak. I stared at him in silence.

'So we travel together,' he said. 'You're very young. What are you doing in this truck?'

I told him my whole story, my indignation rising again. The stranger listened attentively, nodding from time to time, the nods meaning it was exactly as he had expected it to happen. 'Where do you intend to go?' he asked after I had finished. To Buenos Aires, where my brother was. That wouldn't be easy, as goods trains aren't like passenger trains. Our truck might be detached from the train in Neuquen, or the train could remain there for days. Besides there was such a thing as railway police, and if a railway man found us he could either kick us off the train or hand us over to the police. 'But you can count on me,' he smiled. 'I know the ropes.' And I who had, to put it mildly, been let down by Achaval put my complete faith into the stranger. As if to prove that I wasn't mistaken this time he took a parcel from his pocket, unwrapped it, a big chunk of boiled beef appeared, and with his knife he cut it in two, offering me one half which I devoured, mumbling my thanks.

Then he told me his own story, speaking like one who was almost ashamed of his humdrum existence. He had worked the whole winter on a sheep farm about a hundred miles south of Zapala. With spring in the ice cold air he felt the need to run from the snow, perhaps as far as Misiones or the Chaco in the hot North, though first he wanted to blow his earnings in Buenos Aires, for life being short it had to be enjoyed. Why didn't he travel in a passenger train? He preferred to spend his money on putas. He gave me a cigarette, and only then did I realise that Achaval and his accomplice had taken even my packet of cigarettes.

Our journey to Bahía Blanca, lasted for two days. When the train stopped in Neuquen he got out to reconnoitre, telling me not to move till he came back. He returned, beckoning to me to get out as our truck would stay behind. We slunk beside the trucks in the dark, then I followed him into a truck with plenty of straw in it. 'Better not to smoke in here,' he said. He had spoken to a railway man who took him for just any ordinary person making inquiries, and gathered from him that the empty goods train was bound for Bahía Blanca, dropping trucks here, picking up new ones there. So all we had to do was to watch out not to be left behind. The train pulled out before dawn, shaking and rocking, but I became accustomed to this. At a stop next morning the trucks were shunted from one line to the other, and the engine banging into our truck to send us careering down the line till we banged into another truck was a noisy and frightening experience. Then the trucks were immobilised as though for good. My new friend went to reconnoitre again, and on his return an hour later (I began to fear I had been left in the lurch) he told me we hadn't a worry left in the world as he had given a few pesos to the man in charge of our truck. We were to start in a couple of hours, meanwhile he would take me to a nearby fonda. Refreshed we came back an hour later, and before the train left a railway man looked in on us, exchanged a few words with my friend, and then locked the door from the outside. 'Nobody will worry us,' said my friend, settling down on the straw.

The next evening as we approached Bahía Blanca he said we would have to hop it when the train stopped outside the town because once inside the goods station our protector couldn't do anything more for us. 'I don't care for jail, and I'm sure you don't care for it either.'

We left the train at the goods station, and walking beside him on an empty road leading into the town centre I expected him to say that here we parted, and good luck to you, young man. 'We'll take the night express to Buenos Aires,' he said.

'You know I've no money,' I said.

'We travelled together from Zapala, so we'll continue together till

Buenos Aires. I pay your fare.'

And he paid it, and we sat in a compartment opposite each other, he hardly able to sleep with the money he would spend on drink and putas burning wide holes in his pocket. In the morning in Plaza Constitución he shook me by the hand, wishing me well, then on second thoughts he gave me ten pesos before disappearing from my life. My confidence in mankind was restored.

'I'm not surprised,' said my brother when I told him about Achaval. 'I'm not surprised either,' he said when I spoke about my travelling companion.

'I was surprised in both cases,' I said.

That was the difference between my brother Ivan and me.

I moved into the boarding house where he had stayed on his arrival in Buenos Aires. It was run by Italians, the wife enormous and doing all the work, the husband slim and spending his time in the cafés.

I had spent some months after the second world war in Cyprus with Margaret, and to Kyrenia, where we rented a house in the Turkish quarter, came a bogus philosopher from London, an amusing man in every sense. He related a story about a Chinese philosopher who one day gathered his disciples together, and told them they would visit another Chinese philosopher who lived at a two years' distance. They set out, they walked for two years, the philosopher discoursing on philosophy, the disciples listening enraptured. At the end of the second year the other philosopher's house came into view and the disciples stopped to let the master move forward. The master stopped on the threshold, the disciples craned their necks, and after a few minutes of deep thought the master turned round without having knocked on the door, and said, 'We are going home.'

They marched for two years, the master discoursing on philosophy, the disciples listening enraptured. As their home town came into view one of the disciples, taking his courage in both hands, asked the master why he hadn't knocked on the other philosopher's door.

'Because the Spirit didn't move me,' was the answer.

I felt the same when I returned to Paris then to London from my journey to Auvergne. I had enjoyed it, had seen a lot, yet I remained unmoved by the Spirit. How right was a solicitor of whom I saw a lot in those days when he said emotional security meant more than financial security to me. At that time I had no emotional security left whatsoever.

42

As proof of it I came to part from my dog Jamie. Our relations that had lasted for ten years were a relationship à trois. With Margaret no longer one of the three the bottom was knocked out of it. There was a vacuum which the two of us couldn't fill however hard we tried. Besides, I went abroad too often, and one quarantine is enough in a dog's lifetime. So I took him to live in Old Windsor with the dear woman who had bred and given him to me in 1942. When in London I would go to visit him he was always pleased to see me, would accompany me to the gate as I left, then he would trot back to the house. He died in 1955 while I was in Spain, and I have never had a dog since, though I could almost write my life round the dogs I had, Porky in Kenya, Dodo on the Butte-Montmartre, and Jamie in Great Ormond Street, Suffolk and France.

In Buenos Aires I went back to the café where I had met Achaval. The bird-like Mexican vicomte was present, so were the students who included Achaval's younger brother. I told him how his brother had treated me. He rolled his eyes, said the family had given him up long ago, and in order to show his compassion he offered me a whisky. I gratefully accepted, and his brother wasn't mentioned again.

One of the medical students suggested I go to the Provincia de Santa Fe which was full of English estancias where I would surely find work. I saw no reason why I shouldn't. My brother gave me the railway fare to Rosario, and I was only too pleased to leave the Italian boarding house whose primadonna so to speak was a hefty girl from Turin called Silvia, a private tart whom all the male lodgers coveted. As I could speak to her in her native tongue the lodgers looked at me like daggers, and made my life insufferable.

Reaching Rosario I was told in a café that the real English centre was the market town of Venado Tuerto. Overhearing us, a tall man with a heavy gold chain that spread over his large belly observed that he knew an English estancia manager called Roy with whom he had business relations, also some people called Miles who were American, devastatingly rich and bred polo ponies. He gave me his card, saying all I had to do was to show it to Mr Miles or Roy, and one or the other would certainly give me work. He advised me to get off at a small station before Venado Tuerto as it was nearer to their estancias. Argentine at the end of the nineteen-twenties still had a lot of humanity and generosity. I set out the next morning.

In the only fonda of the little township, whose name I have forgotten, I was told the Miles family lived eighteen miles away. How was I to get there? The innkeeper lent me a horse, and I the unknown newcomer rode away on his small Criollo horse, promising to be back in the evening. While I rode to the Miles estancia I fell in with a redhaired, gingermoustached man on a black horse, and as he was going in the same direction we stayed together till he pointed out the monte (a small hill with trees, windmill and the residential building) where the Miles lived. Before we separated he gave me the story of his life, the most important event of which had been the killing of his unfaithful wife in Corrientes. 'So I had to come south, but I still miss the puta she was.' He made me a present of a packet of Camels.

The Miles were nice Americans who seldom ever went to America, living in the lap of luxury, he a famous polo player, his wife the mother of several goodlooking daughters. I was given an excellent lunch, was shown the polo ponies, then was told they had no job for me. In the afternoon I rode back to the township. The wheat harvest was in full swing. At the inn I related my lack of success to the innkeeper who said he would send a message to Roy who lived only a league away. Early next morning Roy arrived in his car, and took me to the estancia he managed for an absent landowner. I believe it was a company. He had been a gunner in the 1914–18 war, and was a slim, likeable man, looking every inch the officer and gentleman. He declared straightaway he had nothing to offer me, but his brother-in-law whom I would meet the following day in the English club in Venado Tuerto needed a tallyman for the harvest on his estancia. He was sure to employ me.

Roy's house was long and low, furnished like an English cottage, and if you forgot the endless flat land covered in wheat you could imagine yourself in England. His bookshelves had only English books, his pointers hailed from England. A German woman, tall and forbidding, served us at the meal, Roy saying she was his housekeeper. Her behaviour was deferential, nearly servile. My bedroom being next to his, I was woken up in the night by the shaking of his bed and the words of passion he shouted well nigh at the top of his voice. Then I heard the German woman's guttural voice telling him she didn't care for him at all. He nearly whimpered as he repeated he loved her. I felt deeply ashamed though I wasn't sure why. The German woman served breakfast as deferentially as the meals the day before. In the English club, the walls heavy with hunting prints and the rooms full of leather armchairs, I met Hugh the brother in law, a large New Zealander who engaged me on the spot as tallyman for the harvest which was to start in three days' time. He would take me back to the Mariposa, the name of his estancia, that same evening.

Hugh had a double chin, rosy cheeks and pale blue eyes. He patted his protruding belly as you pat a dog you are devoted to. He drove me to the Mariposa in his Buick, and there I met his wife Gladys who was Roy's sister. She was pretty and as pleasant as Roy. I was given a room in a small house about five hundred yards from theirs, the other inmate a lanky Australian whose every second word was bugger. I don't know exactly what he did on the estate, and we met only at breakfast, bugger it. For breakfast we usually had ox tongue, which he thought a real bugger. After breakfast he got on a bugger of a horse whom he would bugger as long as the buggering day was long. In the evenings he was up at the house, thus I was left alone to read whatever I could lay my hands on before turning in. Once the harvest started Hugh made it very clear that I was the apuntador de cosecha and nothing else. Gladys continued to treat me as a human being which, I am sure, was the cause of my undoing, if there was a cause at all.

My job consisted of checking the weight of every sack of wheat, that is controlling the team of harvesters who came with the peones and threshing machine, and were paid by the weight. Two Gallego brothers (for the Argentines every Spaniard is a Gallego) ran the team, and we had continuous rows about the weight. I stood in the shadeless flat countryside beside the threshing machine that sent out dust and heat from daybreak till sunset. I was covered in straw and stank of petrol fumes, and even after my evening shower I still felt prickly and smelled of petrol. The brothers, whose waggon was near the threshing machine, used to ask me in at the beginning, and offer me beer. When they saw that I remained adamant about the weights the beer ceased, and thirst was my daily companion. I rode a bay gelding called Lili. Years before in Italy I had ridden a gelding called Carmen, so I found nothing wrong about a gelding being named Lili. It was a friendly horse, and on the first Sunday I rode it to the township, where I visited the fonda, remaining for lunch. A commercial traveller dressed like a townsman sat at a nearby table. As I bit into an apple he haughtily observed that apples were eaten with knife and fork. I laughed so loudly that he took offence, and I couldn't appease him since it would have been difficult to explain who Miss Rosy was. Even she wouldn't have objected to my biting into an apple in the back o' beyond.

When Dylan Thomas came back from his first American voyage I asked him what impression America had made on him. 'Big,' he said. Of the Argentine campo all I can say is that it was vast, the sky as much as the endless fields, and in that vastness you felt almost non-existent.

Now and then Hugh drove out to watch the threshing and to exchange a few words with the Gallegos, then he would leave without having addressed a word to me. A female cousin of his came to stay with them, a whiteskinned redhead of eighteen summers, pretentious and visibly proud of her flesh. She and Gladys rode to the spot where we were working towards sunset, and on some occasions I rode back with them, Gladys chatting with me, the flesh-proud cousin ignoring me. On the fourth Sunday Gladys asked me to the house as Roy was coming over. Roy and Gladys were amiable, whereas Hugh and the cousin pretended I didn't exist. Roy left in the afternoon, dropping me off on his way. To my surprise Gladys turned up as I sat reading in my room. The night was coming fast, her pretty face was wet with tears.

'I came to tell you it isn't my fault,' she sobbed. 'Don't think badly of me, that's all I ask. I must rush back.'

I had no idea what she meant.

I quickly found out the following morning when Lili and I arrived at the threshing machine. Hugh stood beside his car, chatting with the Gallegos. On catching sight of me he shouted, 'Get off my estancia at once.'

'What do you mean?' I stupidly asked.

'Get off my estancia. I don't want you here a minute longer. You dared to say that my cousin looked like a sack of potatoes. Off you go.'

'I never said that.'

'My wife doesn't tell lies.'

'I want to be paid if I must go,' I said, feeling squashed.

'Bob,' that was the Australian, 'will pay you, then drive you to the station. Now get out of my sight.'

I mounted Lili for the last time, then rode back to the small house, where the Australian was waiting for me.

'Well, you buggered it up, you stupid bugger,' he said.

'Honestly I don't know what it's about,' I said.

He laughed in my face, saying I was too clever a bugger by half.

'I must see Gladys,' I said. 'There's a misunderstanding which, I'm sure, I can clear up.'

'No misunderstanding, no clearing up. You've got to bugger off, and it's my buggering job to pay you and take you to the station.'

46

Till the last moment I hoped that Gladys would appear, declare it was a ghastly mistake, and then I could get on Lili and ride back to my work. Gladys didn't appear.

Since then I have often thought about the sack of potatoes and Gladys' tears of the night before. My only explanation is that in her dislike of her cousin-in-law, which was evident every time I met them together, she said to her that she looked like a sack of potatoes, and in order to give it more emphasis she added that somebody else had said so too. Who was that somebody else? The young tallyman. The cousin rushed to Hugh, and the result was my being kicked off the farm. Hence Gladys' tears when she saw that she would be the cause of it.

As the train took me to Rosario in my youthful conceit I decided that Gladys was in love with me, and Hugh had sent me packing because he had noticed it, the sack of potatoes being just a flimsy excuse. Her tears had been caused by losing the man she loved.

The story doesn't end there. In 1942 when my *Death and Tomorrow* became a bestseller I received a letter from Scotland. It was from Hugh who had come from the Argentine to join up. 'To read a good book,' he wrote, 'is a pleasure, but if the good book is written by an old friend it is doubly a pleasure.' He went on to say that Gladys was in Edinburgh, and she too would be so happy to hear from the old friend.

I shamefully confess that I didn't answer his letter.

After the journey to Auvergne I mooched about in London for two long years which remain a haze from which not a shape, not a single voice emerges. Then one day Cyrus Brooks of A. M. Heath & Co, my friend and literary agent, asked me whether I were willing to write a travel book about Spain. Peter Baker MP, who ran and owned The Falcon Press, badly wanted a book about Spain. Cyrus thought it would be a good idea, especially as it would lift me out of the rut. I said I didn't feel like going away, nothing surprising about my saying that since once in a rut, you want to stay put. Cyrus persisted, and I gave in without any true desire to leave my soulless routine. On the day before I left I went to see him, to say that on second thoughts I saw no reason why I should go to Spain or anywhere else. He reminded me that I had signed the contract with Peter Baker that same morning.

I left for Paris the next day, and instead of taking the night train to Irun I lingered in Paris for nearly a week, for Paris was as much my past as London. I went to see Nancy Mitford who urged me to go to Spain. 'It'll be a new start for you,' she said. I dined with Robert Naly, the painter who has been my close and staunch friend since my Butte-Montmartre days and still is, and I said I had no wish to go to Spain. 'How long is it now?' he asked, meaning Margaret's death. He had been her friend too, and was in at the end.

'Four years in two months' time,' I said.

'Time you started a new life,' he said.

'Where?' I asked.

'At Trafalgar,' he laughed. Then more seriously. 'It's most impressive.'

My last adventure in Argentine was rustling cattle across the River Paraná north of the town of Posadas. It was while trying to find work near Santa Fe that I came upon a man who knew somebody who knew somebody else who took cattle from the Paraguay side of the river to the Argentine side, where cattle sold at a better price and the lack of customs duty added to the profit. I rustled cattle for only one night, which is probably the reason why it remains like a dream, and something from Hans Andersen's Tales, the dark river flowing mysteriously, the shape of a ship in the distance, and then the firing from the Paraguayan bank.

We were taken, a number of us, across the river as night fell in a long flat boat, and were told to keep our traps shut. On the other bank I was given a Criollo horse which I would swim across the river. I was in the company of a man who had rustled cattle across the Paraná several times. He was Italian by birth, but when I addressed him in Italian he said he had forgotten it long ago. His advice was to follow a cow into the water as Criollo horses instinctively follow cattle. I should hold on to the horse's mane while crossing the river, and leave everything to the horse. There was no moon, the Southern Cross looked less like a cross than ever before, and the cattle began to arrive. We got on our horses, my companion moved away from me, calling out that I shouldn't forget to give the horse free rein.

The cattle was driven fast to the river, the first stopped, and out of the darkness appeared mounted men who hit them till breathing hard they entered the stream. The rest followed. I took my horse to the edge of the river to flank the beasts, and when a heifer entered the river straight in front of me I urged my horse forward. He took to the water like a duck. I hadn't expected the current to be as fast as it was. We and the cattle were almost swept along. The horse was game, I held on to his mane, letting him take me where he and the river wanted. The cattle sighed, the horse too, and suddenly in the distance I saw upstream the navigation lights of a ship, her shape just discernible, large and big enough to send us to the bottom. Then I heard firing behind us, shouts too, and as if he understood what it was about my horse seemed to swim faster. The firing stopped, the shouting continued, and great was my joy when the horse began to rise from the water. My companion was waiting for me.

'They caught some of them, the damned customs men,' he said. 'Lucky we were paid in advance, eh?'

'What do we do now?' I asked.

'Wait here till the boss and his drivers come. We've nothing to fear on this bank. The cattle is in the Argentine, so we're all right.'

Two men arrived in a Ford, the shorter of the two complaining bitterly about the Paraguayan customs men whom some traitor must have tipped off, and woe to the traitor if he ever caught him. At least five of his men had been arrested, not to mention about sixty head of cattle. He gave us our bonus, telling us to push off. I asked whether he would employ me again. 'Not for some time,' he said. So I pushed off with my mate to leave our horses with a fonda-keeper about twenty miles away.

We rode for a while, then slept near a long wall, our horses tied to a tree. When we awoke it was daylight, and looking over the wall I thought I saw men and women moving about, their faces covered with dark cloth. A leper colony, I said to myself, which added to the dreamlike quality of the adventure. We left the horses in the fonda, I parted from my companion and took a train to Buenos Aires. For that one night's work I was paid twice as much as I received from Hugh in a whole month.

My brother had lost his job at the agricultural college. They gave no reason, simply telling him that his services were no longer required. He was in the Italian boarding house, and I moved in too. Now the Argentine lodgers could be jealous of both of us since Silvia spoke in Italian as much to him as to me. We both tried to find jobs. In answer to an advertisement in the *Buenos Aires Herald* I called on an insurance firm that specialised in dowries, dotes para niñas. With a lot of pamphlets under my arm I sallied forth to persuade mothers to take out an insurance policy in order to give their daughters a handsome dowry on the wedding day. Not only did I not succeed in persuading any mother, but one threw me out, shouting that her daughter was pretty enough to find a husband without a dowry. The following evening I called it a day. My brother fared no better with sewing machines. Apparently every able-bodied housewife in Buenos Aires had a sewing machine.

Here enters the piano manufacturer.

His name was Emcke or Emke, and his father manufactured pianos in Germany. I had met him on the *Madrid*, but lost sight of him after our arrival in Buenos Aires. He was twenty-three, thus very much my senior. None the less, he had unburdened himself on the ship with tears in his eyes, for his was a sad tale. He had fallen in love with a girl whose father was one of his father's workmen. He wanted to marry the girl, his father put his foot down, proudly declaring that no Emke or Emcke (I will stick to Emke) made a mésalliance. He packed his son off to the Argentine to visit his agents, to see whether the sale of pianos could be improved. Obedient Emke submitted, came out to Buenos Aires, sighing like the young Werther, and wiped his eyes moaning for his girl way back in Germany. He had shown me her photograph, and I couldn't understand what the fuss was about: she couldn't have looked plainer.

My brother and I ran into him in Florida, and he expressed great joy at seeing me again. He took to my brother, asked us to lunch and in the course of the meal told us he was off to Brazil to organise the sale of his father's pianos in Rio de Janeiro and São Paulo. He was short and round, and his little eyes oozed kindliness. I said we were at a dead end in Buenos Aires, to which he replied that Argentine was saturated with immigrants, whereas Brazil was still virgin land with immense opportunities. We ought to go with him to Brazil, where he knew influential people who were bound to give us jobs. In the same breath he told us that his heart was broken, every particle of him longed for his girl, and the distance between became more and more insupportable. My brother and I looked at each other, we had just enough left to pay our passage to Rio, we both nodded, then said to Emke we were ready to go to Brazil as long as he travelled third too, our financial position forbidding us to travel in a superior class. He said that a German liner the *Sarmiento* was sailing to Rio in a few days' time. She carried only third class passengers, and the three of us would voyage together. Neither my brother nor I was loath to say goodbye to the Gran País.

During the six days' voyage Emke constantly spoke about his sweetheart in faraway Germany. If he were a man he would stay on the liner till Hamburg, face his father, then take his inamorata to the nearest Lutheran church. Frightened, I said he shouldn't even think of it, but if he had to think of it he should wait till he found us jobs. He assured us he wouldn't dare to go home, his father being too much of an ogre and he too dutiful a son. Then he sighed, and shed tears, moaning for his Gretchen. The bay of Rio de Janeiro with the sun rising was as fine a sight as I ever saw. 'You'll see we'll make good here,' I said to my brother.

We went ashore with Emke who took us to a German restaurant in the Avenida Rio Branco, introduced us to the proprietor, asked him to give us lunch at his expense, and he would come to collect us afterwards. We left our luggage with the German, Emke went off to see the agent and we walked about in the glittering heat, our shirts sticking to our bodies, cars and trams making an earsplitting din. When the hour of lunch came we returned to the German, and fed on Viennese escalopes washed down with Antartica beer, German like the Quilmes in Buenos Aires.

Lunch was over, and no Emke came. He was delayed or too busy with his agent, to whom he had probably mentioned us, so we didn't worry. However, we began to fret towards four o'clock. And when four went by I had a sudden and awful thought. 'Come with me,' I said to my brother after asking the German where the *Sarmiento*'s agents' office was. It was near the restaurant. I inquired from a fat German clerk whether the ship had sailed. At three o'clock was the answer. Had a Herr Emke sailed on her for Hamburg. The clerk looked at the passenger list: indeed he had. 'But,' I said, 'he told us who were his fellow passengers that he was staying on in Rio.'

'That's right,' said the clerk. 'However, he changed his mind because he came here at noon to book his passage as far as Hamburg.'

I thanked the clerk.

'What are we going to do?' my brother exclaimed as we left the office. 'First go back to the restaurant. We've enough to pay for the meal, then we'll see.'

The German restaurantkeeper told us that Emke had paid for our meal in advance. 'He wasn't so bad,' said my brother. I agreed with him.

We spent the night in a cheap hotel run by an Italian. It was in a square, facing a Baroque church, whose bells kept us awake most of the night. The Italian proprietor, like most Italians who make good in South America in a small way, was a disillusioned man, as if the struggle to survive had taken all the strength out of him. In his opinion there wasn't a hope in Rio, we should leave at once for São Paulo, where we would have a better chance. We left the next evening.

In São Paulo we took rooms in a cheap boarding house run by a pretty Austrian woman who was as hard as nails. 'Here one pays in advance every evening,' she said, though only after we had moved in. I have recently looked at photographs of São Paulo today, and was hardly able to recognise the town my brother and I had known, though I made out the two hills on which the town was built and the bridge that joined them. I don't think it is the same bridge any more. Still, it was a busy and soulless town already, full of people trying to survive.

My brother, who understood mechanics which, alas, I never did, found a job with International Harvesters. The American foreman started the day's work telling the workmen he would take the piss out of them. To judge by my brother's tiredness in the evenings that foreman was a man of his word. I walked the streets, entered offices and shops only to be told no work was available. On the fourth or fifth day I saw a plate outside a door that tickled my fancy. Fazenda la Jamaica, it said. Why Jamaica, I wondered, and went upstairs, where I was received by a Chinese-looking man with a long jade cigarette holder. His name was Almeida, his mother came from Tahiti, and his father, he assured me, was of pure Portuguese descent. He himself had spent years in England. He said 'tophole' at the end of every sentence; often at the beginning, too. He had several business interests that included the Jamaica, a large coffee fazenda on the edge of the Matto Grosso. The majority of the shares belonged to an American company. Race horses were bred on the fazenda, and when I asked whether he could give me a job he said the Englishman who ran the stud needed help, so he saw no reason why I shouldn't be that help. Right away he gave me the fare to a place called Alvarem (I think) which was eighteen hours distant by train. He would wire the Englishman to tell him to meet me at the station.

'Leave tonight,' said Almeida.

'I'll leave tonight,' I said.

'Tophole,' said Almeida.

I sat on a hard third class railway bench for nearly twenty hours. In the middle of the night a dwarflike man came down the carriage, offering to sell a gold watch for a ridiculously small sum.

'You stole it,' said a passenger accusingly.

'That's why I'm selling it so cheap,' answered the dwarf.

Standish, the Englishman, was at the station when I arrived. He had come in the estate lorry. He was short and lithe like a jockey, and his wrinkled face showed no pleasure at meeting me. 'So you came,' he said, 'to push me out of my job.' I protested in vain, and he remained convinced that Almeida and I were intriguing together against him. On our

52

way to the fazenda he made me a bitter speech which he was to repeat till he turfed me out of my job on which he never even let me start.

'It's easy for you,' he said. 'You're young, life is before you. You have never had any disappointments because at your age disappointments are unknown.' That's what you think, I said to myself. 'Yet you come here to take my job. Almeida is a bloody Wop, so instead of telling me he wants to be rid of me he sends you here to push me out of my job. What did you do in the war?'

'I served in the mounted prams,' I said.

'Don't try to be funny with me. What did Almeida exactly say to you?' I told him, pointing out that I had met Almeida only once and by sheer chance. 'Tell that to less intelligent men. I'm too intelligent for both of you.'

I couldn't move him.

The house was large. It had been built at the beginning of the century by the first owner of the fazenda, a Briton with a large family, to judge by the enormous nursery wing. I was given a bedroom where, I am sure, some little girl had slept and grown up thirty years before. About two hundred yards from the house loomed the virgin forest. What astonished me was that nobody thought of entering it, nobody ever bothered about that unknown curiosity. They found the virgin forest when they came there to plant coffee, and they left it as they found it. Anyhow, it was too thick and there were too many snakes, the Brazilian foreman said.

'You'll clean your own room,' said Standish. 'I'm not putting my servants at your disposal.'

'What about food?'

'That's your business, not mine. I don't feed my enemies, got me?'

'What will be my job?'

'Wait till Almeida notifies me officially that you're my successor.'

It was an untenable situation, yet I stood it for a fortnight since I had no alternative, hoping against hope that the man would come to his senses.

In a house on the fazenda lived the son of a selfmade baronet, a hefty young man, wealth his only topic. The baronet owned shares in the fazenda. I asked the young man, who was about my age, to try to persuade Standish that I wasn't there to steal his job. The young man said that it had nothing to do with him; in my place he would return to São Paulo; and when I explained that I couldn't return to São Paulo because I had nowhere to go he laughed, observing that having nowhere to go simply didn't exist. He, for example, had four houses to go to in England alone.

An American lived in another building, a horse-faced Texan with ice cold eyes, the business manager of the fazenda. I appealed to him too. He said that he and Standish hated each other enough without my making their relations worse. The foreman's cook agreed to send me two meals a day to the house which I took in the nursery bedroom. I had absolutely nothing to do, and spent my time reading George Meredith and George Eliot whose complete works were in a bookcase in the room next to mine. And I couldn't resist the tangarines thick on the trees right outside my window. Now and then I saw Standish riding past on a thorough bred stallion, a fine chestnut who had won many races in England. Standish's peevish expression didn't change even on horseback.

I became as friendly with the foreman as was possible on that fazenda. He mistrusted the mostly halfcast labourers, saying any of them would murder for a small sum. I also gathered from him that Standish had twice tried to stop his wife from sending me food. What was I to do? On the fourteenth day Standish provided the answer. He came to me, his face radiant as he showed me a telegram he had received from Almeida to send me back to São Paulo and pay my fare. 'You see it didn't work,' he said. 'Pack your things, I'll pay the foreman's wife for your food. The train leaves in an hour's time.' It was well timed.

'You were wrong about me,' I said at the station. For I was young and inexperienced enough to believe that you could sway your enemies.

'I'm never wrong,' he said.

I sat on a hard bench for twenty hours again. The only incident during the journey was a fat countryman complaining that his wallet had been stolen. At São Paulo station a woman sobbed and shouted that her basket had been stolen while she slept, the basket containing all she possessed. A tout accosted me as I left the station, offering me forged lottery tickets. However, I had been warned about them before I left Rio de Janeiro. I went straight to Almeida's office.

'Tophole,' he said. 'But why are you back?'

'You sent Standish a telegram calling me back.'

'I never sent him a telegram,' said Almeida.

'He showed it to me.'

'He must have got some friend to send it. He's a clever chap. Do you want to go back?'

'Never.'

'Tophole.'

'Can't you give me some other job?'

'Not at this moment. Anyway, I'm going to London to meet my board. See me when I come back in three months' time. May I offer you a Turkish cigarette?'

'I don't smoke Turkish.'

'Tophole.'

I wasn't surprised when I heard a few years later that the whole Jamaica setup had gone bust, but I am sure that Almeida fell on his feet. I liked him.

As it was evening my brother would be back in the Viennese boarding house. I rang the bell, the Austrian woman appeared and refused to recognise me till I insisted on my being my brother's brother.

'He's been taken to hospital,' she said, 'nearly a fortnight ago.'

She banged the door in my face after adding that he was in the Santa Casa, the hospital for the poor.

The train I had taken from Paris to Spain was the Paris-Madrid express. As Madrid wasn't on my itinerary I stopped off at Irun for the night. I walked about the small frontier town, and looked into shop windows, had a glass of beer here, a glass of sherry there, and a bottle of valdepeñas with my dinner, watched the people, overhearing snatches of conversation, a strange sort of peace descended on me. I felt it even more strongly when I reached Burgos next morning. In the cathedral it gripped me. It was March 19, the feast of San José, so all the banks were closed. I mentioned to the Castilian hotelkeeper that I couldn't cash my traveller cheques. He immediately lent me the money I needed. Thus began my three years in Spain.

4

At the Santa Casa they refused to let me in because it was too late, but I did gather that my brother had jaundice, nothing to worry about. Yet I worried the whole night in a mean room in a mean hotel near the hospital. I was back at the Santa Casa in the morning, and was told that my brother was well enough to leave. Even the entrance hall, where the news was imparted, smelt nauseatingly. It wasn't difficult to imagine what the smell was like in the wards. I hung around till my brother appeared, emaciated, his hair long, his cheeks sunken, and the yellow aura of jaundice around him. He looked like a cross between St Sebastian and Harpo Marx. 'How do you feel?' I asked.

'Better,' he said. Then he described his twelve days in hospital. He had been lucky in that he had had a bed. On a paliasse next to his bed lay a Japanese, who had been in there for five years. The poor young man was completely paralysed, yet his stoicism and courage deeply impressed my brother who chatted for hours with him in English. My brother had made the acquaintance of a Jesuit, Father Alvarenga who told him to call on him in the House of the Jesuit Fathers when he left hospital. Between my brother and me we had hardly ten escudos left.

We went to see Father Alvarenga who received us surrounded by Chinese converts. On the wall of the waiting room was a bad but pious painting of the Canadian Martyrs of the Society of Jesus. Father Alvarenga listened to our long tale of woe, then sent us to a Brazilian nobleman, a descendant of a courtier of Dom Pedro, Emperor of Brazil, a deeply religious and charitable man, Father Alvarenga assured us. The nobleman, whose Christian name was Manoel, was only a few years older than us, and lived with his mother and many sisters in a house that was the essence of poverty and past glory.

Manoel was a sad young man, lacking vitality, speaking only about his ancestors and their great days. He knew nobody who could give us a job, he sighed. He was out of touch with the evil present which he abhorred. However, he would send us to a boarding house, kept by a decent Christian who would let us stay there till we were able to find work. And he, Manoel, would give us lunch before we set out for the boarding house. He rose, we rose with him, and he took us to the kitchen at the back of the house, telling the old cook to serve us lunch in the pantry. 'Give them the same food,' he said generously, 'as we're going to eat in the dining room.' I blushed, my brother nearly burst into tears of humiliation. None the less, I devoured the food, whereas he ate only little being weak and ashamed. In the afternoon we moved into the boarding house, where he got straight into bed, apologising for not feeling well.

I toured the town in search of a job. With my banking experience I called on the staff manager of an American bank who with true American bonhomie held out hope he knew perfectly well didn't exist. The hope lasted for three days; on the fourth he refused to receive me. The boarding house was draughty, and whenever a door opened wind blew through every room. My brother got better, our morale lower. Manoel came round one day to give us a little money. 'My personal charity,' he said, 'but I can't do more.'

'We're down and out,' said my brother as he left.

We had come to South America to make good: now we were down and out.

I think that in our heart of hearts we felt that we hadn't reached rock bottom yet, and without reaching rock bottom we wouldn't ever rise. So one day we informed our landlord that being unable to pay the rent we would leave him because it was unfair to keep him waiting any longer. He said he was willing to wait, we said it wasn't fair on him, would leave our little luggage with him, and we left to prove to ourselves that we were truly down and out.

We slept that night in a park, where hundreds of other down-and-outs gathered. We sat on a crowded bench because we had come early. Otherwise we would have lain on the ground which was crowded too. Suddenly a shape appeared: I thought at first it was a dog. Then I saw it was a man who had no legs; he pulled himself along on two small wooden contraptions tied to his hands, his belly sweeping the ground. He couldn't look up, so the stars weren't for him; I bent down and saw his face, his expression serene, and I thought he was smiling. That night I learnt that the poor are always with us. To my governess-instilled prudish horror I saw a couple copulating a few feet from me. I expressed my horror to a quiet Italian sitting next to me. He had been a schoolmaster in Piedmont, and was unable to find work in São Paulo.

'There's no question of their being shameless,' he said. 'They're just roofless like all of us.'

From Burgos I went to Valladolid, a town full of students, the walls full of black-lettered slogans, ordering Britain to give Gibraltar back to Spain. That was shortly after the Queen's visit to Gibraltar. My next stop was Salamanca, a town of great architectural beauty, and I found the people amiable. And sitting on a heavy wooden bench on which his students had listened to Fray Luís de León I said to myself that I had wasted four years of my life; my mourning for Margaret was not its cause but my pride. For I had considered her death my failure, instead of accepting and submitting to God's will.

From Salamanca I travelled to Cáceres in the night train. When I mentioned my intention of going to Cáceres all present in the station buffet strongly advised me not to take the train. It was a bad line, said one, a very bad one, said another, their voices implying that the bad line was caused by the line's fundamental wickedness for which no human could be held responsible. I braved the bad line, reaching Cáceres the next morning. Estemadura was the cradle of the conquistadors, a dour country, and moving in the harsh wind, dour Estremadura I repeated endlessly.

My next stop would be Seville, and there being no railway line, bad or good, between Cáceres and Seville I took a coach in the early morning to reach Seville in the evening. Next to me sat a notary who was returning to Seville from a business trip in Cáceres. He had been to London, had been taken to Wheeler's and Simpsons in the Strand, and assured me that English food was the best in the world. Did he know France? Under Napoleon the French had not only occupied Spain but had foisted a foreign king on them. Pepe Botella, he said scornfully. Joseph Bonaparte had been a wine merchant before his younger brother took him under his wing.

I fell asleep in the afternoon, so did the notary. I awoke to the sounds of singing and clapping of hands, and my nostrils filled with the scent of eucalyptus. 'We are in Andalucia,' the notary said proudly. The breeze blowing in through the coach's open windows was full of promise of flamenco and corridas. The notary's wife awaited him at the coach station in Seville. When he caught sight of her he hastily bade me goodbye, and as I alighted he ignored me. I had reached the country where girls belong strictly to their mothers and wives obediently to their husbands. I was to lunch one day in Puerto de Santa María in the house of the local poet who took a coach afterwards to Córdova. His wife and I accompanied him to the coach. Before the coach left a middleaged woman appeared, and whisked the wife away the second the coach left, as though to protect her from my criminal intentions.

In Seville I admired the Giralda, the vastness of the cathedral, and was enchanted by the Barrio Santa Cruz. Here I am, I said repeatedly to myself, among people who had never seen or heard about Margaret. I couldn't bore them with my pain since she was unknown to them.

My next stop was Jerez de la Frontera, though only for the day. Later I was to know the town of sherry inside out. In the travel book I wrote I called Cadiz a ship, Jerez a horse, and Seville a beautiful woman.

On reaching Cadiz the same evening I came to the end of the journey I had outlined for myself, and now the writing had to start. I must find some quiet place for it. In a café it was suggested I should have a look at Puerto de Santa María on the other side of the Bay of Cadiz. The levante, that evil wind that brings the sand of the Sahara along, was blowing fast, shepherding orange-coloured clouds as I took the small boat to cross the bay. The boat was crowded with singing, clapping and drinking young men, recruits on their last spree before joining the colours. 'I think,' said a fellow passenger with Andalucian fatalism, 'that the ship will turn over, and we'll all drown thanks to these noisy sons of the big whore.' We reached the Puerto safely.

I was struck by the symmetrical white elegance of the town in the estuary of the Guadalete. Having learnt from long experience that a café or a tavern is the best place to make inquiries in an unknown city I entered one at random, Providence, I am sure, guiding me. The cafékeeper had a round face and blue eyes sparkling with a private joke he refused to share with anybody. Cayetano became as good a friend as I have ever had, an eccentric who as I was to find out opened his café when he felt like it, and if he enjoyed his clients' conversation remained open till daybreak or after. At a table sat intelligent faces immersed in a game of dominoes. When I started to put questions to Cayetano they rose, and came to help him with their answers, plying me with fino, the sherry wine of the Puerto. Thus I made the acquaintance of Don Luís, Don Pedro, Don Dionisio and Don Joaquín who became my friends and close companions during my long stay in the Puerto. Not to tempt Providence again I took the train back to Cadiz that night. Next day I moved into the Puerto's only hotel, and my new life began.

After the night in the park that proved in every sense that we were down and outs my brother and I went to hear early Mass in the Jesuits' church. After Mass one of the Chinese converts advised us to do as he did, namely clean trams in the sheds of the São Paulo tram company. He knew about sixty words of Portuguese, I roughly forty, yet he managed to make us understand that there would be no difficulty in being taken on. We went to the sheds, and were told by a foreman to turn up well before midnight, since the cleaning would last till dawn. Having jobs, so no longer being down and outs, we returned to the boarding house. 'I was worried about your not coming back last night,' was all the landlord said.

My brother worked for two nights with me, but as he hadn't got rid of his jaundice he couldn't rise the third night though the poor fellow tried hard. In the morning Father Alvarenga sent a doctor who ordered my brother to stay in bed. They shouldn't have discharged him from hospital so soon we learned. My brother lamented his weakness, I told him not to worry since he had helped me enough in the Argentine. Now it was my duty to look after him.

The work at the tram sheds was easy and dirty. The floors of the trams were heavily spat over despite the notice in every tram, declaring that spitting and whistling were vulgar. My colleagues were Italians in the same condition as I and halfcasts from the provinces, most of them unable to read or write, a quarrelsome lot, and one night one was knifed in the course of a fight. The pay was negligible, yet it just kept my brother and me alive. He joined me a week later.

Manoel came to see us. He had news for us: notwithstanding his keeping aloof from the emperorless world he was forced to live in he had heard that an American meat packing company was looking for young men first to train, then to employ as clerks. We should go to see the staff manager whose office was in the centre of the town. The works were ten miles out of the city. Sick and tired of cleaning trams, and feeling the enmity of the other cleaners because we didn't steal soap and whatever else you could lay your hands on, we went next day to see the staff manager of the meat packing company. He was a cleanshaven bland Quaker who never stopped beaming while he spoke to us.

To start with we would live in the company's hostel next to the works.

Lights out at ten because the company wanted all employees to keep fit. Reveille was at seven because vigorous, healthy young men rose early. We would start our training at eight thirty, lunch at noon in the canteen, further training in the afternoon with a short tea or coffee break, and in the evening the gymnasium and the library were at our disposal. 'Can't one go out?' I asked, thinking this would be worse than the ordered home life we had escaped from.

'You can,' laughed the manager indulgently, 'but you won't want to. The work is so absorbing that you'll think about it even after you knock off, and you might have some great ideas how to improve your training or even some original ideas about meat packing. You won't want to be away from your companions who'll all be your pals. And,' he smiled like a brothelkeeper offering some fresh goods to an exacting customer, 'we've a baseball team and there are theatricals every weekend. It's a grand life, boys, you'll love every minute of it. In time you might become a manager like me. Ours is a great organisation. Once you're one of us you'll want to remain with us for the rest of your lives.'

He gave us two questionnaires to fill in, and told us to come back early the next week. We took them away, and in our windswept room studied them. The rules of the hostel were enclosed. You had to pledge yourself not to smoke or bring in drink.

'Never,' I said.

'Never,' said my brother.

That night in the sheds I couldn't find my mop and scrubbing brush. Of course they had been stolen. I complained aloud and bitterly. On that two of my colleagues set upon me, and if the foreman hadn't intervened I would probably have been knifed. I was given a fresh mop and scrubbing brush, but the other cleaners made work practically impossible for me and my brother who had rushed to my rescue when I was attacked. Leaving the sheds at daybreak we both knew that it couldn't go on, and if we tried it would end disastrously. What were we to do?

We didn't care to look each other in the eye, for each of us guessed what the other was thinking. On Sunday night we capitulated, and signed the questionnaires.

My only correspondent in Europe was my sister to whom I had given Poste Restante São Paulo as my address. As I hadn't heard from her for some time we went to the post office on our way to the staff manager. A large, thick envelope was waiting for me with a Swiss stamp. I read the long letter from a Swiss lawyer, and while I read it I knew that a different I would emerge at the end of it, one who had almost lost contact with his down and out previous self. For my mother's friend, who had come to see us in Montreux and who gave me the money to sail to South America, had died, leaving me about twenty thousand pounds. Thus my misery ended as in a fairy tale. If the thought came to me of ending a novel with a letter from a lawyer announcing that an unexpected fortune was left to the down and out hero I would sternly dismiss it as not worthy of a conscientious novelist.

A fat draft for my passage back was enclosed with the letter. 'What is it?' asked my brother.

'We're saved,' I said. We tore up the questionnaires and went to the Jesuit church.

I gave Father Alvarenga, who seemed pleased to see the last of us, a small donation for his converts, paid our landlord who said, 'You see there was no cause to worry,' and moved into the best hotel in São Paulo. That night we went to the park to find the legless man whom at first glance I had taken for a dog. He lay on his belly, his head resting on the wooden contraption tied to his right hand, his eyes on the ground. I bent down, put three large banknotes beside him, then tapped his shoulder. He woke up, slightly raised his head, I pointed at the banknotes and quickly left. We repaid Manoel, and asked him to lunch with us. The finest store in São Paulo was Mappin's, like Harrod's in Buenos Aires. Mappin's had a roof garden restaurant, and there we entertained Manoel. Already I was keen on good food, so carefully chose the dishes, starting with cold consommé.

'I don't want any tea,' said Manoel in his gloomy voice. 'I'm not English.'

It took us an effort to persuade him that the consommé wasn't tea.

A week later my brother and I sailed on the *Avila Star* of the Blue Star Line, first class passengers only. We embarked late at night, each of us slept in his state-room, and at breakfast we ate our way through the bill of fare, from bacon and eggs to pork chops and mash. We shared a table with the ship's doctor, a Scotsman. He had a healthy hatred of the Americans, and kept saying, 'We should celebrate the fourth July, not they.'

We had clung to our dinner jackets, though on many occasions their sale would have helped a lot. We sat at night in the dining room and danced on deck like any well-to-do wellgroomed passenger. A pretty woman with long fair hair, after having listened to some of my adventures, observed to my brother, 'He's a perfect romancer, he ought to write books.' She added, 'I said romancer, not liar.'

'We failed,' my brother frequently said during the voyage.

'What does it matter,' I said on the crest of the wave.

'All my life I'll be ashamed of having signed the questionnaire,' he said. 'The lowest form of surrender.'

'What does it matter,' I repeated.

Failure or no failure South America had taught me a lot, whereas for my brother it had been a shameful failure which haunted him for the rest of his brief life, turning him into an austere man, shunning other people's company. Our roads parted when I went to Kenya; shortly after he married a woman ten years his senior. They went to live in Wiltshire, where he farmed, growing mushrooms and keeping a market garden. On every visit I paid him after my return from Kenya I found him more aloof, more distant and devout, in his devoutness abhorring other people's frolicks and laughter, I probably the first among them. 'My poor Peter,' he used to say. Now and then he spoke of South America, repeating that it had been a ghastly failure. 'Think of all those who managed to make good. Yet you and I who call ourselves intelligent failed completely. An illiterate Italian from the Mezzogiorno would have done better.'

My last visit to him was with Margaret soon after our marriage. He gave us bacon sandwiches for lunch, and no drink as though we were in the meat packing hostel. His wife who was on war work in London came down on the Saturday, and there being little room in the cottage Margaret and I moved to a hotel in Malmesbury for the night. Next morning he and his wife arrived in his gig to hear Mass in the Catholic church. He and she were in the first pew, Margaret and I far behind them. The next time we met in the church he was in his coffin. It was his thirty-fourth birthday, and I sadly thought that his life had ended on the day we sailed from South America.

I was one of the pallbearers, the others were the land girls, both short, and a man who worked on the farm, short too. Being tall I felt I was carrying the whole weight of his disillusioned life. But when the coffin was lowered into the grave I was as near to him as we had been in childhood and South America.

'Que te vaya bien,' I called to him. I have no fears on that score.

'Now you're all that's left me,' I said to Margaret, leaving the cemetery. My sister had died while I was in Kenya.

Cayetano's tavern was called Alegría, where every afternoon I met Don Luís, Don Pedro, Don Joaquín and Don Dionisio to play dominoes, the idea that no fino was drunk before the end of each game, the loser paying the round, the reason that thus one would drink less than standing at the counter, necking down the good sherry wine. Often the game stopped on account of excited talk about Spanish history, the usual topic the Armada and its defeat about which they argued as though it had taken place the day before. If it wasn't the Armada then it was the Peninsular War, Wellington ignored, only the Spanish resistance counting. They were no xenophobes, just Spaniards thinking with ferocious love of Spain. Though not one of them was a phalangist they all admired the Caudillo. We were joined one afternoon by a Castilian who had been in the División Azul, the Blue Division, that had fought with the Germans against the Russians in the second world war. 'Because you were anti-communist?' I asked.

'Because I fell out with my father,' the Castilian said, 'but I can assure you I never fired a shot, God be praised. I wouldn't kill a fly however obnoxious it is.'

'Then why bother to go to Russia?' inquired Don Luís who was the local librarian, a Madrileño, mocking the Andalusians in secret. Isn't there a Madrileño saying that from Madrid one goes straight to Heaven as it is the next stop?

Dionisio was from Old Castille, all the others natives of the Puerto, Don Pedro in every sense the caballero andaluz, a man of great learning and with perfect manners. He was friendly with the police chief, and accompanying me to have my permit renewed I expressed the wish to him and the comisario to see the detention cells. 'The prisoners are in the patio,' said the chief, opening the window giving on the patio. A couple of prostitutes, two gipsies and a bearded tramp lay on their backs, basking in the sun. They began to struggle to their feet when they saw us.

'Don't bother to get up,' said Don Pedro. 'Pray, remain seated.'

He was fifty-one years old, yet like a true Spaniard had declared himself an old man whom one had to tolerate because of his advanced age. He had five daughters and three sons, the eldest twenty-six, the youngest two. The most prolific father was the watchmaker who had fourteen children, he like a rake, his wife a barrel. Don Joaquín was a widower, and had fourteen years before won a fortune at the lottery. Since then he bought a ticket every week, feeling insulted and conspired against because he didn't win. In fact, he never won again, yet he didn't give in. I

64

went to see him one afternoon in his office. His secretary said he was out, and bade me wait in his room. A few minutes later Don Joaquín arrived. I heard his secretary saying that someone was waiting for him in the next room.

'It must be the lottery man bringing me the good news,' he said.

'It's only me,' I called.

Another unforgettable person was Manolo who had before the Civil War called himself a royalist without king. He was tall, emaciated and a bit of a fool. He had in his youth fallen in love with a prostitute next door in Puerto Real. She asked him not to lay her because she had syphilis. 'Makes no difference to me,' said that latter-day Romeo. 'I love you too much.' He laid her, lost his hair and teeth, suffered a lengthy cure, and behind his back he was called el sifilítico romántico. His sister was a schoolmistress, he had mildly represented a local bodega, then lost his job, and in his disappointment moved into his sister's flat, and went to bed. He stayed in bed for eighteen months, refusing to rise, his suit being too old, his shirts in holes, his hat deformed by age. His sister got fed up in the end, and bought him a suit and shirts. 'Now you can get up,' she said.

'Not before you buy me a new hat,' said Don Manolo.

I met him in the full glory of his new suit and hat.

Don Isidro, a fat man with a round face, had seen better days. He had to sell his car at the time I arrived in the Puerto. He bought a Vespa, but as he didn't trust himself on it alone he retained his chauffeur, and it was an imposing sight to see the Vespa spluttering past, the uniformed chauffeur in front, fat Don Isidro hanging on to his shoulders for all he was worth. (Needless to say, all that was before the economical miracle of Spain.)

Don José was a rich old miser who owned several houses in the poor quarter of the town. Now and then he came to play dominoes with us, his aim, we knew, to have a free coffee. If he wasn't the loser he drank it with relish, taking his time over it; if he lost he paid for our drinks with a miserable countenance, and took no coffee. He wanted to get rid of a tenant who was a bad payer. To evict a tenant was a difficult task as tenants, especially poor ones, were protected by the law. There was a long tussle in front of the judge, and when at the end of it the judge decided in favour of the tenant in his fury and disappointment Don José dropped dead in the court room. I saw from the Alegría his body wrapped in a grey shroud being carried to his residence. 'We die before the judgment,' observed Don Luís. 'Don José during it.'

The limpiabotas, the boot-blacks, were an integral part of Andalusian life, considered the lowest yet the most necessary profession since not even servants deigned to clean shoes. Among the limpiabotas Caneco stood out. He was a gipsy who should have been a great gentleman in some bygone age. He was given to drink, and when he appeared without the wooden box that contained the utensils of his trade it meant that he was in his sherry cups. We were playing dominoes one afternoon when Caneco staggered in box-less. 'I'm standing these caballeros a drink all round,' he called to Cayetano.

'You've no porcelain,' said Cayetano, porcelain in his language meaning cash, 'so I won't serve you.'

'All right,' said Caneco, 'if I can't offer them a drink I'll clean their shoes free.'

And he was as good as his word. He rushed to fetch his box, then cleaned our shoes with even more care than when he was paid.

'If you stand him a drink he'll be offended,' whispered Don Luís.

I nodded as I had understood that from the start.

Then there was the Tula who had been a prostitute till age stopped her from exercising her profession. In her despair she threw herself in front of a train, luckily suffered only light injuries, and was taken to the town's hospital run by nuns. In Spain suicide is a fearful crime, and she would have been flung into jail the moment she left hospital if the good sisters hadn't taken to her. They found her a dear, innocent creature, her past notwithstanding, and felt deep pity for her. She remained on the hospital's register after she left, thus she couldn't be arrested. Of course the police knew the situation, but closed their eyes to it. Tula was small, frail and bird-like. She was in many ways a happy creature when I came to know her. She slept in a disused bodega, none the less she was spotlessly clean. She turned up at night in the Alegría, and I and whoever was present stood her drinks which she accepted, joy filling her dark eyes. Her conversation consisted of laughing and asking God to go with you. One night I asked her what she would prefer, five pesetas or a bottle of fino. 'Fino,' she said. I gave her the bottle and five pesetas. She refused the money, I insisted, so she said in a heartbroken voice, 'If I must take the money I have to return the bottle and won't be able to drink it, ay Madre de Dios.' I stopped insisting.

I went to England for three months, she saw me in the Alegría on my return, and immediately ran to the disused bodega to put on her Sunday apron.

Another of my favourites was Chumi, a Velasquez dwarf with a voice that curled to the stars when he was in the mood to sing flamenco. It wasn't often, yet when he was he would stand beside the counter, his head lower than the top, beating time with his hand hitting the counter (if in a street he beat time hitting the wall).

The Puerto was a town of aficionados, the inmates had bullfighting in their blood, and during the season toros, toreros and corridas were the main topic of conversation. If you don't understand what bullfighting is about you find it a cruel pastime; if you do understand it is a great art and fair in every sense since the dice is loaded against the torero. But I repeat you must be contaminated by the bullfighting spirit. Outside Spain I wouldn't dream of going to a bullfight; in the Puerto I was swept along with the others. I went one day to Cadiz, where I was to meet a member of the Puerto police who was going to take me to a corrida. With him I wouldn't have to pay. Our date was outside the plaza de toros. For some reason I can't remember he didn't turn up. I didn't mind since it was only a novillada. In any case I wouldn't waste my money on it. I was just going to leave when the first novillo entered the bullring. I heard rhythmical clapping and shouts of olé. I whipped out a hundred peseta note, and rushed in.

Our local matador was Miguel del Pino, more or less at the end of his career though still a fine performer with the capa. He was a quiet, modest man. On the eve of corridas the bullfighters came to the Hotel Loreto (spelled with one t), where I was staying. Early in the mornings I could see their banderilleros pressing their shirts and blazing suits. Towards eight in the morning the municipal band marched through the streets, playing pasos dobles, the sun of Andalusia beat down on the white houses, and the air vibrated with the excitement of the corrida to come. The cafés and taverns were crowded with aficionados, and in that atmosphere I felt in communion with them.

Now and then I was taken into the burladero. The first time I asked what would happen if the bull jumped in. 'You'd jump into the ring like the rest of us,' was the answer.

I saw some of the greatest matadors of Spain in the Puerto's bullring and as fine and heavy Miura bulls as any aficionado could wish for.

In 1929, shortly after my return from South America I went to meet my fortune in Geneva in complete ignorance of money matters. No pocket money in my early youth and the struggle for a few pesos were of no help. I was fair game for anyone, and the bald headed Swiss lawyer, who looked after the inheritance, took advantage of me and made me sign papers I didn't understand a word of. He was helped by my going down with typhoid fever. I had to stay in a nursing home for a hundred and eleven days. (As will be seen a hundred and eleven days of confinement were to recur.) None the less, I had the lion's share of twenty-thousand pounds at my disposal when I rose weak and no heavier than a leaf from my sickbed. Luckily part of the inheritance I couldn't touch at the time.

I went to Paris, not the Paris I was to know, understand and love later, but to the Paris of fashionable restaurants and nightclubs full of Americans and rich Argentines. One morning I entered the Place Vendôme: two Italians looking like gangsters with their borsalino hats entered it simultaneously. I stood gazing at the splendid architecture of the square: the Italians gazed too. One observed, 'What an admirable square with all the banks and jewellers.'

I went to London, bought a red Bentley, and roared down to the Riviera, for fundamentally I was at a loose end, having no vocation and no ambitions, since I didn't yet know what I wanted. Crossing a bridge of the Rhône I had to stop because a large flock of sheep appeared at the other end. The shepherd ordered me to back, I backed to the bank, then the shepherd and his dogs turned the sheep round, and left the bridge, leaving it free for me. I swiftly shot forward in fear of their coming back.

I took a room in a hotel in Juan-les-Pins, and my Riviera career began. It was on two levels, the levels joining each other at the end.

I took myself to the casino in Cannes as every street led to it. I played chemin de fer at low stakes, the month being early December when the winter season hadn't yet got going. I won regularly, and when Christmas came and the stakes were larger I continued to win. I considered it my due, for wasn't my childhood awful and my South American venture an undeserved defeat? That was one level.

On New Year's Eve I met Peggy, my American love to be. She was tall, had fair hair and blue eyes and seemed to step out of *The Girls' Realm*, a magazine which my sister used to read under Miss Rosy's guidance in our teens. Peggy was a snob and oozed purity. Life for her divided into two: what is done and what isn't done. She wouldn't even glance at what wasn't done. I thought that I had found in her the woman of whom Miss Rosy would wholeheartedly have approved. That was the other level.

On that New Year's Eve she, I and some mutual acquaintances dined in the Ambassadeurs, the casino's restaurant. After dinner we looked into the gaming room, where under her approving eyes I won about five hundred pounds. 'You're a clever, intelligent player,' she said. When I started to lose in February she discovered that she abhorred gambling. Women like success, and luck seems to be inspired success. I played at the big table in the company of the Maharajah of Kashmere and similar players with unlimited resources.

Dawn was approaching when I left the casino, Peggy had retired earlier, inviting me to lunch in her mother's villa the next day. I motored with my pockets bursting with counters (I was to have a safe later in the casino) to the Winter Palace Hotel in Menton, and called for breakfast to be served on the terrace. The sun rose in his Mediterranean splendour, and I saw it as a pledge to my radiant future. I would marry Peggy, win a large fortune and dedicate my life to hunting, shooting and doing whatever I liked. The idea that history might interfere with even so useful a life couldn't occur to me in my state of euphoria.

I lunched with Peggy, won that night again, and I knew that nothing could stop my triumphal progress.

Experts say you can't dedicate yourself to loving and winning simultaneously as each should take up all your time. On the one hand I dined and danced with Peggy, on the other I sat at the big table raking in money. Once I bancoed seven hundred pounds. The woman who gave the bank was the bejewelled widow of a scent manufacturer. She turned up an eight, her smile more brilliant than her earrings. I turned up a nine, and the smile went. 'How clever you are,' said Peggy.

By then we had decided to get engaged, and marry in the summer. Her taste for purity held her aloof from my vehement courting. Still, she would now and then let me kiss her in my car when I drove her back from the casino at night. In her eyes there wasn't too much wrong with being kissed by her future husband. One late night we sat in my car on the edge of the road not far from her mother's villa. Suddenly two gendarmes appeared, one shining his torch into the car, and saying in a strong Corsican accent, 'If you can afford such a car you can surely afford to take a room in a hotel.' I thought that funny: Peggy felt insulted.

I became like most gamblers a creature separated from the real world. Money didn't count as cash, only as counters, hence the sums you won or lost were so many counters more or so many counters less. Winning proved you were a better man than your neighbour: losing showed you were a poor fish. The counters piling up didn't stand for a house of one's own or a trip round the world: they were a weapon to win more. Strolling along the Croisette I loked into Van Cleef & Arpels' window, where a gold cigarette case took my fancy. I went in, and asked what the price: about a hundred pounds, if I remember rightly. Too much, and I hurried to the casino ready to lose twenty times as much without batting an eyelid.

To win was a matter of pride and selffulfilment, also a form of ecstasy. You were above other mortals, Providence smiled on you, and the sun of victory, like the sun of Austerlitz only stronger, picked you out as if the rest of mankind were in darkness. And eyes too were focused on me, the boy with the golden wand. The casino inspectors and the croupiers on whom my tips rained looked at and treated me with admiration. Perhaps, they thought, I would be the great exception, the one who defeated the gamester's usual fate.

I gave parties, would ask a dozen people to dinner, kept champagne flowing, yet deep within me I felt I lived on borrowed time which gave it all an extra kick. I thought of buying a second car, but did nothing about it, saying to myself I was in no special hurry. I had no activities outside parties and the big chemin de fer table. Now and then I said to Peggy that I would stop gambling when I doubled my capital, and then I would buy a country house in England. 'I love English lawns,' she sighed. I hired for one night the Brummell, the casino's nightclub, and entertained my guests with two orchestras, one of them Pisaro's Orquesta Típica, thus I could hear *La Cumparsita* and *Adiós Muchachos* in somewhat different circumstances.

Among the down and outs of the casino was a fat American woman, Paula. She had come to Cannes a few years before me, first winning then losing, and shaking with gambling fever she remained in Cannes, her husband and family trying in vain to persuade her to return home. Having won once she was sure she would win again. Past glories are the lifeblood of the gambler. She haunted the casino, standing behind or beside players, and would say, 'If you win give me ten louis.' The gambler is too superstitious to say no. If it was a win she took the ten louis to a cheaper table, only to lose them. Dressed by Worth, Peggy used to arrive in the gaming room towards seven. I would rise from the table, and we'd go to the bar to have dry Bacardis. 'How can you leave the table with your luck,' Paula would whisper fiercely if she were near me.

I grinned at her because I could take loving and winning in my stride.

As though he were the avenging angel of gamblers the knight arrived in the casino. He was short, fat, and bald, and sported a fierce white moustache. He wore a grey flannel suit and owned several big stores. He was surrounded by deferential hangers-on. Our first brush was purely accidental. The scent manufacturer's widow gave a bank that won eight times. I was no longer playing extravagantly because like most fools who touch cards I began to limit my winnings, considering two hundred pounds sufficient unto the day. The only intelligent way to gamble is to limit your losses rather than your gains. When the widow's bank was put up to auction I didn't bid for it first. However, the knight did. 'Why don't you bid for it?' asked my neighbour. 'You're always so lucky.' I outbid the knight who then bancoed, and I lost a substantial sum, but not yet a fortune. This shouldn't have happened to me, I said disapprovingly to myself.

The Hotel Loreto was the only hotel in the Puerto. The next best place was the Posada la Rueda to which you could bring your horse, mule or donkey, and straw was provided for man and beast. Most of the customers were peasants and gipsies. Rosario, the Loreto's proprietress, was a round middleaged woman with rolling eyes. If in the dining room a customer wanted lemon with his fish she sent out the waiter to buy one lemon. When the next customer wanted a lemon she sent out the waiter to fetch a lemon again. One night there was a noisy fight between the night watchman and a drunk in the patio, and some of the hotel guests complained in the morning about the noise. Seeing me approach Rosario thought I would do the same. Before I could open my mouth to wish her good morning she cried out with rolling eyes, 'Don Pedro, what are we going to do?'

I rather prided myself on being called Don Pedro till I discovered that behind my back I was referred to as Don Mister.

The hotel was in a long, white street, rebaptised General Mola, its original name Calle del Ganado (cattle street). Facing my window was the elementary school, and the noise was deafening during classes. The schoolmaster used his rod far from sparingly, which only added to the din. Next to the small school was the centre of the blind lottery vendors, whose cry was 'Tengo siete íguales'. The blind were invariably accompanied by boys aged around ten, and they would enter shops, taverns and bars, the boy holding the blind man by the arm, and practically everybody bought a ticket. The draw was every night, really a bagatelle as you could win no more than a hundred pesetas. In short, it was a form of charity that kept the blind busy and alive.

The thirteenth of December is the feast of the blind, Santa Lucía being their patron saint. The blind lottery vendors of the Puerto gathered in the centre in the morning, where they were given cakes and fino galore. Through my window I saw them drinking and eating, then leaving the centre happy and swaying to and fro, laughing and embracing each other in the street, while the boys who guided them waited patiently beside them.

On my side of the street was a small café, where I used to have coffee in the morning. I don't take sugar with coffee. An old beggarwoman, who stood at some distance from the counter, said to the cafékeeper, 'I've never before seen anybody taking coffee without sugar.'

'This caballero,' said the cafékeeper, 'never takes sugar.'

'Very interesting,' said the beggarwoman. 'If ever I have a little peseta I'll try it out myself.'

Naturally, I offered her a coffee which she drank, assuring me that it was excellent without sugar. Days went by, and I noticed that the beggarwoman hadn't turned up in the café again. I asked the proprietor whether she was ill.

'No, she isn't,' he said, 'but she doesn't want to come here in the mornings because she's afraid you might think you're forced to buy her a cup of coffee.'

I promised I wouldn't, and next day she was back. Grand was Andalusia before the economic miracle of the sixties.

Now and then I took a boat or train to Cadiz, where I loved strolling from sea to sea. You entered a street with the sea behind you only to find the sea at the end of the street again. Walking in one of the narrow streets I was hailed one day by a man with a small moustache and red cheeks whose face was vaguely familiar. 'I think I know you,' he said in English. 'Weren't you and your wife in Antibes in forty-eight? Of course, you were, and your wife did me a great favour. How is she?'

There it was again, though less so since Andalusia had come into my life.

I told him she had died four years before, he consoled with the right words and expression, we sat down on a café terrace in the Plaza San Francisco, and slowly it all came back. He was a Canadian, his name was Barry, he had before the war been John Barrymore's secretary, and when Margaret went for a few days to London from Antibes she brought him some tool he needed for engraving (he wanted to become an engraver at that time), which you couldn't find in the South of France. Hence Barry's gratitude.

I attached no importance to our meeting, he accompanied me to the boat, and we agreed to have a drink the next time I came to Cadiz which would be after my journey to London. He had settled in Cadiz, and lived by giving English lessons, mostly to the military, for hadn't he been a captain in the Canadian Army during the war?

I was impatient during dinner because of the knight's impudence in beating me at the game. Losing is akin to defeat. I listened without the expected and accustomed respect to Peggy's highfalutin' talk, waiting for the moment I could leave the Ambassadeurs to challenge the knight. In every sense I was out of luck that night.

The casino of Cannes was run by André who also owned the Cercle Haussmann in Paris and the casino in Deauville. His locum tenens in Cannes was a M. Weill. Only a few days before I had told him that as I had no desire to lose back the vast sums I had won he should never cash more than a hundred pounds the same evening. At my first encounter with the knight M. Weill wasn't in the casino. His assistant was unaware of our arrangement, and I, with my rising gaming fever, which in my case was offended vanity, was the last person to tell him. After dinner I cashed another fat cheque, sat down at the big table, Peggy stood behind me as usual, waiting for me to win as usual, and I attacked the knight, whose hangers-on were massed behind his chair, cheering him, as it were, whenever he won. And he won all the time. It was hopeless. If I turned up an eight he was bound to have a nine. I, who had for a month been the boy with the magic wand, couldn't help noticing that in the other punters' eyes the boy's hair was rapidly turning grey, and the wand had lost its magic. Since gambling contains a good deal of being luckier-than-thou I played as foolishly as I could. Yet during my winning days all and sundry, Peggy among the first, congratulated me on my intelligent playing. Success is considered a sign of intelligence.

'I can't stand watching this,' said Peggy. 'See you tomorrow.'

'You see,' whispered Paula after Peggy had left. 'Didn't I tell you one can't do the two things at the same time?'

When Paula saw my losses mounting she moved away, and took up her new position behind the knight's chair, but the hangers-on made short shrift of her. The inspectors and croupiers eyed me less favourably. Soon they wouldn't eye me any more. That night half of my winnings went. I felt like a pricked balloon. I suffered as an innocent suffers when condemned to hard labour.

During the next fortnight I lost most of my inheritance. However ludicrous that may sound I had no conviction left when I touched the cards. The glamour was gone, and without admitting it to myself playing, that is losing, bored me. It was a sort of ritual that ceased to have any meaning. And Peggy was tiring of me as fast as my money went. A failure is no Apollo, and certainly not Eros. How can you trust a man who gambles his fortune away? I didn't weep for the fortune I lost, for luckily I am not one who cries over spilt milk even when there are bucketfuls of it. But losing Peggy broke my heart.

She told me it was the end between us, 'One of us must be strong'. I was too much in love to have any strength.

I moved to the smaller tables, where I sat with elderly women who lived in pensions de famille, trying to win their pocket money for the day. If I won I hurried to the big table to lose my winnings in a jiffy. The knight left for London, and I overheard one of his hangers-on asking him the night before whether he had enjoyed his holiday. 'Had quite a good flutter,' he answered. I consoled myself with the thought that whereas he was short, fat and old I was tall, slim and young. There must be compensation in this world I said to myself without much conviction. Paula, who had received numberless louis in my heyday, now ignored me.

Peggy didn't care for the idea of her discarded suitor frequenting the same places and breathing the same air as she. She feared nothing more than appearing ridiculous. She found it undignified to meet me at parties and with mutual friends. She summoned me into her presence to tell me that I should leave the Riviera. 'Your continued presence here is humiliating for me.' Like so many broken hearted lovers I erroneously believed that if I fell in with the loved one's wishes my stocks and shares would rise again. I said I would do whatever she wanted, but where should I go?

'Go to Kenya and shoot lions,' was her surprising answer.

My going to Kenya and shooting lions in my desperate attempt to forget her would save her from her present humiliating position. Probably she had seen in a film some unfortunate lover with his love's photograph in one hand, a rifle in the other being mauled to death by a lion while whispering her name. None the less, I am as grateful to her for her suggestion as I am to the knight for taking my money. Without them I wouldn't have found my road.

'I'm going to Kenya,' I said, nearly adding, 'Where is it exactly?'

Immediately she produced a baronet, thirty years older than I, who had been in Kenya during the 1914–18 war. The baronet spoke eloquently about the colony, I hardly listened since if you are determined to go to a place you will find out about it on your own when you get there. He told me a joke that was much appreciated at the time. Are you married or do you live in Kenya? I looked at Peggy with reproachful eyes. (Many years later a mutual woman friend of ours said to me, 'Young people have no sense of humour, look at yourself loving Peggy.')

I went to Geneva to see my lawyer, got some money out of him, returned to Cannes to take leave of Peggy, whom, I was convinced, I would win back if I followed her instructions. I looked into the casino for the last time. 'There is a vacant seat at the big table,' said M. Weill.

'I don't gamble any more,' I said.

M. Weill turned his back on me.

My goodbye dinner in Peggy's mother's villa was a heartbreaking event for me. Her mother, of whom I was fond, expressed the opinion that I would get somewhere in life. Hopefully I looked at Peggy: she seemed uninterested. We were left alone in the drawing room after dinner. I declared my love again, she repeated it was finished between us. I rose like one starting for the scaffold, said stiffly, 'Goodbye for ever,' and turned to the door, hoping she would call me back. She didn't, and a year later married the old baronet.

The next time I saw her was during the war. She wrote to me after *Death and Tomorrow* came out, congratulating me on the book. Roger Senhouse, who knew her well, arranged a lunch at the Ivy. Margaret was there as well. 'How young you look,' said the old man's wife as we shook hands. 'It couldn't have worked,' she said to me in a low voice while Roger and Margaret were chatting. 'I couldn't agree more,' I said. She had remained the Peggy of yore. When Roger spoke about the war effort in general she said one had to do whatever one could to win the war. 'Our butler is in the Home Guard. We feel the war acutely, especially at meals when he serves us in battledress.' She reminded me of an amusing little incident during my winning days. I leaned over to pick up cards, and the ash of my cigar dropped into the bosom of a seated corpulent woman in evening dress. 'I'm awfully sorry,' I said.

'That's not enough,' said her equally corpulent husband.

I turned to Peggy, asking her in a low voice, 'What does he expect me to do?' I still wonder.

Roger was the first to leave the Ivy, Margaret, Peggy and I went out together. Peggy told the porter to fetch her a taxi. Margaret was going to the Air Ministry where she worked, and as I wanted to accompany her to the Ministry I took leave of Peggy at the same time as she.

'You ought to have stayed with her till the taxi arrived,' said Margaret as we walked away.

I finished the travel book about Spain in the velvet-like air of the Puerto. The day I finished the book a man called on me. His name was Walton. He lived in a converted baker's van, and his life consisted of going from one corrida to the other, spending the off-season in Gibraltar. He was a true aficionado. His income was small, and when talking about the different towns during the bullfighting season all you got out of him were the varying prices of meat, vegetables and fruit. He never slept in a hotel, and had never entered a restaurant on the Peninsula. I sat on the only chair of my whitewashed room in the Loreto, he on the bed while he told me the story of his life. His wife had died four years before, which snapped the last link with his English existence. He had had two sons, both killed during the war. 'Two expensive public school educations killed with two cheap bullets,' was the way he put it. He had come to see me, he said, because he had read some of my novels. We chatted about bullfights for a couple of hours, he full of knowledge and enthusiasm. When he left he declared he had seldom enjoyed a conversation more and made me promise to keep in touch with him. I didn't see him again, but he did write to me when The Shorn Shadow, my novel about a torero, appeared. The letter was posted in Valencia.

Taking the typescript of the book on Spain with me I left the Puerto determined to come back as soon as I could. My companions of the Alegría saw me off at the Puerto's charming station, and loaded with bottles of sherry they had given me I travelled to London. When I entered my agents' office Cyrus Brooks and Mark Hamilton, his son-in-law, told me without looking at me that Falcon Press had gone bust, and Peter Baker was in prison. 'It must be a terrible thought to have worked in vain,' said Cyrus Brooks. I assured him I hadn't worked in vain, for in Spain I had found the peace of mind of which I had been bereft for four long years. I nearly wrote to Peter Baker to thank him for the opportunity he had given me. The book was published by another publisher a year later.

I sailed from Marseilles to Kenya on the *Grantully Castle,* the oldest ship of the Union Castle Line. Some of the passengers were convinced that she was the same *Grantully Castle* that had taken Sir Charles Warren's expedition to Bechuanaland in the 1880s. The passengers talked to me as you speak to a member of your club. Their chumminess at first astonished me, not realising that in a sense I was already in East Africa, where white men stick together, and consider each other friends merely because of their colour. On the other side of the portholes was the town of Marseilles, whereas on the ship we were already past Suez. The first person to speak to me was a grey-haired man with hurt brown eyes. His name was Price, and he was returning to Nyasaland where he was resident engineer. 'I'm glad my furlough is over,' were his introductory words. 'You look a worldly sort of young chap,' he went on, 'so you might be able to shed light on the strange mystery my life has become.'

I was flattered, so we had a couple of gimlets. The mystery consisted of his wife refusing to have sexual intercourse with him. (He dropped his voice to a whisper as he said sexual intercourse.) His wife had been out with him, but had gone back to England a year before him. 'We part as real lovers, never a nasty word, I arrive home and she refuses her wifely duty. I just can't understand. What can be the reason?'

'Perhaps there's another man,' said the worldly young chap.

'You don't know my wife. Out of the question.'

That is the only conversation I retain from the voyage. The passengers were mostly civil servants on their way back to East Africa. They talked only shop. On the twenty-third day our liner sailed into Kilindini Harbour, the air moist and on fire. I took a train to Nairobi the same night, and entering the dining car I saw a printed notice, NO CREDIT, my first impression of Kenya.

I had two letters of recommendation, one to a businessman in Nairobi, the second to a settler in Kitali. Naturally I called on the addressee of the first letter; the second letter I never sent off. I often wonder what my life and road in Kenya would have been like if I had got in touch with the Kitali settler and not with the businessman. Such sort of speculation is like the ifs of history: it gets you nowhere.

The first thing the businessman told me was that settlers and civil servants didn't fraternise, the settlers considering the civil servants their worst enemies. He took me to the Nairobi Club, frequented only by businessmen and civil servants. A local lawyer he introduced me to drove me to the Muthaiga Country Club, where only settlers gathered. As it was past six we had whisky at the club. 'Two sundowners,' said the lawyer. He explained that gin alone was drunk in the morning as whisky fired your blood under the midday equatorial sun. He explained too that when one came to the Colony and intended to become a settler (one didn't say Kenya: one said Colony) one usually went as paying guest on a farm till one acquired the art of being a settler. I said that would suit me.

The lawyer was well acquainted with a settler whose farm was between the townships of Rumuruti and Thomson's Fall. He would write to him. In the meantime I should go to Lake Elmenteita to stay a few days with Boy Long and his wife Ginesta. Boy Long was straight out of a Michael Arlen novel. I observed that I didn't know Boy Long. 'Doesn't matter,' said the lawyer. 'Just say I sent you.'

My initiation as a settler began in Boy Long's large house. On the lake lived flamingos by the thousand, and they were like a pink cloud on the water at dawn and at sunset, both short and quick in tropical Africa. Boy Long had been the tutor of Lord Delamere's son. Lord Delamere was Kenya's Grand Old Man who opened up most of the country at the beginning of the century. When the First World War came Lord Delamere got Boy a commision in the Guards. Boy had an excellent war record, and after the war he married Ginesta, an heiress, with whom he returned to Kenya. They bought a lot of land and built a house, probably the largest in Kenya, and Boy hadn't a worry left in the world. He was tall, handsome and noisy, she quiet and well mannered.

Boy had a legend which he himself cultivated as if he were the flower and the gardener too. He once rode into Government House on horseback in the middle of a party, saying he was sorry to be late. On another occasion he threw a woman who cheated at bridge from a first floor window into a cactus, observing she deserved a lesson. On the day of my arrival he asked where my personal boy was. I said I hadn't a personal boy.

'You can't live in Africa without a personal boy. I think I can find you a good one.'

He found one called Saidi, a Malgache who couldn't speak French, but had a smattering of English. He was a Muslim, so wore a fez, and was quite young though he didn't know his exact age. He remained with me till almost tthe end. I had brought with me Porky, a nine months old Sealyham bitch whom I had acquired in Nairobi. and never had I a braver companion in my life. As a Muslim Saidi wouldn't touch a dog, yet he brought her her food and went to look for her if she strayed too far. In their own way they didn't mind each other, though kept their distance. Saidi's first act as my personal boy was to wash a pair of white flannel trousers with the result that I couldn't wear them even as shorts.

The Longs' greystone house could have competed with a manor. In the separate guest house I had a room with a bathroom next to it. You had your first drinks when the sun set. Then you separated, had your bath, put on dressing gown and pyjamas in which you dined. The quality and colour of your dressing gown gave away your social position. Boy wore a Charvet dressing gown: so did I, hence he and Ginesta found nothing wrong with me. He farmed on a large scale, possessed cattle of every conceivable breed, and had fourteen dogs from deerhound to Kerry Blue and while I stayed with them Porky went hunting with them at daybreak.

On the Sunday Lord Delamere came to lunch. He seemed half as old as time. He said it was clever of me to come to the Colony. 'Here lies the future.' On the Monday I received a letter from the solicitor, telling me that his friends, the Mayhews, were willing to have me as pupil and paying guest. On the Wednesday I entrained with Saidi and Porky at Nakuru for Thomson's Falls.

Thomson's Falls is nearly two thousand feet higher than Nairobi. The grass is green, it is a world of rolling downs and cedar forests which turn lilac as the sun kisses them goodnight. One evening I saw three buffaloes lollopping across the road in front of my car on their way to the lilac forest, and five minutes later it was night.

At Thomson's Falls station a tall man of my age came up to me. 'Are you de Polnay?' I said I was, he said his name was Robert Kuhne, and he drove a lorry between Thomson's Falls and Rumuruti on Wednesdays and Saturdays, the two days in the week when the train came and brought the mail. He was to take me to Rumuruti, where Alan Mayhew was waiting for me in the Laikipia Gymkhana club. Robert and I became fast friends, and after leaving Kenya our roads often crossed. I ran into him and his aged mother at the Bristol Hotel in Beaulieu-sur-Mer the last winter before the war; we were both in Aix-les-Bains on the day the second world war broke out; we met by sheer accident at Fortnum's during the war; and the last time I saw him was in a Paris bus long after the war. His half-brother who farmed in Laikipia was the son of Hudson's Soap.

Robert was the only person of my age in the district. I sat beside him in the lorry and, he explained that almost every settler was far older than us two, nothing surprising about that since most of them came out on the Soldiers' Settlement Scheme in the early twenties, receiving ninety-nine years' Crown leases practically for a song. They were captains or majors or colonels, all sticking to their temporary wartime rank, but the two generals who lived on the slope of the Aberdares at the height of nearly eight thousand feet, were the real stuff.

'You'll learn that the great excuse here is altitude and latitude,' said Kuhne.

'The great excuse for what?'

'Going mad. We're all slightly mad. You'll go mad too.'

I asked what the Mayhews were like. He thought Alan rather ridiculous, but Constance, his wife, was a dear though a little precious. Alan maintained he had been to Winchester, though everybody knew that it wasn't true. So when one day an honest-to-God Old Wykehamist appeared they pounced on him, and took him to the Gymkhana Club in order to expose Alan. The Old Wykehamist made mincemeat of him. After he left Alan quietly said, 'That man's never been to Winchester.'

'What's daily life like on a farm?' I asked.

'One sits in the sitting room, reading books sent from the Nairobi lending library, and thinks one is farming. On mail-days one goes into the township to collect one's mail, usually bills and month old newspapers and weeklies, that is *The Tatler* and *the Bystander*, perhaps *The Field* or *Country Life* if one's relations at home are rich enough, then comes the shopping. There are three stores in Rumuruti, one belonging to an Englishman, the other two to Indians. One is in honour bound to shop at the white store, but most settlers slink to the Indian dukas because the Indians slash prices, which is easy for them as they lend money at a high rate of interest to their compatriots, ten to fifteen per cent a week. Anyhow, one owes as much money to them as to the Englishmen. Ours is a very broke district . . . We're crossing the Equator.'

It makes me laugh when I hear people boasting about having crossed the Equator several times. I crossed it twice every time I went to Thomson's Falls.

I asked about the big game in the district. Being a newcomer I was fascinated by the beasts I had only seen in zoos and circuses. Laikipia, Robert explained, was lousy with lions, but they didn't roar, too clever to give themselves away in spite of the scarce population. The number of rhinos, buffaloes and leopards was legion. Elephants seldom crossed the flat country, preferring the forests higher up, especially the Leroki Valley. In his opinion buffaloes were the most dangerous because first they bolted, then made a detour, and charged you from behind. Generally, wild beasts kept their distance, but it would be foolish to count on that. 'Otherwise they wouldn't be wild beasts.'

We reached Rumuruti, the flagpole was flying the Union Jack. It stood between the district commissioner's house and the police station. The askaris' mules were grazing on an anaemic yellow grass patch near the post office. The three stores were in a row, there were a few huts in the distance, and that was all. Alan Mayhew was waiting for me outside the post office. I was immediately struck by his lack of personality. During the years I lived on his farm my opinion didn't change. He had bursts of energy that amounted to nothing.

He was fat, his hair yellowish with streaks of grey, his eyes pale blue with little expression in them, and his vulgar joviality made you wince. 'That's a nice dog you have,' he said. 'I have four.'

Walking to the club he told me his story, stockbroking before the war, rising to the rank of captain during the war, and then the Soldier's Settlement Scheme. The one great adventure had been the war which took him as far as Salonikai in the Machine gun Corps. We entered the club's bar where the barman was a Malgache too, so Saidi wouldn't be friendless in Laikipia.

Being sundowner time the bar filled up. Robert was right in that every settler carried parcels of old newspapers. There was the Colony's daily paper, *The East African Standard*, but those from home were somehow different, and stale news was better than fresh. To my astonishment the conversation at the bar wasn't about farming or game: it was about the 1914–18 war. One settler said the shrapnel splinter in his right knee was hurting again. 'Where did you get wounded?' he was asked probably for the hundredth time. He got it in Flanders going over the top. 'When exactly?' In seventeen.

'At that time I was in Palestine, riding with Allenby,' said a greyhaired man with a moon face.

Another settler had been in a destroyer during the battle of Jutland.

'I was in Salonikai,' interjected Alan, but nobody heeded him. The battle of Jutland about which the ex-naval person had recently read a book was discussed in detail, some saying it had been a draw, others maintaining that it was a victory since the Germans never poked out

81

their noses again. They argued loudly, and they spoke as if the battle had taken place just recently. Whisky was drunk heavily. I was fascinated by a frog-like retired major of the Indian Army. He farmed eighteen miles away, and asked me to go and see him at the first opportunity I had. Alan said in his screeching voice that he prefered Jellicoe to Beatty. As nobody took notice of him he told me it was time to go to the farm.

While we drove along in the darkness, the headlights picking out a gazelle here, a hare there (known as rabbits in the local language) Alan chatted about his happy school days at Winchester. It was cool, almost cold. As we bumped over a pighole Alan exclaimed, 'Steady the Buffs,' and we took the short escarpment leading to his house he cried, 'Up she rises'. Already I had learned his favourite witticism, 'Everybody his own goat'. (Chacun son goût.)

The lopsided moon was up, picking out his coffin-shaped house. His dogs arrived barking, the barking lessened as Porky replied, and ceased as she jumped out of the boxbody car. 'They won't fight,' said Alan, 'as she's a bitch.' He burst out laughing. 'Do we fight bitches, fellow-me-lad?' The house-boys appeared with hurricane lamps, Alan took me indoors, then went to call his wife. A log fire was burning in the sitting-room; fires were lit every night in the Kenya Highlands. I looked round the room: no chintzes, the armchairs were covered with Somali shawls, a bronze Buddha stood on the chimneypiece, Japanese prints and daggers hung on the wall, a buffalo head rather out of place among them. The two bookcases contained the works of Freud, Jung, D.H.Lawrence, Aldous Huxley, Henry James and Stendhal, and I couldn't help wondering what Alan's wife was like.

'Here's the missus,' said Alan with a loud, vulgar laugh as Constance appeared in a kimono.

Her skin was slightly ravaged by the African sun, yet her profile was sensitive, her hair black, her eyes hazel, and she spoke in a strange affected voice, looking past you. It would have surprised me had I been told that she would play an important part in my life. She showed me my room which was at the end of a small passage. The house had been built by Alan with the help of an Indian fundi (carpenter). When their son Martin was born three years before they added two rooms, one of which was to become mine. Those rooms were built of timber. Constance was fourteen years older than I, Alan twenty.

We had drinks in the sittingroom, then I went to have my bath in a zinc tub filled with hot water by the house boys. We dined in pyjamas and dressing gown, and I found it almost embarrassing to sit with such an illmatched pair. Constance spoke to me about Ravel and Debussy, Alan listened proudly, and said beaming on us, 'I don't think there are many round here who know who those blokes are.' The hyaenas were hooting; the dogs ran out to bark their challenge. Alan took himself to bed shortly after dinner to read one of John Buchan's novels perhaps for the fiftieth time. 'I don't care for that nonsense,' he said, pointing at his wife's books. Constance put on the record of the César Franck symphony. Thus began our uninterrupted evenings together which were to last for three years, neither of us going to bed before two in the morning.

In London I became every day more impatient to return to the Puerto. I needed the new strength it had given me, and which I feared to lose if I stayed away too long. I went to see Jeffrey Simmons of W. H. Allen, who is still today my close friend and publisher, and told him I had at last found an idea for a novel. He asked what it would be about. I said it would have nothing to do with the years the locusts had eaten after Margaret's death, in fact the action would take place before the last war. He wished me luck, and I returned to the Puerto, where I fell into the same life I had enjoyed before I left for London.

In the morning I worked in my hotel room on the novel which I eventually named *Before I Sleep*. I stopped when I heard a blind woman coming down the street, singing a cante jondo atrociously. 'She has art but no voice,' said the experts. I went out into the sun which was in evidence as much in winter as in summer if the Levante didn't blow. I strolled beside the Guadalete or in the streets which had hardly any traffic. There weren't many cars in the Spain of the early fifties. At one o'clock Don Luís left the municipal library, and we went to Cayetano's. The amigos arrived, and we sat down to play dominoes. That would last till three o'clock when the amigos went home to lunch, leaving me either to lunch in one of the three restaurants of the Puerto, or, which was more often the case, to Cayetano boiling me eggs in his Heath Robinson coffee machine and ponderously cutting me sandwiches, lifting each slice of bread to the light to see whether it was thin enough, then shaking his head, cutting another. He was a caterer with a mother's instinct. Some of the amigos returned twenty minutes later as Andalusians aren't heavy feeders, and when they speak of food it is mostly in the abstract.

On feast days the routine was different in that we would go to lunch out of town at Gabriel's Ventorillo. Out of town is one way of putting it since the Ventorillo was just a few yards beyond the boundary. There were no outskirts, the street ended, the town ceased, and you were in the country. In front of the Ventorillo was the single track railway line to Rota, a tomato-growing district which two years later the Americans took over to build a base. The slow little train with its time-old coaches was known as the Rota Express. Now and then (a real expedition) we took the Rota Express to lunch in Rota and came back at night, then to talk about that venture into the back o' beyond for days.

I became convinced that I had found the ideal existence which would end only with my death.

5

Robert Kuhne was right about the local farmers, at least where Alan was concerned, though I didn't find much activity either on other farms I visited. Alan rose early, so Constance and I rose early too. The sight from the veranda was magnificent. The Aberdares were to the right, still shrouded in darkness, Mount Kenya in front, its shape not yet visible. The sun rose, turning the landscape into mellow brown, for brown was the colour of the long stretch of thorn trees rolling with the plains towards Mount Kenya. Slightly above the plains was a reddish-yellow circle, the bamboo forest burning on the slope. Then the sun lit up the eternal snow on the mountain top, first lilac and blue, then as white as a virgin. Clouds lifted and sailed slowly away. Heat would fill them, there would be thunder in the afternoon, but no rain. The sun was a frying red ball full of the fire of devastation. In the boma the cows lowed, in the sky hovered vultures, and carrying a stick like any bona fide farmer Alan walked to the lowing cows, stood for a while in deep meditation, then poked a cow with his stick, and strolled back for breakfast. After breakfast he sat in an armchair, reading.

The idea was to upgrade native cattle. He had three Shorthorn bulls to do the job. However, it would take generations of cows to achieve that, perhaps one of the reasons why Alan never seemed in a hurry. On the weekly dipping day he went down to the dip, staying there near the swamp till all cows, bullocks and calves were dipped. The bulls came at the end; by then he had lost interest and climbed up to the house to read a five weeks old *Daily Mail* from beginning to end. The land near Rumuruti was poor, you had to reckon eleven acres for one beast. Alan had about six hundred on ten thousand acres.

After a while I entered into an arrangement with him, and remained on the farm, my main reason being that I enjoyed Constance's company. She was an exception among settlers' wives, for you could talk to her. She wasn't brilliant, but was full of understanding and lived only for music and literature. Her favourite opera was *Pelléas and Mélisande*, the records of which she played on her gramophone almost every night. She belonged to a generation that had grown up before the first world war, and was laden with taboos. She had neither the courage nor the strength to rid herself of them. She separated the existing world from the world her thoughts and predilections conjured up, books and music her only escape, D. H. Lawrence her prophet, Aldous Huxley the guiding light. There was a comic element in her deadly serious devotion to books, and it was fascinating to watch a person who, in spite of her blind attachment to convention, could liberate herself in her reading and in talking about what she read. It was all immensely personal, yet in no manner did she let it interfere with her humdrum life on the farm. She had a copy of Benvenuto Cellini's autobiography. I discovered that a page was missing. When I drew her attention to it she confessed she had torn it out because she found disgusting his description of the worms he had vomited during one of his incarcerations.

Psychoanalysis morbidly interested her. She tried, as it were, to analyse herself, one night discovering an Oedipus complex, the next God knows what. She, who never for a moment thought of leaving a husband she despised, worshipped Freud, and was convinced that sex was all powerful, and explained every human action. She was an agnostic, finding it the easiest way out. I tried to convert her, but having no personal doubts I got nowhere with her. Hilaire Belloc had said that faith is like having an ear for music. Constance was stone deaf in front of God. If God existed, she said, why doesn't He show Himself to her? I quoted Pascal 'You wouldn't search for me if you hadn't found me already.'

'Pascal is too austere,' was her answer. Then she took Walter Pater's *Greek Studies* to read in bed, and forget austere Blaise Pascal.

Hospitality was boundless in the Colony. If anybody turned up you put him up for the night. On one occasion a stout party with a cavalry moustache arrived at sundown on his way to the Northern Frontier, where he would stay with a friend of his in the King's African Rifles. We had shepherd's pie for dinner, so it was a Monday. He was a loquacious man, and his loquacity didn't cease after Alan went to bed with a work by Dornford Yates.

'You two don't look like the ordinary run of settlers,' said the stout party. 'I'll tell you a story which happened to me in Jersey. I was staying there with a cousin last time I was home. It was a hot summer night, I couldn't sleep, so I crept out of my cousin's house, and walked down the street. The moon was shining, there wasn't a soul about, and suddenly I had to stop because from a garden, at the end of which was a long, low building, cattle were advancing towards the street. I waited to let them go by. They were all white and there were dozens of them. They came two by two, and the procession seemed endless. When at last they were gone I walked back to the house. In the morning I asked my cousin who owned all that cattle. As far as he knew nobody in the district had more than half a dozen cows. I took him to the place where I had seen them. "Oh this," he said, "is the slaughter house."'

I glanced at Constance, and she, who refused to believe in the immortality of man's soul, was ready to accept that cows and bullocks possessed it. 'How wonderful,' she breathed.

It shouldn't be imagined that she was a sedentary woman, spending her time reading and listening to gramophone records. Though she went to bed at two she was up at six, and didn't relax before the evening. Cheese was made on the farm, a sort of cheddar, and she spent long hours in the cheese shed which Alan seldom visited. Yet if I suddenly wanted to play tennis in the midday heat she came without a murmur, and if I felt so inclined that meant six or seven sets. She served underarm which, of course, dated her, but her movements were graceful. She ran the house efficiently, which is saying a lot in a country where verbal communications were difficult owing to Swahili being the government established language. The boys on the farm were mostly Kikuyus who had their own language, hence spoke very little Swahili that was as alien to them as to the settlers.

Twice a week we drove to the post office in Rumuruti to collect the mail. I had bought an old Dodge for a fiver, a come-down after the Bentley, but that didn't sadden me. In my novel *Indifference* one of the characters makes a purseproud man say on the Day of Judgment, 'Lord, treat me gently, for I had a Rolls Royce on earth.' After the post office came the club, and slowly I became acquainted with every settler in the district.

They were without exception certain that the British Empire would last for ever, and to be a Briton was a special gift of the Almighty. They didn't boast about it, they took it as their due since they had proved Britain's greatness during the world war. Look at Laikipia with only one white policeman and a handful of askaris, yet never any trouble, the Union Jack on the flagpole in Rumuruti sufficient to protect them and the Empire. My country right or wrong, but my country could never be wrong. Surrounded by them for over three years I myself imbibed their faith in the Empire, feeling as sure as they about her eternity on earth. Perhaps that explains my attitude in 1940 at the time the Germans marched into Paris.

Among the members of the club were many eccentrics who probably hadn't been eccentrics before they came to Kenya. With your nearest neighbour twenty miles away you have to fall back on yourself, thus discovering your hidden resources like the major did who asked me on the day of my arrival to call on him. His name was Taylor.

His farm was on the other side of Rumuruti, the road only a track, the land flat and covered with thorn trees and bushes. I saw a lone buffalo, but it took no notice of the car. Taylor received me in khaki shirt and trousers, his face large and bloated, his spectacles goldrimmed. The house was a ramshackle building, his servants went about in torn kansaws (the long white or yellow robes servants wore). In Kenya you judged the white man by his black servants. If they were a slovenly lot their master wasn't highly thought of, and if they didn't stay long on a farm it was considered their master's fault. Almost everybody on Alan's farm had been there for at least a decade.

Saidi snorted in the back of the car, where he remained till the end of my call. The walls in the house were covered with buffalo and antelope heads, on the floor and chairs were lion and leopard skins, and a bookcase was crammed with books on India. The major said he disliked and despised almost every settler in Laikipia. A house boy brought in a bottle of whisky and a jug of water.

'I'm going to show you something,' said the major. 'I don't show it to every Tom, Dick or Harry, but as you're young you'll appreciate it.'

He pulled from a shelf a book that looked like a family album. He brought it to me, and I groaned inwardly expecting to see old photographs, his mother, his father, he as a subaltern, he on shikar, he pig sticking. I opened the album, and stared at dozens of pornographic drawings, all executed by Taylor himself. It was filth without art, and I couldn't help thinking that solitude wasn't as uplifting as some people thought. The only interesting feature of those obscene drawings was that there invariably were animals in the background. A man and woman copulated on a sofa with a lion looking away, a man and two women on a floor with a bushbuck moving away from them, and the best was two women in close embrace beside a pecking hen. 'What do you make of them?' Taylor asked.

'I think they're very good,' I said.

'I draw one or two every evening. I've got hundreds.'

'Do they give you a kick?'

'Shows how young you are. They express my loathing of the flesh.'
He paused to listen: we both heard a car approaching. 'Quick, give them back. That's Major Barton. I don't want that old lecher to see them.'

Major Barton lived only twelve miles away, so he looked in on Taylor every second day. He was thin, the face long, and was inordinately proud of an uncle of his who was an archdeacon. A few weeks after my call on Taylor Barton had an unpleasant experience. One of the two generals came down from the slopes of the Aberdares to spend the night with Taylor who invited Barton to share the military party. Barton set out without rifle or servant. One became slack after a time. As he drove along an elephant loomed up in front of him, taking up the whole track. Barton stopped the car and waited; so did the elephant. The elephant was the first to get tired of inactivity, and slowly approached the car. Barton didn't care for the way the elephant's ears were flapping. It might charge the car, and with sudden decision Barton jumped out and climbed the nearest tree from which he watched the elephant smashing up his little car. The more it smashed the angrier it got. The elephant lingered on though nothing was left to destroy. Time went by, and Barton shivered in the tree. Eventually the elephant moved off, but Barton didn't dare to come down in case the elephant remained in the vicinity. He gave it another hour, then in the darkness, falling into ruts and pigholes, scratched by thorn trees, blundering into bushes, he made his painful way to Taylor's house. Taylor and the general had finished dinner, in fact were having their nightcaps.

'You're late,' said Taylor, 'damned late.'

'An elephant smashed up my car,' panted Barton.

'That's not an excuse.'

Even Constance was impressed when she heard that.

Among the eccentrics was a young man who stammered, yet managed to convey to the woman he was to marry that he wanted to spend the honeymoon in a flat-bottomed boat in the local swamp which was full of pythons and similar horrors and where the mosquitos made life impossible. It was his insistance on it that stopped the woman marrying him. 'I'm well out of it,' he said. 'She wasn't my sort at all. We'd nothing in common.'

The summer in the Puerto ended with the feast of Our Lady of the Miracles, the patron of the Puerto, hence every second woman in the town is called Milagros. The autumn set in with the summer sun still beating down on the white houses, as though it disregarded seasons. On a golden autumn day I went to Cadiz, and the first person I ran into was Barry whom I had once again forgotten.

'Let me take you to John Lodwick,' Barry said. 'Do you know him?'

'I don't, and I haven't read any of his books.'

'Now you'll know him. Come along.'

John Lodwick rented a large house belonging to José-María Pemán, a famous Spanish writer who had endeared himself to the Andalucians by predicting that the horse would outlast the motor car. Barry and I were received by the pretty housekeeper who was also John's children's governess. He had a son and a daughter, nine and ten years old. Their mother was dead. The housekeeper said that John couldn't receive us because he was writing, and when he wrote nobody was allowed to disturb him. 'We'll come back later,' said Barry. On our return an hour later John himself opened the front door.

He looked like the naval officer he had intended to be before the war. His head was large, and he was broad, though there was little fat on him. He asked us to stay for lunch, we had several glasses of fino, then during lunch he talked about his writing, and I saw and heard that he took his vocation far more seriously than I. Whereas I like to be as normal in my behaviour as the next man John considered the writer far above the usual run of people, an annointed, privileged being, who is entitled to ignore and despise the unannointed masses. He considered it his duty to his talents to lead a life above the rules and regulations that had been laid down for others. He would have a meal if the fancy took him, not caring a rap whether it was four in the morning or five in the afternoon. He told me that now and again he went for a walk at midnight, and only the day before he had slept throughout the day.

He considered his writing like a priest the Mass. The first thing he did when he had realised he was a writer was to throw his dinner jacket from Waterloo bridge into the Thames. He seldom went to England, lived mostly in Spain without having much affection for the Spaniards. He had practically no Spanish friends, and with the exception of Barry and the delightful Vice Consul, Bruce Scott, he saw nobody in Cadiz. I promised before I left to look in on him whenever I came to Cadiz.

'Beware of his temper,' said Barry as we walked away.

My first encounter with big game came a fortnight after my arrival in Laikipia. Alan drove me in his Oldsmobile to see a settler who lived about ten miles away. Halfway to the farm I spotted a herd of impala not far from the road. The buck had a fine head. Alan stopped his car, I got out and walked towards the herd, the thorn trees hiding me more or less. The impala slowly moved away, I followed, they reached the plain beyond the trees, and flitting from tree to tree I advanced towards them. Suddenly the herd bolted, but it wasn't because of me: a large shape covered in sand had appeared on the plain. A big warthog, I thought. Then as the shape turned towards me I saw it was a rhino. As I had only softnosed bullets I had no wish to meet it, so I tried to make myself scarce, unaware in my ignorance that I was upwind from the rhino. It charged as it veered, a sand-covered railway engine at full steam. Because of the soft-nosed bullets I let it come about forty yards, then sending up a prayer I fired. The first bullet, as we discovered afterwards, killed it, but I fired a second because that heavy mass continued to slide towards me. My sensations were pride and astonishment. I have killed a rhino, I said to myself, a rhino, and saw before me the jacket of a book I had read in my childhood, the glorious hunter standing on the beast he had killed. However, that one was an elephant. I went to fetch Alan to impart the great news. He called me a bloody fool because I shouldn't have risked it with soft-nosed bullets.

'But the rhino risked it,' I laughed.

My next victim was a lioness. I was on the farm that adjoined Alan's. His owner was often away and allowed me to shoot over it. On my way to the swamp I pushed through some bushes, and there before me were a lion, a lioness and two cubs. The king of beasts took to his heels with the cubs; the lioness turned and charged me. I killed her, poor faithful mother. A few weeks later I shot a lion with a black mane.

In time I lost the love of killing, and no longer considered every dangerous animal that I shot as a new feather in my cap. Besides, as somebody so rightly put it, it takes too much out of you.

Till the end of my stay on the farm leopards refused to leave me alone. It wasn't a case of affinities or dislike at sight: the reason was Porky, who was just the right size for a juicy dish. Since I spent most of my late afternoons beside the swamp the leopards that lurked in the vicinity were aware of my intrepid Sealyham. Speaking of her intrepidity I can still see a long plain with two buffalos making off with a little white ball rolling along behind them. When going to the swamp I often heard leopards moving behind the curtains of papyrus reeds.

The swamp was my personal delight before dusk when mallards and teals were up in the air, or rocketing to the clouds if I caught sight of them in one or other of the many pools. Now and then spur-winged geese would appear in the sky, whistling, their necks craned, their wings like sails. On such an evening I shot a wild goose which I saw dropping into the swamp. Saidi and I searched for it till nightfall. I returned to the house, regretting the goose as it had been impressively large. As I sat in my bath Saidi burst into the bathroom, carrying the goose.

'Elephant bird,' he said admiringly.

It weighed fifteen pounds. It had fallen practically at the feet of a squatter working on his patch in the swamp.

Often Constance accompanied me to the swamp. Alan, though a good shot, seldom came with us, preferring to sit in an armchair with the memoirs of some general of the 1914-18 war.

He came alive only when it was a matter of cricket. He was an excellent slow bowler, belonged to a team based in Nairobi, and he would go off to play cricket in distant parts of the Colony, leaving Constance and me on the farm. However, came the day when he and Constance went to Zanzibar for a fortnight. I decided to take advantage of my solitude, in that I wanted to find out whether I had the stamina to be alone. For the first ten days Saidi was the only person with whom I exchanged words. I didn't even go to the township to fetch the mail. I had a horse called Kiwi, and when I went riding I remained within the boundaries of the farm. Slowly I discovered that I was perfect, a man without faults. The silence round me aided my discovery. On the ninth day a settler I didn't care for turned up, I gave him drinks, we had an argument which ended in a stupid row, and when he left I woefully admitted that I was a long way from perfection.

Three days before Alan and Constance's return my solitude was shattered. There lived on the edge of the district a man who was only a few years my senior. He was called Derek, and was referred to as a remittance man, also an adventurer, because he was a gay dog and kowtowed to no one. His fat income made many a settler jealous. He came to see me, saying he had heard I was alone, and suggested I accompany him to friends of his in Nyeri. They were delightful people and we would have the time of our lives. First I refused, but he pressed me till I gave in. We went in his car, Saidi sat behind, and Derek promised to bring me back the next day. Though I pretended to the contrary I was glad to leave solitude behind. We motored through the thorn covered plains to Nyeri with Mount Kenya constantly in front of us. We saw a large family of baboons tearing up maize on a small plantation.

Derek's friends were called Newton, the husband short, the wife tall, and she immediately disliked me. I dried up, and before going to bed I asked Derek not to forget to drive me back to Laikipia in the morning. He promised he would. After breakfast I repeated my request. Derek said we would leave straight after lunch. I walked the four miles to the club in order to kill the morning. At noon I returned to the farm. At once I sensed that something was wrong: hardly a boy was visible in the compound. I went to Derek's room: his suitcase was gone. My host and hostess remained invisible. Saidi found out from one of the boys that Derek and Mary, the wife, had left in his car soon after breakfast, and an hour later Charles, the husband, had left in his.

I was furious at being stranded, cursing myself for not having come in my car. Saidi fried me eggs, I counted the minutes and felt like one abandoned on the strangers' farm. At midnight I went to bed, telling Saidi to wake me at six. I woke up several times, and once I thought I heard a car. There was no car. 'What are we going to do if they don't come back this morning?' I asked Saidi. He rolled his eyes, and had no suggestion to make.

At ten o'clock we walked to the club, I resolved to offer the first person I met there the price of the petrol if he drove me back to Laikipia. Not a soul appeared at the club. It was nearly noon when I heard a car stopping outside the clubhouse. I rushed out with my best smile which quickly froze as I set eyes on Charles, the husband. He looked taller, as if wretchedness had made him grow.

'I thought you were here,' he said. 'The boys told me you went for a walk.'

He spoke as if it were the most natural thing to desert a guest for a day and a half without giving him a reason. I said I must go to Rumuruti, and where was Derek?

'I'll drive you to Rumuruti straight after lunch.'

He tossed down the pink gin, took me to his car, Saidi got into the back, and we drove to his farm. Twice more I asked him where Derek was, and twice he ignored my question. We went into the sitting room, where a framed photograph of Mary stood on the chimney-piece. He pointed at it as he muttered, 'She's gone off with that bastard.'

'I'm so sorry,' was all I could say.

'You've no cause to be sorry. It's I who owes you an apology for having left you here without an explanation. I was foolish enough to chase after them.'

She had left him a note, saying she would marry Derek the moment he gave her back her freedom. She hoped he would as she had been a good wife to him for twelve years. Immediately he chased after them to Nairobi. In Torr's Hotel he was told that they had booked in but were out. He waited for them in the hall till seven o'clock when they came in like a pair of love birds. 'She laughed in my face, he tried to pat my shoulder, like a couple of jolly chums together. I bashed in his bloody face, the other people in the hall separated us, she hurled insults at me while I was led to the door.' He lifted Mary's likeness, threw it on the floor, stamped on it, then hurled it into the empty fireplace. On second thoughts he pulled out the photograph, saying, 'I don't want the boys to know. I'll tell them the memsahib's gone to England. Let's try to eat.'

'Where do I come in?' I asked during the meal. 'Why did he bring me here?'

'To cheer me up after they left, I suppose.'

After lunch he begged me to stay on for a couple of days. I suggested he came to Rumuruti with me, and remain on the farm for a few days. He said he didn't care for Alan; I explained that Alan and Constance and the son were away, and in the end he accepted the invitation. He drove me back, remained for three days on the farm, and I did my best to cheer him up. So Derek's scheme hadn't been a bad one. Frankly, I enjoyed his company, and when he left I was sorry to see him go. We didn't meet again. Six months later I heard that he had sold up and returned to England. I never found out what became of Derek and the irritating femme fatale.

When Alan and Constance came back from Zanzibar I informed them that as no fortune could be made by cattle breeding without a large capital I had hit on the excellent idea of starting a chicken farm. Constance thought it a good idea too. An Indian fundi built the chicken coops, and I threw myself with zeal into the world of chicken runs, incubators and foster mothers. I began with six dozen Rhode Island Reds and six dozen White Leghorns, convinced that I would have at least a thousand laying hens within a year. In two years' time I would supply the entire Colony with eggs.

My first client was the district commissioner's wife, the second the

English shopkeeper in Rumuruti, then as the number of my laying hens grew I sent the eggs to Nairobi. The mortality rate among the newly-hatched chicks was disappointing, but that, I thought, would be remedied in time.

On my second visit to John Lodwick I asked him to the Puerto to meet my friends and lunch with us on the edge of the town in the Ventorillo. He said he would come the next Tuesday. On the monday he telegraphed he couldn't come because he was too busy writing. He came the following week accompanied by Barry. They took the boat, I was on the pier to receive them, and led them to the Alegría, where my friends were waiting. On the way I pointed out a fine Baroque house. 'Being interested in painting is enough for a writer,' said John. I asked him what he meant.

'It would be detrimental for a writer's talent for him to be interested in everything. I'm interested in Spanish painting, so I see no reason to be interested in Spanish architecture. One interest is enough for a writer.'

'Even so you could glance at it,' I said.

He didn't.

The luncheon in the Ventorillo went off splendidly. John and Barry were much liked by the Quixotes of the Alegría as my amigos liked to call themselves. The Rota Express thundered by at ten miles an hour; the prawns of the Bay of Cadiz were enjoyed by all. John spoke fairly good Spanish which was as much appreciated by the amigos as the fino we drank. Walking back to the Alegría I mentioned to John that I was writing a novel, *Before I Sleep*, a difficult task with the amigos waiting for me at the corner. John suggested I stay with him for a week or so in Cadiz, where I would have all the peace I needed. I accepted his invitation.

'I don't think it will work out,' said Don Luís when I told him that I was going to spend a week in John's house in Cadiz.

None the less, I turned up on the following Monday. 'Johnny is working,' said the housekeeper.

'I'll lunch at a nearby restaurant,' I said.

'Oh no,' she said. 'I'll have your meal ready by two o'clock.'

The house was vast and as cold as an iceberg. There were a few fire pans, but their heat wasn't sufficient to heat even the smallest room, and most of the rooms were large. I lunched in the vast dining room with the housekeeper standing beside the table. When I asked her why she didn't sit down she said she sat down only when Johnny was in the room.

'Where is he now?' He had had a big meal at ten in the morning, so he wouldn't eat again till the evening. 'Is he working?' She didn't know because she wasn't allowed into the study. 'There he wants to be alone,' she said with pride.

The room she gave me was vast and filled with cold air. The stone floor sent up its special brand of cold; the fire pan smoked in the hope that the fire would die out. 'If you want anything just shout,' said the housekeeper. I sat down at the table, the silence was like death, nothing and nobody moved (the children were at school), and after an hour of shivering I went out to a café, where I was sure to meet Barry or the vice-consul.

'You were unwise to accept the invitation,' said Barry. 'You'll see you won't be able to work in John's house.'

'It's only for a week,' I said.

As meals in Spain are taken at a much later hour than in England or France, I turned up in the house a few minutes after eight. I had been given a latchkey. I let myself in only to find the house in complete darkness. I switched on a light, looked into the dining room, not a soul there either, then when I went into the patio the housekeeper called from the first floor that Johnny had had his evening meal at five, and was sleeping now, and of course he couldn't be disturbed. 'You know what great writers are like,' she added.

I had a good mind to tell her that I hadn't a clue.

I left the house, had a meal in a restaurant in the calle San Francisco, and regretting that I had accepted the invitation, I didn't sleep much that night in the frozen house. There was an enormous bathroom full of pipes that now and then gurgled, but no hot water, and cold water not always willing to flow.

In the morning I found John in the patio. 'Why did you dine out? You're my guest,' he said aggressively.

'When I came in the house was in darkness, and the housekeeper never said I could have a meal.'

'Come back at half past eleven. We'll have a meal then.'

'A bit early for me.'

'Just an excuse to fuck off to a restaurant.'

I protested. To meet me halfway he said that lunch would be served at twelve-thirty. 'I'll lose an hour's work,' he said.

I went out, returned punctually to the house only to be told by the housekeeper that they had lunched at half past eleven, and as I wasn't in they thought I was lunching in town. 'Where is John?' I asked.

'Working, so he can't be disturbed.'

However, he was present in the evening, working his charm on me most successfully in that I decided to stick it out till Saturday. During dinner he explained that Cadiz was but an interlude as his real home was in Barcelona, and he would return there with his children in the following autumn, his main reason to be near José Janés, his Spanish publisher and an intimate friend. He asked who published my work in Spanish, and when I said Calleja in Madrid, he promised that when he went to Barcelona in the autumn he would persuade Janés to take some of my books. We spent an agreeable evening, both went to bed long after midnight, and the next day I didn't see him, the same the day after, and early in the afternoon I sent him a message through the housekeeper that I was going back to the Puerto. Lodwick's son went to the nearby cab rank to get me a cab to take me to the station.

The cab was already on its way when John stormed down the stairs, then danced like a boxer in front of me, saying my leaving was an insult, I had said a whole week, and the week wasn't up. Malachy, the son, arrived panting, the cab was outside. 'If you go I'll never speak to you again. Is this your repayment of my hospitality?' I told Malachy to send the cab away. John and I moved into the sitting room, where he lost his temper again. I wasn't a friend, I had come to his house only to denigrate it, and there was nothing writerish (his word) about me. I called to Malachy to find me a cab. It was terrible to live in an alien land, John continued, and when at last he met a writer writing in the same language the writer (he pointed at me) considered that his hospitality wasn't good enough for him. I tried to explain that the reason I was returning to the Puerto was to work in the surroundings I had become accustomed to. He was the first person who should appreciate that since he himself had evolved his own routine too. Then why had I come? Because I hadn't thought that I was such a slave of habit. John swallowed that, we became friends again, and I asked Malachy to send away the cab. However, the burst of friendship didn't last long, and Malachy was sent to the cab rank to fetch another cab. By the time he returned John and I were chatting about matters unconnected with my stay in his house. I had managed to make him see that my leaving was no insult to him. Malachy was told to send the cab away. When the hour to take the train approached it was he who told Malachy to fetch the cab. When I came out into the narrow street there stood five horse-drawn cabs in a row. For every time

Malachy was told to send the cab away he ordered a new one. I had a good mind to get into the first and let the others follow in its wake to the station. As I paid off the four coachmen I wouldn't need, John lost his temper, saying the whole scene made him look ridiculous, and he stormed back into the house. I went off determined not to continue our relations.

A fortnight later he sent me two of his novels and a letter that would have moved a rock, as if he had known that he had a vital part to play in my life. I went to Cadiz, and our friendship flourished once more. It was to flourish several times.

I was left alone on the farm with Constance because Alan in pursuit of some nebulous scheme had gone to the gold-fields of Kakamega, and he was still there when I left the Colony. Constance's love of books had contaminated me. I had always been a voracious reader, though without her almost religious devotion to the written word. Every week two or three books came from a lending library in Nairobi, and now and then her mother in London sent her books the mother thought Constance would like. Her mother's taste wasn't the same as hers, and she gave away most of them, as if their presence in her bookcase were an offence to her.

It was November 1932, the lopsided moon was lighting up the world of thorn trees and bushes, and Porky and Constance's dogs were outside, barking at the hooting hyenas. To their hooting was added the hysterical and mocking laughter of a laughing hyaena whose body, I was sure, had dissolved into laughter long ago. Like the Cheshire cat. The Buddha on the chimney-piece smiled, the fire burnt brightly, and when the laughter ceased for a few seconds a hyrax groaned like a soul in torment. The dogs came in only to rush out at once.

Constance was lying back on the Somali shawls covered sofa, I sat in an armchair reading the last pages of a novel about people who wintered abroad. It was the great period of novels about hotels and boarding houses, such an easy way of bringing people together. When I finished the novel Constance asked what I thought of it. In my opinion it was a poor imitation of Aldous Huxley's *Those Barren Leaves*. Constance agreed. 'I too could write a novel about wintering abroad,' I said.

'Why don't you?'

'Don't be silly.'

'I'm not being silly because I'm sure you can. At times I feel that you've more imagination than is good for you. Why don't you put it on paper?'

'After all, I did live on the Riviera, and saw those wintering people by the hundreds.'

'You ought to try,' she said.

At two o'clock I went to my room with Porky who slept at the foot of the bed, but when I fell asleep she wriggled up, breathing on my face till I awoke and pushed her back. Then the game would start again. She had another game in which she indulged while I read in bed. She was fed in my room so as not to have fights at feeding time with the other dogs. She seldom finished her meal, and through a hole in the wall the same rat slunk in nightly to nibble at the remains. When the rat appeared Porky ignored it, but if the rat started making too much noise pushing the tin about she flew off the bed and at it. The rat disappeared through the hole, Porky jumped back on the bed, then a few minutes later the rat reappeared and the procedure was repeated.

On that night I didn't lie down at once. I pulled a chair up to the table near the window, put the hurricane lamp on it, then looked for paper. All I found was my poultry account book into which I entered the number of eggs I sent to my customers. Only the last four pages were blank. I took a pencil and began to write. A strange sort of excitement got hold of me, partly ecstasy, partly fever that brings shivers, excitement I hadn't experienced before, yet it wasn't strange to me. It was the excitement words alone can give, for words have muscles, likes, dislikes, and can give the sensation of drunkenness, euphoria, sadness and even death as they fall on paper. And a young man with a moonlike face appeared, hailed a taxi, and the taxi took him along the rue d'Antibes in Cannes. That young man was of my making, and that young man would meet at the end of the taxi ride people who were of my making too, and the same went for the house which not bricks but my words were building. When I had filled the four pages I lay down, the excitement remained with me, walking in and out of my dreams. When I woke up in the morning I knew that I had been waiting for it since I had started telling myself stories as a small boy. My whole life, I felt, had worked in that direction. If I hadn't lost my fortune on the Riviera and if Peggy hadn't sent me packing I wouldn't have come to Kenya, and if I had sent off the second letter of introduction on my arrival I wouldn't have met Constance. One likes to hope there is an explanation and a key to one's life. I found them both in the last four pages of my poultry account book. One of my first reactions was to feel sorry for Constance, the agnostic who accepted leaving this unexplained Universe some day for the darkness of nothingness. My faith was stronger that morning than ever before.

I showed Constance the four pages. She said I should go on, for which I was grateful, though by then nothing could have stopped me, not even if she had called it rubbish. Some people's hair goes white over night. I lay down without a vocation and woke up with one, roughly the same idea only the other way round.

I drove to the store in Rumuruti, where I bought half a dozen exercise books. I sat in Alan's office, writing the whole day. When I finished the first chapter Constance observed, 'If you ever get published you'll never hear from me again because my usefulness will be over.' It took me six years to have a novel published. It was in fact, the fourth I had written. By then I was far from her, but I wrote to tell her. My letter was un-answered, and truly I never heard from her again, which is one way of being remembered.

That first unpublished novel wasn't bad altogether. The best in it was the hotel proprietor sticking a hotel label on the coffin of a hotel guest who had died in the night. I mailed it to Jonathan Cape who returned it saying it was 'witty and amusing, but too frothy and short.' I was pleased with witty and amusing but horrified by short. We quickly counted words in several novels, reaching the disheartening conclusion that mine was only half the usual length. The result was my writing a boringly long novel on Kenya which was neither witty nor amusing. Yet I didn't lose hope, since nothing could deter me any more.

I had come to Kenya as an aloof visitor, expecting to stay only a little time as my heart was left behind in Cannes. Then Kenya and Constance prepared me for my vocation, and then they withdrew from my life be-cause I had found it, Kenya as much as Constance.

I lay in the ditch of my daydreams, the first to suffer from it being my chickens, for I lost interest in poultry farming, which I think would have turned into a failure even if my ambition hadn't lain elsewhere. You must have a special gift to keep chicks alive and hens laying. I lacked it. Ninety chicks or so would be hatched by the incubator, all put round the foster-mother, a pleasant sight to see the wet little things, so innocent and sweet, clustered round the lamp they took for mother hen. Then in the night the foster-mother would smoke for some inexplicably wanton reason, and you counted forty dead chicks in the morning. Still, fifty sur-vived to grow daily weaker, eventually perishing from different diseases. The district cattle inspector, a Rhodesian with an imposing red moustache, had a look at my fowls one day. 'This isn't an occupation for a man,' he said, turning his back on them. I agreed with him.

'You'll leave much sooner than you expect,' said Constance when I had finished my first unpublished novel. 'Your heart is no longer here.'

It is possible that I wouldn't have left Kenya till a year or so later if the disastrous drought of 1933 hadn't come. The long rains of 1932 hadn't been long enough, the short rains missed Laikipia, and the grass was dry and burnt by the sun when it became evident in 1933 that the long rains were late. The cattle started dying, the swamp dried up almost completely, only a little muddy water trickled through the furrow, and the river bed was nearly empty. The native squatters lost their sheep and goats, no maize grew in their shambas, and the hopelessness of it all undermined their courage, even their wish to live. Vultures sat on the trees near the boma, waiting to swoop down on the dying cattle. Every morning the herdsmen came to report the number of deaths, and I would go out and 'post mortem' the poor beasts to send swabs to the laboratory in Nairobi, unnecessary since they had died of starvation.

As if the drought weren't enough, the locusts came. They appeared by the billion, the corrugated iron roof of the house reverberating under the impact of their onslaught. They settled down to feed on the plains and anywhere else where grass was left, an ugly brownish carpet stretching from one end of the horizon to the other. Locusts go early to bed, and bunches of them rested on branches in the evening. There were so many of them that some of the branches broke under their weight. The squatters marched up and down, banging tins together, a sound locusts are supposed to abhor. A cohort or two would rise, but the legions remained. When they had devastated the farm they moved on. Before we could count our losses the wind changed, and they were back to put an end to all hope. It was useless to move the cattle as nobody else had any grass left either.

The extent of the disaster came home only when the shorthorn bulls died. I had seen them every day walking ponderously down to the lucerne patch; I had visited those fine majestic beasts daily in their shed. The first to go was the roan bull, the second was the Lincoln Red, the white seemed to hold out. If the white survives, I said to myself, I will stay on. Then the white bull died too.

Spring came to the Puerto, the short Andalusian spring, just a stepping stone to summer. Holy Week was celebrated with fervour and barrelfuls of fino. The taverns remained open the whole night. The daily processions were moving and impressive, and on Good Friday the small clad in blue statue of Nuestra Señora de los Milagros was carried through the town behind a high silver Crucifix, a band in front and followed by the penitents in their hoods and cloaks. Many saetas were sung to the Milagros whenever the procession halted. I stood with Don Luís in front of the ayuntamiento (town hall) in a large crowd, before us the palms of the square and above us the singers' voices rising to the diamond-like stars in the velvet blue sky. Suddenly Don Luís turned round and hissed to a tiny spectator who stood behind me, 'Go away or I call a policeman.' The tiny man slunk away. 'What did he do?' I asked.

'Why do you think a small man like that chose to watch the procession behind you?' I said I had no idea. 'To pick your pocket. I mean to cut your hip pocket open in case your wallet was in it.'

We then hurried to the Priory to see the procession arrive. I saw the tiny man in the crowd: he made off when he caught sight of us.

The feria followed Holy Week, the whole Puerto turning out for it, the booths filled with happy drinkers on the first day, less happy drinkers on the second, and only singing and clapping outside the empty booths on the third.

On the third evening coming back from the feria to the Alegría I was told that an Englishwoman was looking for me. She had gone to the Antigua de Cabo, the restaurant next door. I went there, and found an unknown young woman with ginger hair and brown eyes. She said that somebody she knew (she gave the name but it meant nothing to me) had told her I was in the Puerto, so she wanted to meet me. I asked her to have a drink with me in the Alegría when she had finished dinner. She appeared a few minutes later, took several glasses of fino, then wished me good night. I offered to accompany her wherever she was going so late at night, but she refused, saying she didn't want to be accompanied, besides hadn't far to go, and she walked out of the Alegría never to be seen or heard of again. I would long have forgotten her if she hadn't suddenly complained while we were at the counter of a dignified retired local judge who stood on the other side of her for pinching her behind.

'Pretend you don't notice it', I said.

'I pretend as hard as I can,' she said a few minutes later, 'but he's still pinching it.'

Antelopes and gazelles were dying too, the duck left the swamp for Lake Victoria, and as I watched the downhearted squatters trailing round the farm it dawned on me, rightly or wrongly, that Africa was the enemy of man, be he white or black.

All of a sudden the rains came with great violence. The sheets of water made visibility practically nil, the land between the swamp and the ridge became a marsh. The duck were back, but the cattle died even faster. I saw a vulture on the back of a cow, starting to feed off the poor beast though it wasn't yet dead.

The last straw was Saidi's betrayal. Before the rains a bush fire broke out on the boundary, on the other side of which farmed a South-African Dutchman (as the Afrikaners were called in my time in Kenya). One used to suspect one's neighbour of fire-raising because setting fire to the bush was considered by some farmers a good way of making grass grow faster after the old grass had burnt. Constance and I were pretty certain that the Afrikaner had set fire to the land. Anyhow, more of his grass was burnt than ours. He came round one day, and hurled accusations at Constance who with admirable dignity ordered him out of the house. Then with the coming of the locusts it was all forgotten.

At the end of the rainy season both Constance and I received summonses to appear in court in connection with the fire. We appeared in front of the district commissioner who took a poor view of the Afrikaner's accusations. The Afrikaner ranted away, and when asked whether he had any witnesses he said he had one waiting outside. He was called and my jaw dropped as I beheld my faithful Saidi who only a few hours earlier had brought me my shaving water. I exclaimed, 'Saidi, what are you doing here?' I was told to be silent. Quietly, without glancing in my direction he declared that he had sat in the back of the car when Constance and I drove to the boundary to set fire to bush and grass. It was difficult to keep silent in the circumstances, for you don't have to be a seeker of decency to feel as disgusted as I did. He left the witness box, Constance was called, she looked and was honesty and truthfulness themselves. I followed, spluttering my indignation. The case was dismissed. As we left the court Constance's head boy told us that Saidi had removed his belongings straight after breakfast. But why had Saidi, whom I believed to be devoted to me, betrayed me so outrageously?

I find no answer to that. Was it the Afrikaner bribing him or some grievance I never knew of that turned him against Constance and me from whom he had received only kindness? It remains beyond my comprehension. Two years later Constance wrote to say that she had received a letter from Saidi, telling her he was without a job, asking her to employ him, adding that she knew what a good and reliable personal boy he was. He also inquired how I was keeping.

After the betrayal I saw no reason to linger on. I decided to leave for Nairobi, and wait there till I found a ship for Europe, a ship that had to be cheap because I was nearly broke. The remaining bits and pieces of my inheritance continued to trickle in, though only at intervals, and I had to wait another four months for the next one. So I sold all I could sell which included the car and my guns, not to mention the chicken coops, incubators and foster-mothers which I sold to a new settler in Lai-kipia, a chap of my age who had arrived full of hope and ambition. I felt condescendingly sorry for him.

My last two days on the farm were like visiting a cemetery in which every tomb contained a part of me. I stood here one day when a lion poked its head out of a bush; there, walking with Alan, we put up three young lions that made off as fast as their legs could carry them; over there I had watched an oryx moving through the trees, ready to believe it was a unicorn; and yonder I was followed by a pack of wild dogs as I rode on Kiwi back to the house at sunset.

I observed to Constance that on leaving Kenya I would leave behind the 1914-18 war which was crammed down my throat daily. I would be returning to my own generation. 'You didn't waste your time out here,' she said.

Then it was time to leave. Constance and I set out in the harsh moon-light, and as I looked back at the house picked out by the moonbeams it seemed like an enormous coffin again. Yet in that house my life had changed. The hyaenas hooted, the hyrax groaned, and burning eyes appeared on the road only to disappear as the car approached them. The night air was cold, Orion scintillated above us, the Southern Cross farther away, and the car chains rattled. We used chains because some of the roads were still muddy.

I hadn't been to any town for nearly two years. Thus, when on approaching Nairobi, I saw the first two-storeyed house it took my breath away. In Nairobi I stayed with Porky in a hotel, Constance and her son with friends. Porky wasn't happy in Nairobi, and hated collar and leash. She must have felt that I was leaving, and since for dogs every separation means oncoming death it was a woebegone Porky that trotted at my side.

It was out of the question to travel first class, and anyhow most of the settlers I knew prefered tourist class on the boats of the Woermann Line, German shipowners who were reputed to do you well. I booked my passage on the *Usumbara*, one of their smaller ships. Porky would be taken after my departure to Thomson's Falls to a dear woman friend who was fond of her. And with her Porky remained till the end of her life. In 1942 I spoke one night on the BBC Overseas Service, and some weeks later I received a letter from the friend in Thomson's Falls, saying Porky was still alive, though she had lost an eye fighting a honeybear. When she had heard my voice on the radio first she had whimpered, then barked, wagging her stump of a tail. 'She is the best and bravest dog I ever had,' added the friend.

When I had arrived in Nairobi nearly four years before, a piper had been playing on the railway platform as the train pulled in. Now there was a piper again. Constance came to see me off. 'If you become a writer,' she said, 'I'll believe in God because then I'll understand that there is a pattern.'

It wasn't the moment to tell her that that wasn't the right approach to faith, but I did tell her that without her I couldn't have found my road.

Next day when the anchor winch of the *Usumbara* began to work I leaned over the side to look down at the widening breach. The water was such a dark dirty blue that you couldn't have spotted a shark. To my astonishment I felt pain and giddiness and a sense of being torn away as the distance grew between the ship and the country I was leaving and which I was resolved never to visit again because I had outgrown it. I felt like jumping into the sea, sharks or no sharks, and swimming back to the past four years. I went to the tourist class bar.

6

Rumour reached me in the Puerto that a drunken Englishman had moved into the Posada la Rueda, and slept on the straw with tramps and vagabonds. One morning while I was shaving Rosario appeared in the doorway of my room, rolling her eyes as she announced that an unspeakable drunk wanted to see me. Before she could finish the sentence a red-faced middleaged man with bloodshot eyes, wearing an overcoat but no collar burst in. He said his name was Billy Bilson (it wasn't quite that though it sounded like it), he was staying at the Rueda, 'very typical, very typical', and we had some acquaintance in common in London, hence his call. Rosario withdrew disgusted, Billy Bilson explained that he was a sort of remittance man, his wife being sick and tired of his drinking in her presence had sent him to Spain, the cheapest country to get sloshed in. 'She counts the money, counts the money, but it's her money.' When I had finished shaving and was dressed I took him to the nearest café, where he gulped down a few finos, said his turn would be the moment his next allowance arrived, shook me warmly by the hand, then slunk away. Now and again I saw him in the distance, and if he caught sight of me he waved and hurried off. Apparently, it wasn't his turn yet.

In Andalusia you send telegrams only when there is death in the family. 'A telegram for you, Don Pedro,' called Rosario on a May morning from the other side of the door. I bade her bring it in, and in she came ready to condole with me. The telegram was from John Lodwick. 'Go at once to the Posada la Rueda, pay Billy Bilson's bill, have his belongings sent to the Consulate. The least you can do. Lodwick.' I didn't care for the least you can do. 'Bad news?' asked Rosario. I shook my head, then went to telephone Bruce Scott the vice-consul in Cadiz. (Lodwick had no telephone, not even in his Barcelona flat. 'I hate telephones,' he often declared.)

Billy Bilson, Bruce Scott explained, had been on the binge in Cadiz, and fell on the quay where the *Galicia*, the Spanish battleship, was tied up, breaking his shoulderbone. The Spanish sailors took him into the sickbay, and the admiral in person telephoned the consulate to tell Bruce that they were looking after a fellow countryman of his. Bruce found that most generous and handsome, went immediately to call on the admiral, saw Billy, and made arrangements for him to be transferred to hospital. That took place the day before. In the evening he met Lodwick, told him about Billy who incidentally Lodwick had never met, and said he, Bruce, would see to Billy's luggage being taken to the hospital. 'I mentioned of course that he had stayed in the Puerto,' Bruce added.

'Now I understand,' I couldn't help smiling, for there was Lodwick in a nutshell. The poor, unknown Billy had broken his shoulder, I hadn't broken my shoulder, so the least I could do was to get his luggage to him.

The luggage went off, I wasn't annoyed with Lodwick, the next day came a long letter from him, apologising for the tone of his telegram. He had feared that I might not go near the posada considering such a place beneath my dignity, hence the least you can do. Billy Bilson left hospital about a month later, turned over a new leaf, wore collar and tie, eventually returning to London, where he found a job in a library. He wrote several times to Lodwick and me.

By then Lodwick and his family had moved to the Laguna, the long sandy strip that connects Cadiz with the mainland. He took a small chalet a few yards from the sea, and the best hours of our friendship were lived in the chalet. I used to come over from the Puerto to spend the night there which consisted of sitting up with him in the garden, chatting till dawn. It was mostly a matter of answering his questions. 'We've got to May 1942,' he would say. 'What did you do in June?'

One night he remembered that the plants in the window hadn't been watered. For some reason or other the water was cut off, so he took the gin bottle from the table, and poured the gin on the plants.

He was returning to his flat in Barcelona in the autumn after a voyage to the Spanish Sahara about which he wanted to write a book, and in fact had been commissioned to do. Why didn't I go to Barcelona in the autumn too? He spoke about José Janés, his Barcelona publisher who fascinated him in an almost uncanny manner, and repeatedly said that a trip to Barcelona would be worth my while, for he was certain that he could persuade Janés to buy the Spanish translation of some of my books. After warmly praising Janés he would suddenly run him down, calling him ostentatious and vulgar. Nobody really worked in his office, nobody knew anything about anything, the only exception the Señorita Carmen, the daughter of a famous Spanish actress, whom I must meet, and if she liked me Janés would do whatever she suggested. I could stay with him in his flat till I found a flat for myself. It would be proof of my not caring for him if I said no. 'I might,' I said. 'I don't know yet.'

The fact was that my life in the Puerto had become too much of a routine, and after a time all routine irks me because it begins to look endless. Then there was Don Luís who often said I was wasting my life living in a backwater like the Puerto. Soon, he warned me, the building of the American base in Rota would start, and the Puerto would fill with riff-raff, looking for work with the Americans. And then the Puerto would cease to be even a backwater. He strongly urged me to go to Madrid, a town I hardly knew, but which he as a Madrileño was sure I would love.

Lodwick left for Africa, on his request I travelled with him from the Puerto as far as Jerez (he mentioned that in his book), and once more he insisted on my going to Barcelona. 'I'm going to Madrid,' I said.

And to Madrid I went at the end of September. I put an ad into a Madrid paper in order to find a flat. I received a number of replies, one from a Señorita Picasso. Finding her name irresistible I took a flat in her house in the Barrio Salamanca on a monthly basis. She was tall and fa and no relation of Picasso.

At the time I was writing *The Shorn Shadow*, my novel about a bull fighter who finds an English wife. The two people I knew in Madri were away, thus I roamed the town with nobody to speak to except the paintings in the Prado, but they were too busy to hear or answer me And I ate a lot of suckling pig, which the Madrileños consider the choi cest dish under the Madrid sky. It can be quite revolting when fried in bad olive oil. I was homesick for the Puerto and the amigos, and when heard flamenco on the radio my heart was heavy because the amigo could hear it too in the Puerto.

I called on Calleja in the Ronda de Valencia who had published thre of my novels in Spanish. I was asked to show them my latest work, and meeting was fixed for the following week. On the appointed day received a long letter from Lodwick who was back in Barcelona. He re newed his invitation, urging me over four pages to join him. He ha spoken to Janés about me, and he was sure he would take my books; an what about our great friendship? I'm going to stay on here, I said t myself as I set out with two books under my arm for Calleja's offic Chateaubriand in his *Mémoires d'outre-tombe* often speaks about la main d

Dieu, the hand of God. I must have felt it on me as I reached the Ronda de Valencia, for suddenly I turned on my heel, took the books back to the flat, then went to speak to Señorita Picasso to tell her that I was leaving that night for Barcelona, thus wouldn't need the flat the next month.

In the evening I took a train to Barcelona; in the morning I took a taxi to Lodwick's flat in the calle Príncipe de Asturias. We were delighted to see each other. Immediately he rushed out to Janés in his office in the calle Muntaner, coming back an hour later to announce we were lunching with him at two.

Janés was and looked exactly as Lodwick had described him, both when he ran him down and when he praised him. He was of medium height with long hair, more fat than thin, his complexion pale, his voice filling any room. He was ostentatious, often vulgar yet had charm and streaks of kindliness. His relationship with John was curious to say the least. They would be extremely rude to each other, hurl insults, then it was all love and friendship till the next insult. At the end of the meal without having read anything I had written Janés promised to take at least one novel of mine. Lodwick paid for the lunch.

'This is the first time John has paid for a meal in his life,' said Janés as we rose.

'How dare you speak like that you damned Catalan?' Lodwick hissed. He wasn't a shouter but a hisser.

'Because I'm saying the truth,' laughed Janés.

Lodwick left in a huff, Janés drove me to his office in his Cadillac of which he was mighty proud, saying on the way that John was the best friend he had, and that he considered him one of the greatest living writers, in fact had signed him up for all his written and unwritten novels. I wasn't five minutes in Janés office when Lodwick arrived, smiling broadly and the two of them nearly embraced. I asked to meet the famous Señorita Carmen of whom Lodwick had spoken to me so often on the Laguna. She was on holiday in Majorca till the following week.

In the tourist class bar of the *Usumbara* a man called Jobson was holding forth. He had decamped from the Highlands, hiding in a lavatory of the train till it pulled out from Nairobi station. He was heavily in debt, and in Kenya your creditors could stop you from leaving the Colony. He travelled down the day before the ship sailed since creditors were more in evidence at boat train than ordinary train departures. Jobson booked into a hotel in Mombasa, and calmly waited for the next day when the

Usumbara would sail. However, that morning to his horror he saw a policeman entering the hotel. Luckily he was alone in the lounge as even the manager was in some other part of the building. The policeman took off his topi, scratched his head and waited. 'Can I be of any help?' Jobson asked.

'I'm looking for a man called Jobson,' said the policeman. 'I've got a warrant to take him back to Nairobi.'

'Do you know him?' The policeman shook his head. 'I don't know him either, but I heard some guests saying that he was sailing on the *Usumbara* today. He must have gone on board.

'Thanks, I'm going at once.'

'As I'm sailing myself could you give me a lift in your car?'

The policeman took him, they went on board together, the policeman asked the purser whether a Mr Jobson had arrived, the purser said not yet, and the policeman and Jobson had a drink at the bar. Then, as the other passengers began to arrive, Jobson mingled with them, but didn't go near the purser from whom every ten minutes or so the policeman inquired whether Mr Jobson had arrived. When it was 'All visitors ashore,' the policeman sought out Jobson to thank him for having tried to help him. 'The fellow must have smelt a rat,' the policeman said.

'You look for him in town,' was Jobson's parting advice. When the policeman had gone down the gangway he went to the purser, handed in his ticket, and was given his cabin. He was treated like a hero by the other settlers, who kept him in drink till Genoa.

'A good place to hide from creditors,' he observed as we steamed past Stromboli.

In the tourist class most of the passengers were from the Highlands, except a sordid Belgian baron who refused to pay his bridge debt when we reached Genoa. The oldest travellers were General Crocker and his wife whose hunger was insatiable. She went to bed every night her canvas bag bursting with sandwiches that were served at nine in the saloon. 'The Hun is a ghoul,' was the general's favourite expression on the German ship. One night cricket was played in the saloon with doughnuts. The few Germans said 'Shame' in German. In Port Sudan the seamen caught a shark, and when it was pulled on board they got frightened of it. 'No English seaman would behave like that,' said the retired commander who was the secretary of the Molo Hunt which hunted jackals. Eventually they came back with axes, and keeping their cautious distance it took the shark some time to die.

As we entered the Canal I threw my terai overboard, watching it as it bobbed away. 'This is the real end of my life in Kenya,' I said to a woman passenger who stood at my side. 'Regret it?' she asked. I said I was just lost and bewildered.

I stood on deck as the *Usumbara* entered the Mediterranean. A cold wind was blowing since we were in January. I loved the cold wind, and when at the second dawn I saw the distant shape of Crete I felt with joyful relief that I was returning to Europe even if represented by the Minotaur. Had I seen him I would have waved to him.

The party broke up in Genoa. Only there did I fully realise that if I wanted to hear hyaenas hooting again I would have to live near a zoo. The same woman passenger who saw me throw the terai into the dark waters of the Canal accompanied me to the station, chatting about a farm her brother intended to buy near Nakuru. I listened politely, smiling and nodding, my mind full of the Italy I had known in my early youth. 'I'm taking the train to Milan,' I said. I would spend the night in the town I had often visited while living in Cernobbio. Milan wasn't near Nakuru, so it meant nothing to her. We swore to meet again in London, the train pulled out and I never saw her again.

The train sped through snowcovered fields. I couldn't take my eyes off them, but when I did I beheld a delightful sight straight out of an Aldous Huxley novel. A tall Lombard sat opposite me, his beard red, his nails exquisitely manicured, and he was reading a score. My eyes went back to the first snow I had seen for four years. Snow wasn't white: it was, I discovered, light blue. Oscar Wilde had said that nature imitated art, the de Goncourt brothers went further, saying they enjoyed nature only when it reminded them of a painting. Many years after my journey from Genoa to Milan I saw a wintry landscape by Vlaminck in a friend's house. The snow outside Genoa immediately came back. In my enthusiasm I turned to Red Beard.

'The snow is beautiful,' I said in Italian.

'It is beautiful, signore,' he said, bowing.

This is perfection I said to myself. However, perfection fell to pieces when he embarked on a long tirade, enumerating his grievances. He was a member of the Scala orchestra, the conductor picked on him, so did his fellow musicians, especially a flautist who had then run away with his wife. That swine and bandit had moved to the San Carlo in Naples in the company of the putana his wife was. 'He knew that if he stayed on in Milan I'd kill him.' I refrained from pointing out that there were no difficulties entailed in travelling to Naples.

In Milan I looked into the Duomo, then at the Cenacolo, walked through the Galleria Vittorio Emanuele, and remembered the principessa who resided in Milan. She and her prince were in Cannes while I was winning in the casino. The prince wasn't which put him into a rotten mood, his vast fortune notwithstanding. She often scolded him for his sulky looks, telling him to laugh as I laughed. When I had lost most of my inheritance I couldn't help thinking that in the long run the prince had more cause for laughter than I. If I rang her she was sure to ask me in. I didn't ring because I considered social intercourse beneath the writer-to-be, which just goes to show the pretentiousness of the beginner.

I took the night train to Paris. In the same compartment was a vast Frenchman who turned out to be a journalist, and an Italian girl in a black silk dress and patent leather high-heeled court shoes. I chatted with the journalist, explained that I was a writer and intended to write an outstanding novel. 'To write one needs peace and inspiration,' he said. 'Go to Majorca. It'll inspire you, and you'll find all the peace you need.'

I decided that after seeing my brother in Wiltshire I would go to Majorca.

The journalist went to dine, leaving me in the overheated compartment with the Italian girl. She smiled, I smiled back, and she said she was going to Paris. I asked whether it was a pleasure trip.

'Not at all,' she answered. 'I'm officially a dancer, but I really earn my living on my back. Why make a secret of it?'

I said I couldn't agree more, thinking that I was truly back in civilisation. The journalist returned wiping his moustache, the deuxième service bell tinkled down the corridor, I went to dine, and when I came back there was neither journalist nor Italian girl in the compartment. A little later the journalist appeared looking as replete as he had after his meal. The girl followed shortly, as placidly bovine as when she had spoken to me. Next morning a seedy Italian was waiting for her at the Gare de Lyon.

'So you failed again,' said my brother who drove to Swindon to meet me. I declared I hadn't failed in Kenya since I had become a writer there. 'How can you call yourself a writer?'

'Because I am.'

During my stay with him in his austere cottage I told him that I would go to Majorca. Why Majorca? Because a man in the night train between Milan and Paris had suggested that Majorca was the right place for a writer. 'You must be mad,' sighed my brother. 'And, pray, what will you do when your money runs out?'

'I will be earning my living with my pen by then.'

And so I was.

It is difficult today to imagine the Majorca I knew in the year before the Spanish Civil War. The island was still the gem Chopin and George Sand had known. I made Puerto de Pollensa my headquarters, and when I took the bus to Palma now and then the driver lost himself in the higgledy-piggledy streets of the village of Pollensa. Life was dirt cheap, hence a number of Britons who couldn't afford the South of France since the pound had gone off the gold standard had moved into the island, about a dozen of them renting villas in Puerto de Pollensa. They were the same sort I had known in Kenya, though less interesting because altitude and latitude hadn't affected them. Retired army officers and magistrates from the Raj made up the contingent. They often forgot that Majorca wasn't a British possession. On Armistice Day the wife of one of those settlers went round the port with Flanders poppies. She waylaid the old postman, and asked him to buy a poppy. 'What on earth for?' the Majorquin asked.

'For the wounded of the war?'

'You mean the Moroccan war?'

'What a stupid old man,' she said to me later.

A retired cavalry captain who had married a rich City merchant's daughter was the life and soul of the party. Having been poor most of his life he just didn't know what to do with all the money his silly, whimsical wife put at his disposal. He got drunk twice a day, you couldn't enter a bar without running into him, and he loved laying down the law. The others tolerated him because it was preferable to falling back on their own boredom. A retired magistrate lived with an ample woman whom he called his cousin; a shellshocked officer of the world war trotted round with a wife twenty years younger than he; and there was a hard bunch of lesbians who entered bars wishing to sweep out any male present.

I met a London journalist who had come to the island to write a book. His hefty wife liked mingling with the lesbians, one of whom was a sweet young American girl I often saw in the two bars of the port. She lived with a grim Russian woman who never addressed a man. Then one morning the journalist, whom I will call Geoffrey, burst into my hotel room, shouting that his wife had eloped with the sweet American girl. They were on their way to Naples. He was distressed, repeating several times that he could give his wife far more than a woman was able to. The grim Russian woman became grimmer, moving eventually to another part of the island. I was fond of Geoffrey, we saw much of each other, and I missed him after he returned to London, still heartbroken.

During the second world war I lunched with the editor of an illustrated weekly, and in the course of our chat I asked him whether he knew Geoffrey from and about whom I hadn't heard for years. He said Geoffrey was working for him, and he would soon give a dinner party for us to meet again. I should bring Margaret since Geoffrey had remarried, and his wife would be present too. The dinner was in the Ritz, Margaret and I were the first to appear, and my eyes nearly popped out as I saw Geoffrey sailing in on the arm of an enormous lesbian wearing a dinner jacket. 'I'm happy again,' he said to me.

The two bars in the port were owned by Germans, one a socialist doctor from Munich who had left after Hitler came to power, the other a self-appointed Nazi, Fritz by name, who had not returned to Germany since 1914. He had been a planter in British Borneo, where he was interned for the duration. Then he went to America for a time. He was married to a Danish woman whose young sister had come to live with them. Fritz was an amusing liar and a devoted poker player. When in 1948 I landed in Rome airport coming from Nicosia a fairhaired large-bosomed woman addressed me in the customs queue. She was Fritz's wife on her way to Denmark from South Africa. I asked after Fritz. He had gone off with her sister, and she hadn't heard from them since the end of the Civil War. She didn't look disconsolate.

The socialist doctor considered himself a philosopher, and as such approved of his wife going about with the lesbians. 'Widens her horizon,' he would say when she went off to Palma for several days with them.

Then there were the painters, young, eager, keen and unknown, drawn to Majorca by the picture postcard light and the easy life. Turning their backs to the light they painted rocks, pines, fishing boats and fig trees. As far as I know not one of them made the grade, but they were enjoyable companions for a beginner. They could discuss suffering versus sacrifice, and whether good was the antithesis of bad. Pictorially speaking they added. In their heart of hearts they wanted to become Raoul Dufy.

I tried to lead the life I imagined a writer should: long walks by the sea, longer walks inland, wine drinking with the natives in dark taverns, and fishing with the local fishermen. And my work amounted to little.

Summer came with heat and Anglo-Saxon tourists with whom the residents didn't mix, for settlers keep to themselves. In September the heat was still intense. During the silence of an afternoon I sat outside my small hotel with nothing moving, the only sound the intermittent snoring of an old colonel at a table next to mine. A man slunk past the terrace like a shadow in a hurry. I hardly noticed him though when he disappeared I said to myself there was something wrong or out of the ordinary about him. I came out of my torpor, thought it was only my sluggish fancy, then completely roused I remembered I had promised a tall English painter and his short wife to go to their room in the hotel on the other side of the little square. There was still not a soul about. I entered the hotel which was cool, dark and quiet as if the whole building participated in the siesta. I turned to the stairs, for in that hotel as in mine you didn't ask the porter to telephone or send up the page since they had neither. You went up, and as likely as not you knocked on the wrong door.

Somebody was looking down, in fact was looking at me. Before I could put my foot on the first step, there appeared a man out of the shadows. With his hand on the balustrade he came down so fast that he seemed to be sliding. It was the man I had seen slinking past my hotel terrace. Now I knew what was wrong with him. He wore a collarless evening shirt, not starched, yet unmistakably an evening shirt. His black trousers and dusty black shoes were almost unreal in that world of white shorts and sandals. A waiter off-duty, my mind said. Then I saw the face and knew he was no waiter. It was a sickly pale face, the eyes were colourless behind the gold-rimmed pince-nez. He slid past me like an apparition that humbly knows it isn't there. I started to mount the stairs, he had reached the front door. I took another step, he turned round and was just below me. He had a stoop. He lifted his head, and focused his colourless eyes on me.

'Excuse me,' he said. I stopped, and silence ensued. I might have been mistaken, so I took another step up the stairs. 'Excuse me,' he said. I stopped, another silence, then he spoke, looking at the ground. 'Do you know the bus time-table?'

'I'm afraid I don't, but they'll tell you in the kitchen. I can hear someone moving in there.'

'Thank you, thank you so much.'

From the landing I looked down: he was in the same spot, his eyes still on the stone floor. With a sudden jerk he started for the kitchen. He reminded me of a bat. He moved uneasily, I watched him till he reached the door, then as I was going to turn away he was on his way back, making for the stairs. I bolted, that is I went to knock on the painter's door. They had just copulated, and lay naked on the bed, proof of their being avant-garde and artists.

'We've experienced a new sensation,' she said. 'Right here in bed.'

'I've experienced a new sensation too,' I said. 'I saw a man down in the hall who not only gave me the creeps but was like a bat flying round and round.'

'That's your subconscious,' they both said, then got up, pulled on their shorts and shirts, and we started out for the doctor's bar. The hall was still asleep, but convincing noises emanated from the kitchen. We came out into the glare and a voice said behind me, 'Excuse me.' I knew it was the man. I turned round, and in the strong light he appeared distinctly unsavoury, so white and humble, a Uriah Heep. 'Have you a stamp?' he asked. I said I hadn't. He looked as though he would burst into tears. 'You really haven't?' he said desperately.

'I haven't,' I said impatiently.

'You haven't a stamp,' he said, stating the saddest fact on earth.

I hurried after the tall painter and his short wife, caught up with them, and then couldn't resist glancing over my shoulder. He stood motionless, staring after me.

'He looks like a ghost,' said the painter's wife, 'but we happen to know there are no ghosts.'

We spent the afternoon and evening in the doctor's bar, then dined in Fritz's bar, and as dawn broke I accompanied them as far as their hotel. I wouldn't turn in having an appointment with a fisherman who had lost one of his arms dynamiting fish. The light began to take on the colours of Veronese (in a little while they would become those of Guido Reni), the first fishing boats were chugging out to sea, and in the square between our two hotels I saw a group of people. Two guardias civiles towered above the rest because of their three cornered hats. We hurried up to the group. The guardias civiles stood impassive, their rifles slung over their shoulders. The man in the black trousers and evening shirt lay on the ground in a pool of blood. He lay on his back, a young man crouched behind him holding up his shoulders, as if preparing to lift him, and then perhaps the man would walk away. The distorted shape of the body and especially of the legs made it clear that he wouldn't walk again.

'He jumped out of a third floor window,' said one of the guardias civiles. 'Broke his neck and spine, I think.'

'We telephoned for an ambulance,' said the other guardia civil, adding, 'He's an Englishman.' He said that as an explanation.

The man had either taken off his pince-nez before he jumped or they had fallen when he dived. His pale blue eyes were wide open under fluttering white eyelashes. He seemed preoccupied. Then he saw me, his eyes lit up, and a smile appeared. He looked at me, wedged in the crowd, as you look at an intimate trusted friend of long standing who has come to rescue you in a dark moment.

'Coffee?' he whispered. I bent over him. 'Coffee?'

'You want coffee?'

'Coffee,' he said. 'Give me coffee.'

'I'll get you coffee at once.'

'Coffee,' he said, and he looked contented, for the old friend wouldn't let him down. That was what an old friend was for.

I rushed into the kitchen. The hotelkeeper was in the crowd, but his daughter was already making coffee for breakfast. 'Give me a cup of coffee for the love of God.'

'Is it for the dying man?'

'Yes, hurry.'

I ran out with the coffee, probably spilling half of it. I could have spilled the lot. Shaking their three cornered hats the guardias civiles said the man was dead. The youth had risen, and the dead man now lay flat, no paler than he had been in the afternoon. The ambulance arrived with a doctor who hardly bothered to examine him. 'This man is dead, take him away.'

Neither I nor anybody else succeeded in finding out who the man was. He had arrived with no luggage, no papers were found on him, and nobody ever came to look for him. He hadn't filled in the registration form the hotelkeeper had given him.

On my word I didn't know the bus time-table, I swear I had no stamp on me, and I couldn't have fetched the coffee quicker. Yet I still have remorse.

Another Englishman I knew in Pollensa had also had dealings with the guardias civiles. He was the son of a famous West End store owner, and fell in love in London with a German girl his parents disapproved of. So he married her, and they came to Pollensa to lead an idyllic life, hand in hand and heart to heart. She died, leaving him the most miserable of men. Her death drove him to drink, and on a night of misery he heard her calling him as he lay in bed. He slept naked. He rushed to the window, leaned out, and truly there she was, beckoning to him. He lived in a first floor room above a tavern owned by a thin, slightly hunched elderly man whom the painters referred to as the El Greco figure. The widower jumped out of the window, landed in the garden without hurting himself, thus could follow his wife. He was found in the morning sleeping naked and exhausted in a pigsty a few miles away. The farmer called the guardias who came, took him away, and their doctor put him into the lunatic asylum for criminals. When the news reached the El Greco figure he went to the asylum, and moved heaven and earth to get the widower out. Eventually he was allowed to take him on condition that he remained with the tavernkeeper who would be responsible for him. I came to know him in the tavern. The two men's relationship was touching. I liked the widower, but the one great snag was that he repeated the story of his night in the pigsty every time you saw him.

By November the painters had left, only the settlers remained. They were joined by a hefty man who wrote rousing stories for boys in *Chums*. Meeting him was as near as I got to literature on the island of George Sand.

On Christmas Eve a group of young anarchists tried to break up Midnight Mass in the port. The priest and the congregation threw them out, then the priest calmly turned back to the altar (we were still far from Vatican II), and continued the Mass. In January the island was at its best, las calmas de Enero, sea and sky deep blue, almond trees flowering and snow on the hills. In February I left.

I moved from Lodwick's flat after a week's stay because our relations were too perfect to last. In answer to an advertisement in the *Vanguardia* I found a flat in the Calle Bruch, owned by two Alsatian sisters, one the widow of a dentist, the other selling goods door to door. The widow related her husband's death on the day I moved in. He had died of a heart attack while riding in a tram. When she was notified she remembered that he had had three thousand pesetas in his wallet. Arriving at the police station she searched his pockets at once: the money was safe. 'Wasn't I lucky?' she said.

Lodwick had several friends in Barcelona outside Janés' circle, one a New Zealander who taught at the British Institute, another an Irish girl called Philomena who bitterly complained about Spaniards. If she sat down outside a café immediately she found some male seated at her side. If she pushed the chairs away they brought chairs from other tables. A week after I had moved into the Calle Bruch Lodwick took me to Janés' office to meet the Señorita Carmen back from Majorca.

It is difficult to describe a person who sits near me while I am writing these lines, and who has for twenty-one years been the perfect wife to me, giving me happiness beyond my imagination. At my first meeting with María del Carmen Rubio y Caparó I was struck by her hazel eyes with green reflections and her brown and golden hair. She didn't know a word of English at the time: seventeen years later she published a cookery book, *French Family Cooking* which she had written in English. Her mother Angelina Caparó who was still alive had been in her time one of the most famous actresses in Barcelona, her late father, Carlos Rubio, had been a playwright and actor-manager. There was a marquisate in the family, but they didn't use it.

At our first meeting we chatted about the Dordogne, then as we left her Lodwick said in a grim voice that was a speciality of his, 'With her it's either marriage or nothing.' I looked at him astonished since I had neither in mind. Two days later I returned to the office because the contract they had drawn up didn't include the terms Janés and I had agreed on. The person in charge of contracts hadn't a clue, Janés was out, and I said that as far as I was concerned the deal was off. 'I'll get Señorita Carmen,' bleated the man. 'She'll arrange everything, I'm sure she will.' Thus Carmen and I met for the second time. She did arrange everything, and I asked her to have a drink with me.

We were married on 15 December, first at the British Consulate General at ten o'clock, then at twelve in the church of the Immaculate Conception, a watertight marriage. However, Lodwick wasn't present. He had fallen out with me a fortnight before, the reason Francis Newhorne's visit to Barcelona. Francis had come to stay with me for a few days, brought out partly by curiosity about my future wife, chiefly to show his rich wife who had gone abroad that he too had a life of his own. Naturally, I took him to meet Lodwick, they didn't hit it off, and on top of it Francis dropped his glass which crashed to the floor. The next day I looked in on John alone, he received me, hissing that I had laughed when Francis broke the glass. 'I won't have you laugh at me,' he said opening the front door. Thus the man to whom I owed so much was absent at the wedding.

I couldn't help meditating during the ceremony about the many coincidences (as a nonbeliever would call them) that had brought Carmen and me together. If Margaret hadn't done Barry a favour way back in

Antibes Barry would have forgotten me by the time he ran into me in Cadiz; if Peter Baker hadn't commissioned the travel book on Spain it wouldn't have occurred to me to go to Spain again; if I hadn't chosen the Puerto there wouldn't have been Barry and Lodwick through him; if Lodwick had remained in Cadiz my trip to Barcelona and my meeting Janés, hence Carmen, wouldn't have taken place; and above it all that sudden decision in Ronda de Valencia to go to Barcelona. Today, twenty-one years later I find those coincidences even more miraculous.

We went first to Saragossa, where it was bitterly cold, then to Sitges, where we rented a villa. An old friend of Carmen's, Pedro Pruna the painter who in his youth had worked for Diaghilev, lived in Sitges, and we spent many nights with him, for like a vampire he came out only at night, though that was the only resemblance. Pruna had the shape of a beer barrel. He was of great erudition, his work was much admired, and we would sit and chat with him till the cows came home, leaving him at times at nine in the morning, with him trying to keep us back. Then he slept for three days, and the night sessions began again.

There was Alberto too, a vagabond at heart, earning his living by giving German lessons. He was a German himself, and his story was that he had been in the Waffen SS, had fought at Stalingrad, then deserting he crossed the whole of Europe to reach Spain. The truth was that he had been an army cook in a German unit stationed in the French Pyrénées during the Occupation, and he had climbed the Pyrénées when his unit had started back to Germany after the collapse. The self-appointed SS couldn't have harmed a fly. He enjoyed his hand to mouth existence, and once or twice I assisted at his German lessons which he gave in the back room of a café in the afternoon, usually to small children whom he couldn't control. They rushed around, played, shouted and laughed, and he pleaded with them in vain. The lessons were one peseta per head.

Our other friend was Oderico, a retired Spanish army officer, who came from Cadiz, and I talked to him about my dear Andalusia la baja for hours. Our next door neighbour was a Dutch sea captain who called on us one day to speak about ghosts he and his wife frequented. A lot of them had drowned at sea. He said that as though to prove they existed. 'Quite a few have accompanied me here,' he observed, smacking his lips. We didn't encourage him to come to the villa again.

As a wedding present Janés bought the Spanish rights of two more novels of mine. Carmen and I travelled frequently to Barcelona to see her mother, now and then I looked in on Janés, but never ran into Lod-wick. Two months after our marriage I received a letter from him. He had, he wrote, marked every day in his pocket diary so as to reach the end of two months, thus giving me the time I needed to settle down in my new existence. The two months being over he was free to write to tell me that he would like to see me again. Immediately I took train to Barcelona, and our friendship flourished once more. Yet I couldn't per-suade him to come out to Sitges. He seldom left his querencia, and eight-een months later when he was in London it was I who had to go to see him in the flat he had rented for a fortnight. The only ground he could stand on was his own.

Majorca had disappointed me in that genteel beachcombing amused without inspiring, so in the spring of 1935 I left for Paris. From child-hood onward Paris has meant a lot to me. It stood for complete indi-vidual liberty which I had been seeking ever since I escaped my bonds. On my arrival in Paris I went to a fairly cheap hotel in that still cheap city off the Boulevard de Courcelles, a neighbourhood I wasn't to fre-quent again. Later a woman friend found me two furnished rooms in the flat of some people she knew. Deep in their French small-nobility snob-bishness they would have been horrified if they had heard that I referred to them as furnished rooms, for in their eyes I was the friend's friend who occupied the spare rooms.

The first night I slept there one of the twin sons, Jean-Louis by name, sang the Marseillaise in his sleep. The next day a minister was to visit the lycée where the twelve-year-old twins studied, and they had spent the morning rehearsing for it. The twins slept in the room next to my bed-room. The flat was situated in a large late nineteenth-century house in the rue Lauriston in the XVI arrondissement. It was a quiet street in those pre-war years; the Gestapo was to reside there during the Occupation. The twin's father, M. de Mori, was a Corsican nobleman whose grand-father had moved to Paris. He didn't like being reminded of his Corsican origin. 'Can you see me pursuing a vendetta?' Frankly I couldn't. His wife told me that it was precisely fear of a vendetta that had driven the grandfather to the safety of Paris. M. de Mori drew for fashion maga-zines, and a pasha would have envied his treatment of his wife.

He was a slim elegant man, his well-cut overcoat had a mink collar. His wife wore her late mother-in-law's moth-eaten rabbit coat, which, thin though she was, made her look enormous. While M. de Mori sat in his study, drawing and smoking Havana cigars, she washed and cooked. I remember her as a perpetual washerwoman. Beside the twins they had a small daughter who spent her time running up and down the long passage outside my rooms. When the first of the month came M. de Mori invariably found some excuse to look in. Too proud to mention that the sordid monthly rent was due he chatted away till, in order to get rid of him, I produced the money. The rest of the month I hardly ever ran into him in the flat.

On Sunday mornings the family gathered together. Mme de Mori's mother and sister appeared, and they all went to Mass, M. de Mori leading with the twins, the mother and sister behind them, the rear brought up by Mme de Mori, dragging her daughter along. After Mass they walked the length of the Avenue Victor-Hugo, M. de Mori buying the ritual Sunday cake, then back to the flat, where Mme de Mori took off her Sunday dress to cook the lunch while her husband drank port with her mother and sister.

M. de Mori had a mistress, a little actress on whom he lavished his earnings. Whenever I was asked to an expensive and fashionable restaurant like the long vanished Larue, I invariably saw M. de Mori with his actress, compared with whom his wife was a poor country cousin.

In the rue Lauriston towards the Étoile was an English pub frequented almost exclusively by Britons living in Paris. If a jockey or stable lad came in from Chantilly he went straight to that pub; clerks working for English firms met in there regularly; the well-to-do English residents didn't patronise it. I would look in on my way to the town which in my eyes began at the Arc de Triomphe. It was like being in a pub in Islington except for the nightclub dancers who gathered there in the early evening. Already in the last century English girls were much appreciated by connoisseurs in Paris; the one-way traffic was constant between England and Paris nightclubs and cabarets. In that pub I met Gerda, a fair Cockney girl with green eyes and a likeable laugh. She had come over with a so-called troupe of female dancers. One of the girls had slipped on the nightclub floor and broken her leg, and the agent, who had booked them, declared that in the circumstances their contract was cancelled. Gerda didn't seem to mind. 'Nobody should worry about me,' she told me. 'I always fall on my feet.'

'You won't go far if you spend your time in this pub,' I said.

'I know what I'm doing.'

As a matter of fact she did because she soon stopped going to the pub, and when I inquired what had become of her I was told that she was living with a Frenchman who had all the money in the world. I was pleased for her sake, and forgot her. Many months later I left a party given by some Americans in the company of a Frenchman who had offered to drive me to the Butte-Montmartre, where I had a date. He inquired whether my date was important as we drove away. I said it wasn't, and could ring the person to say I was unable to come. 'Excellent,' the Frenchman said. 'Come to my flat for a drink. I'm living with an aristocratic English lady, the daughter of a lord, a first class catch, I can assure you.'

We motored to the Left Bank, where he lived in a block of flats near the Luxembourg Gardens. Wearing a Lanvin dress, Gerda opened the door to us. She looked at me, said under her breath, 'Keep your trap closed,' then held out her hand with a charming smile. I kept my trap closed in as much as I pretended that we hadn't met before, even asked her when she had come to Paris and what she thought of it. However, when he left the room for a moment she confessed she wasn't happy in her luxurious surroundings and was homesick. 'I'm not made for a life of ease,' she said.

Her lover was proud of her, repeating that every movement of hers showed the thoroughbred she was. They kept me for dinner, and when she saw me off she said, 'I doubt if you'll find me here much longer.' I ran into him at the American's house two months later. I asked after her, he turned his back on me, and I drew my conclusions from that.

I had a dog called Dodo, a Skye terrier bitch with orchid-like ears who, like Porky before her, became my inseparable companion, which meant that we had to walk the length and breadth of Paris when I couldn't afford a taxi because neither métro nor buses accepted dogs. It was worth it. In the mornings I took her to the Bois de Boulogne. At first when I heard something moving in the bushes I half expected a leopard to emerge. Soon I got accustomed to it being either a bird or some dog that wanted to make Dodo's acquaintance.

It was through Dodo that I met Isobel who became in a way responsible for my first published novel. Dodo and I were walking in the Bois, and we met another Skye terrier whom a young Englishwoman was holding on the leash. The two dogs sniffed each other, and the young woman and I exchanged a few words. Her face sparkled with the glow of youth; if she was annoyed or irritated (she often was both) it turned into the face of a hard middleaged woman, and the glow ironed out. We met again, and I found that she was a paying guest in a French family learning the language with which she seemed to make no progress. The dog was theirs. At our third meeting we decided to dine together. She was full of moods, could be bursting with gaiety one moment, and sulking the next. She also brooded over what you had said to her, searching for hidden insults. We could part at night as the best of friends; the next day I would meet a pair of angry, unforgiving grey eyes. After a time sulkiness and insult seeking left her, and all was going well. The people she stayed with were leaving for the weekend, so why shouldn't we go away too? She was all for it, and we chose Fontainebleau. We put up at a hotel facing the Escaliers des Adieux.

Georges d'Esparbès, the man of letters and father of my friend Jean, the painter, had for many years been the curator of the Castle. He was steeped in Napoleonic lore, and on the day of his retirement he dressed up the guides, guardians and gardeners in the gorgeous uniforms of the Emperor's marshals, made them stand on the staircase, and as he came down the steps he shook each by the hand before leaving for good.

I don't think that Isobel would have been impressed by that moving scene. None the less, the weekend was agreeable enough in the hotel filled with similar weekend couples and in the forest resplendent in its red, orange and gold autumn glory. As we strolled along a ride we heard the melancholic sounds of French hunting horns. Half expecting the royal hunt to appear with the King or Monseigneur riding behind the pack, we moved towards the horns. In a clearing about a dozen men in raincoats stood in a circle, blowing the instruments. They were clerks from a Paris insurance company on their yearly musical outing.

On Sunday evening we took a train back to Paris. Isobel sat silent in a corner seat, brooding. The compartment was full of returning weekenders, so I too kept silent. On arrival at the Gare de Lyon Isobel got out before me, but I caught up with her on the platform. She stopped, turned round to face me, and said in an angry voice, 'This is the end between us. I never want to see you again.'

'Then why did you come with me to Fontainebleau?' I asked not too brightly.

'To make sure that I loathed you. Don't follow me, I'm through with you.' (We had been to the cinema a few nights before. 'I'm through with you,' the heroine had said in the film we saw.)

Tossing her head she hurried away. I stared after her. The railway engines were hissing steam; the station smelt of it. Those engines mean business, and you knew that they would haul the trains through tunnels and viaducts, whistling in the night to reach the Mediterranean in the sunlight of the morning. Today trains no longer give that thrill: they look like tapeworms that have lost their heads. I shrugged my shoulders, then Dodo and I returned to the rue Lauriston.

Three mornings later Mme de Mori brought me a letter. It was from Isobel who, unsatisfied with what she had said at the Gare de Lyon, had filled three pages with insults. I became so angry and felt so keenly the injustice of it all that forgetting the writers I had aped in the past I sat down to write my first published novel, appropriately called *Angry Man's Tale*. I switched the action, if action it could be called, to Majorca, which proved that the French journalist in the Milan–Paris express had been right when he said that Majorca would inspire me. What he couldn't know was that Isobel would be needed to get the inspiration working. I wrote as though my pen were on fire. By the time I finished the novel my anger had left me, and I didn't give Isobel another thought.

The Popular Front was in full swing; strikes had become part and parcel of daily life; Hitler looked more and more menacing, yet nobody I met seemed to take any notice of it all. The French as well as the English in Paris were convinced that if Hitler attempted anything they would beat hell out of him, just as they had beaten it out of the Kaiser in the last war. They felt entitled to go about their business behind the safe Maginot Line.

I had decided to leave the rue Lauriston after I finished *Angry Man's Tale*, I had painter friends who lived on the Butte-Montmartre which wasn't yet tourist infected, and many painters and writers who had given the Butte its fame were still among the living, though a number of them had already left the area. The higgledy-piggledy twisting streets fascinated me. I was given the address of a furnished flat off the rue Lepic not far from the Moulin de la Galette. I entered a courtyard full of noisy children, some of them yelling in Italian. (Today it would be Spanish or Portuguese.) The concierge sent me to the second floor, I rang, heard footsteps, the door was flung open, and Mephistopheles appeared in flaming red. I was slightly taken aback. 'Don't be frightened,' he said. 'I'm only trying the suit on. I'll be playing the part at the end of the month.' I explained my errand. 'Come in,' he said.

Disorder reigned in the small flat which was dark because the windows gave on a narrow inner yard, but the ceiling was so high that you almost imagined yourself entering a church, though that was a first impression that swiftly wore off. Besides, churches don't smell of boeuf bourguignon. The door of the bedroom was open, and on the vast bed lay a woman in a transparent nightdress. She sat up as I appeared. 'We've a guest,' said Mephistopheles. She called she was coming, he bade me sit down, not so easy as the one armchair and the two chairs were piled high with clothes. 'Throw the things off,' he suggested. The woman came in with just a shawl thrown over her shoulders. She had a flat face not without charm, and a body with too many curves, all of them visible. 'What can we offer our guest?' he asked.

'We've only got wine,' she said. 'The bottle is somewhere in the room.'

They couldn't find it, so he went out to buy wine in the bistrot on the corner, leaving me alone with the unknown woman who immediately embarked on her tale of woe, her large firm breasts nearly touching my shoulder as she leaned forward to emphasise a point. She was called Paulette, he Raoul, they got on well in bed, he was an actor and an inconsiderate fool in as much as he had too high an opinion of himself. Instead of accepting any part that was offered him he spent his days waiting for his grand opportunity, which she was sure, would never come. The role of Mephistopheles was only for a fortnight; after that they would be without a sou again. Now he preened himself in his stupid get-up, he would stroll about in it till the first night with the entire neighbourhood laughing at him. He had a pleasing singing voice, and knew many old French songs. If he had a little sense he would make up to the restaurant and cabaret keepers in the Place du Tertre to be allowed to sing in their establishments, doing a song or two in each, then passing the hat round, and over one weekend he could earn more than he had ever earned as an actor. But not he. His accursed pride stopped him. She often thought of leaving him, the only reason she remained was his prowess in bed which, she assured me with shining eyes, was beyond belief. I vaguely wondered what all that had to do with my errand.

Raoul turned up with two litres of wine, and while we drank he spoke dreamily of the parts he wanted to play. We had reached the second litre when he asked, 'Didn't you say something about a flat?'

'I was told this flat is to be let.'

'No longer. I've got a fortnight's contract, so I can pay the landlord. We like the place.'

'It's so comfortable,' said Paulette.

They didn't let me go before the second bottle was emptied. I had to admit to myself that they and their way of life had impressed me. All my twenty-nine years I had been ruled by what is done, what isn't and what other people might think. Though I had cleaned trams in the São Paulo sheds the laws of behaviour laid down in my childhood had remained my rules and I was afraid of shocking the polite world despite my so-called freedom. Raoul and Paulette couldn't have cared less. Weren't they freer than I? Only on reflection I perceived that they too had their limitations and frontiers since he refused to earn his living by singing in restaurants. Two days later I moved into a hotel in the rue de Caulaincourt, and my life on the Butte began.

That hotel still exists but it has smartened up, losing in the process the charm it had possessed in my time. My room was on the second floor, and my next door neighbour was a darkhaired young man who, dressed as a woman, danced every night in a nightclub frequented by male homosexuals. Slowly he came to believe that indeed he was a female, told the chambermaid to address him as mademoiselle, and in daytime dressed as a woman too. Going from strength to strength he got himself operated on and became a woman with the obvious result, unforeseen by him, of being kicked out of the nightclub. He left the hotel because he couldn't afford it any more, and the last time I saw her she was a down-at-heel prostitute in Pigalle with all former glamour gone. Next to mademoiselle lived a Belgian journalist, Paul Méral, who had one of the best though twisted minds I ever knew. He was educated in Scotland, and André Gide once quoted a delicious definition of his. 'A friend is a person whom you let down whenever the occasion presents itself.' Paul Méral was to play an important part in my life at the beginning of the German Occupation.

On the floor above mine were two saxophone players who were allowed to practice only between two and five in the afternoon. They blew their saxophones from ten in the morning onward without anybody complaining. I spent little time in the hotel as I was mostly up on the Butte.

My guide and mentor on the Butte was Robert Naly whose acquaintance I made shortly after I appeared on the Butte. As I have said before in this book, he remains one of my dearest friends today, and his wit and brain I continue to admire. So did Margaret, and so does Carmen. His father was a Swiss banker, and the son started his career as a stockbroker in Paris. The Bourse didn't hold him long as his artist's soul rebelled against the rules I had respected for such a long time. He chucked it in, and went to live on the Butte, dedicating himself to painting, and adding to the gaiety of the nations. Through him I met Pedro Creixams, the Spanish Catalan painter, who had the gift of pleasing coupled with a strong personality, and was as admirable a cook as Naly. They were inseparable companions, and it was said on the Butte that Naly made as good as paella as Creixams a fondu. Now that Creixams is, alas, dead his paintings fetch quite high prices. He was four times married, his four wives remaining as devoted to him after divorce as in the heyday of their marriage. Pedro used to talk to me about a Barcelona actress, whose name I didn't retain, with whom he had been deeply in love in his youth despite her being much older than he.

Through Pedro I met Maurice Utrillo who long after his death was to play an important part in my life. You couldn't live on the Butte without being steeped in the Utrillo legend. Here he lay dead drunk in the snow; over there the children of the Butte attacked him while he painted the street; yonder he was arrested for drunkenness and taken to the police station either to be beaten up or ordered by the commissaire to paint a picture for him. The basis of the legend wasn't only his drinking: he had been several times in lunatic asylums. Moreover, on the Butte lived his mother, Suzanne Valadon, an eccentric in her own right, and one of the best female painters there ever was. She said to me one evening that she felt sorry for me because I had such a lot of years in front of me to keep on writing. 'One ought to write or paint just once, and die immediately. Then nobody could say that one hasn't fulfilled one's promise.' Utrillo's stepfather, André Utter, was younger than his stepson. He had started life as a plumber, took later to painting, and if his wife and stepson hadn't towered above him he would have been considered a fine painter. Utter dressed ostentatiously, believing that he looked like a country gentleman, in red plus-fours and white gaiters, and was invariably accompanied by dogs. He became a friend of mine.

At the time I met Utrillo he no longer lived on the Butte. His overbearing, fat harpy of a wife, Lucie Valore, who painted in his shadow, kept him practically sequestrated in a suburban villa, where he worked for her, painting like an automaton to keep her in luxury. Before their marriage Utrillo had done the same for his mother and Utter. Now and again Lucie Valore brought Utrillo to the Butte. She called herself the Empress of Montmartre, and few people were as detested as she.

Creixams had a studio in the rue Gabrielle. One afternoon I looked in on him for a chat. 'Maurice Utrillo is coming here,' he said. 'Don't make any sudden movement or gesture. He's petrified by a sudden movement. It reminds him of the times he was arrested.' Creixams made gestures that would have reminded Don Quixote of windmills, causing him to charge forthwith. Valore, I gathered, was to leave Utrillo in the studio while she attended to some important business connected with an exhibition. She had asked Pedro on the telephone to give him watered wine only. They arrived, I was introduced (her I knew already), Valore went, and Utrillo remained in the doorway, rubbing his hands. He had shaken hands with me on arrival, taking mine in both of his without pressing it or looking at me.

'Come, sit down, Maurice,' said Creixams, putting out his right hand to take Utrillo by the arm. Utrillo recoiled, Creixams stepped forward, Utrillo started backing to the landing. The door had been left open as Utrillo suffered from claustrophobia. Creixams backed to give him confidence, Utrillo came forward, Creixams grabbed his arm, Utrillo jumped, Creixams gave him his huge, warm smile, and said coaxingly, 'I have wine for you Maurice. Good ordinary pinard.'

I remained motionless in the window till Creixams called to me to sit down with them. We sat at a small table, drinking watered wine, but as Pedro was a caballero the wine wasn't too much watered. Now and then he hit Utrillo on the shoulder in his exuberant manner. Utrillo winced.

I had expected Utrillo to look and behave as he did. I don't think there existed anybody on the Butte who didn't know everything that was to be known about him. Only a few days before Francis Carco, the writer, had observed in my presence, 'Utrillo doesn't exist. His legend invented him.' He was, of course, referring to the man not the painter. The man reminded me of an incredibly seedy actor who hadn't seen work for a long time. What struck me most was the essence of him, as though he were made of India rubber, no bones, only rubber. The red ribbon of the Legion of Honour was sewn to his lapel. He was shaved; usually he wasn't. His pale blue eyes were on the open door, he closed them when he drank, and he drank little. His Adam's apple was in evidence. I felt in a vacuum with him.

Suddenly he became interested in me. 'How tall are you?' he asked. I said I was one metre eighty-nine. 'I'm one metre seventy-four.' He returned to the subject a little later. 'One metre and eighty-nine is very tall.'

The next time I saw him he asked me again how tall I was. One day I was lunching at La Bonne Franquette on the Butte, Utrillo sat with

Valore and Naly at the next table. They asked me over, and Utrillo inquired how tall I was. The very last time I saw him, which was in the early fifties, they were in their car in the Place du Tertre, I in a bar, and Valore came in and called me out. I was in her good graces because she wanted me to write her life, her telling me naturally how to write it, which I had no intention of doing. Later we fell out on account of that. Utrillo sat in deep gloom in the tonneau, looking not so much ravaged as savaged by the years that seemed to have no meaning for him any more. 'How tall are you?' he asked.

Sitges in winter was like a zoo, the animals sleeping, grunting, stretching themselves, sharpening their claws as they wait for the morning and the visitors. Most of the hotels, restaurants and bars were closed and the bona fide inhabitants went about their business, praising the quiet life innocent of tourists, yet counting the days before they would descend on them again.

At the end of February Carmen's mother died. In Spain women didn't go to funerals, but sat at home weeping as was expected from them. Carmen, her only child, went to her funeral which shocked many of her friends. 'Now she can just as well go to England,' I overheard one of them saying. It was a beautiful Mediterranean day, and from the cemetery of Montjuich I gazed out to the blue sea above which shone the sun of the spring her mother wouldn't see. With her gone Carmen had no ties left in Spain. Her mother too had been an only daughter, her father an only son, and I often think that our marriage was greatly helped by both of us being unhampered and unencumbered by relations. We decided to stay in Sitges till after Easter.

One day in March we were in a bar in Barcelona, and suddenly I was pushed from behind. I veered round to look into Pedro Creixams' laughing face. He had come to Barcelona for an exhibition of his paintings. I introduced him to Carmen, and it turned out that the actress he had been in love with in his youth was no other than Carmen's mother. My meeting Pedro in Spain gave me a strange sensation. It was a reminder that another world existed outside the country I' had entered two years before. Though an Englishman Lodwick too belonged to the world I had chosen when to escape from my mournful self I had come to the Peninsula. A Spaniard had to dig me in the back to make me aware that I had an existence outside Spain, and my life hadn't begun two years ago with nothing before. As with all my conclusions it took me another year to leave Spain.

Abruptly sunny Sitges became a town of frost. It snowed, it froze, and an ice packed wind howled. Thinking of the harm the frost could do the town's reputation in foreigners' eyes the natives swore that there hadn't been anything like it since the coming of the Romans. Our villa was built for summer, there was no central heating, only a small fireplace, so we moved to the Hotel Colon facing the cathedral of Barcelona till the weather was mild again. Then Easter arrived, and we left for Madrid, where the pictures in the Prado deigned to speak to me since I wasn't alone any longer..

Granada was the next stop in our progress through Spain. On the day of our arrival the Sierra Nevada struck as though it had waited for us. It was afternoon, Carmen was at the hairdresser, and I sat in front of a café, a gipsy shoeblack polishing my shoes. All of a sudden the glass on the table began to dance, then the table joined in, and I heard a noise that sounded like heavy chains being pulled inside the earth. I had a sensation of helplessness. The shoeblack jumped up, his face distorted by fear. 'The spirits are coming out of the earth,' he shouted, a perfect description. Then he made off, leaving his box and utensils. At the other tables the customers threw themselves on the ground, the passersby fled without knowing where to flee, but I remained seated, strapped to the chair by my helplessness. The chains made a growling noise, then, as if tired of it, the table and the glass stopped dancing, the customers on the ground raised their heads, and they slowly got up, the lot of them laughing, the Andalusian's answer to matters beyond his comprehension. The shoe-black returned, finished polishing my shoes, and Carmen appeared. She was under the drier when the earth had started moving. Laughter was general till about an hour later when the radio announced that in an outlying village over two hundred people had been killed by the earth-quake. She noticed nothing till the hairdresser lifted the drier, and pre-sented her with a glass of brandy. 'Because of the earthquake,' he said.

The Alhambra and the Generalife moved us as much as leaving it had moved Boabdil to tears. I had lived too long in Andalusia to be impressed by the sham gipsy gaiety of the Sacro Monte. If tourists approached the gipsies jumped to life, and started singing and clapping exactly as was expected from them. When the tourists left they became their morose selves, counting and quarrelling over the money.

From Granada we went to Seville, and from Seville to the Puerto, where great disappointment awaited me. At the station I saw Caco whom I had known as a poor urchin to whom you gave a peseta when he ran you an errand. Now he was wearing trousers with an American cut and a khaki jacket. He was smoking a cigar. 'I don't think, Don Pedro,' he said, 'that you'll find room in the Loreto. The American engineers are staying there.'

Carmen and I walked through the town I had loved, the streets as it was noon as quiet as before. We went up to the library, where Don Luís received us with a long face, saying, 'You won't recognise the place. Half the scum of the Mediterranean is here. Luckily in the daytime they're working for the Americans in Rota. Cayetano opens the Alegría only towards the evening. It wasn't worth your while to come back.'

It wasn't. Without rolling her eyes Rosario informed me that she hadn't a room for us, everything was booked for a year, and she was seriously considering building a second hotel. 'Besides, the prices aren't the same as in your time.' We decided to move on to Cadiz in the evening.

Cayetano opened only at six o'clock. Within a few minutes the Alegría was invaded and taken over by the American Foreign Legion as the men who worked for them were to be known in Spain, a noisy lot of cut-throats (so they looked), throwing their money about. The din they made was terrific, and they all fancied themselves as heroes of the Far West, though probably not one of them knew a word of English. In a corner sat the amigos, subdued and depressed, playing dominoes as if it were a sad task of the past, making me think of Francis Thomson.

And a ghostly batsman plays to the bowling of a ghost,
And I look through my tears on a soundless, clapping host . . .

There was nothing soundless about the noisy legionaries. That night I said goodbye to the dear Puerto I no longer recognised.

From Cadiz Carmen and I travelled back to Madrid, then went to a delightful village, Piedralaves, a hundred kilometres west of Madrid because I wanted to write a novel for which I needed the peace and calm you find in no Spanish town. Piedralaves had all the peace and calm you could ask for, except for the flies that reminded me of the coming of the locusts in Kenya. One afternoon I swatted eighty-four in our hotel room.

The local white-haired priest, Don Tirso, had been present at the death of Joselito, the legendary torero, at Talavera de la Reina in 1919.

132

'He was drunk already in the train,' he told us. 'When we arrived in Talavera I said to myself I'd better go to the corrida, though I'd first no intention of doing so, because I might be needed.' And he was.

On Whit Sunday the peasants of Piedralaves left their fields to go drinking, eating and singing in the hills, thus leaving their donkeys unattended, and the donkeys had their feast too, racing round in groups, jumping the low walls, gambolling in orchards, paying calls on each other. 'The Pentecost of the donkeys,' Carmen said.

When the novel was well advanced we went to Ávila. Coming through the gate of the ramparts in the evening I was energetically pushed from behind. The crowd moving out of the centre of the town was large at that hour. I looked over my shoulder: it was a donkey, as much in a hurry as the others. An English film company was shooting a picture in Ávila, and I ran into an actor and scriptwriter I had known in London as if to remind me again that there was a world I used to belong to beyond the Pyrénées.

Salamanca was our next stop, and now that I wasn't alone I admired that city twice as much as on the first occasion. We spent the summer in Galicia in a fishing village called Bayona a few miles out of Vigo. In the mornings women appeared one by one, each carrying fish in a bucket balanced on her head. She put down the bucket, out came the hotel-restaurant keeper, and named a figure. If she thought it high enough she accepted, and her peregrination came to an end. If she didn't she continued (the restaurants were in a row on the waterfront) till either she got the price she named or was forced to lower it. If she couldn't get one that suited her she returned to the first bidder who paid the sum he had offered her.

'It took me a long time to learn the art,' said our hotelkeeper who though Gallego by origin was born in Uruguay. 'In the beginning I offered too low a price, and was often left without fish. Then I offered too high and my colleagues laughed at me.'

In our hotel stayed a high official of the Banco de España, Don Eugenio, with an enormous wife and fat stepdaughter. 'I married her,' he said to me, 'when she became a rich widow. In our great Spain officials aren't too well paid.' They seemed to get on well.

We visited the rías between Vigo and La Coruña, and listened to people speaking of the gold and silver buried in the deep bottom in the galleons sunk by el pirata Drake as the Spaniards refer to Sir Francis. When summer ended we took ship to Cadiz, and saw dolphins by the hundred near Cape St Vincent. From Cadiz we travelled by coach to Algeciras, passing Trafalgar on the way. Then came Gibraltar for a day, then Málaga for which I didn't care. If you are well acquainted with the Atlantic side of Andalusia the Mediterranean side leaves you unimpressed. At least so it was in my case.

After a few days in Alicante we boarded the train for Madrid, and took a furnished flat for the winter in the Calle Vallehermoso. Our acquaintances wrinkled their noses because there were too many food shops in the street. As a matter of fact, a poulterer who killed his chicken on the premises was next to our front door. The chickens' agony often mounted if our windows were open.

Madrid was a sort of antichamber to Carmen's and my next move. I ran into my old friend Robin John, Augustus John's eldest son, also into Archy Lyall, who had written two excellent guide books, one about Rome, the other Madrid, and in their company the mild winter of 1957 went by, I feeling less and less tied to Spain, and Carmen wishing to know England which she had never seen. And as our life together progressed I realised that Spain had given me all I could have asked from it. In fact, more.

In March we decided to go to England. It was a great relief to know that I had listened to my own wish at last. We said goodbye to Avelina, our excellent maid, who saw us off at the station. We entrained for Barcelona for Carmen to say goodbye to her friends and for me to see Lodwick with whom I had corresponded during our journey through Spain. In Barcelona we lunched with him and Janés, Lodwick came to the station, and the next morning snow fell on Notre-Dame as our taxi swished by. Two days later we landed in Dover. 'How silent it is,' was Carmen's first impression of England.

Lodwick came to London in the summer of 1958, and took a house for a fortnight in Camden Hill. We were staying with a friend in Dorset, yet immediately hurried to London to be with him. Our friendship was at its climax, and it was the last time I saw him.

On a wet spring day in 1959, Janés, Janés' brother, a cousin and Janés' printer, five all told, motored to a fiesta in the countryside. It had rained hard, and the roads were slippery. On their way back the car hit a tree. They were all killed on the spot except John Lodwick who lingered on for a few more days. I was in the Hastings to London train when opening *The Times* I saw his obituary notice. I mourn him, and often find myself speaking to him.

7

I believe that my formative years were Kenya first, then the Butte-Montmartre. In Kenya I found my vocation, on the Butte I got to know people. By people I mean persons whom I came to understand outside my terms of reference, so to speak. They had nothing to do with my life or interests, they moved outside my orbit, yet rubbing shoulders with them at odd moments I learned the writer's trade, that is to see beyond his own kind.

The Marquis was called Marquis because he wore spats, his concubine was named Douce Colombe (sweet dove) because she was a shrew and made his life intolerable. He was an engraver, and she would go to the studio to throw things at him. She died of a heart attack, and the Marquis went into all the bistrots of the Butte to announce the passing on of the best spouse a man ever had. He implored everybody who was willing to listen to turn up at the funeral. He gave the name of the cemetery and the time of the funeral. Douce Colombe was taken to the cemetery while the Marquis drowned his sorrow on the Butte. On the day of the burial he appeared in the chapelle ardente full of misery and beaujolais. Only one mourner was present, an unknown bearded man, wearing a bowler. The Marquis frowned at the stranger who frowned back. Not one of the friends was in sight.

When the coffin was taken to the grave the Marquis and the bearded stranger walked alone behind it. The glances they exchanged were full of venom. So she had a lover, the Marquis said to himself. As the coffin was lowered into the grave the stranger burst into tears. 'This is too much,' the Marquis shouted, boxing the stranger's ears. The stranger hit back, and the gravediggers had to separate them. The Marquis rushed out of the cemetery, took a taxi straight to the Place du Tertre, where he found the friends in the Choppe du Tertre, drinking like men who had done their duty.

'You weren't there,' cried the Marquis.

'You weren't there,' they answered.

The fuddled Marquis had gone to the wrong cemetery.

I often saw a young man called Jacques. He was twenty, drew well, and the painters I knew thought he would go a long way. He had fair hair, clear blue eyes and the complexion of a country girl. He was modest and a dedicated listener. His father was a rich businessman who lived in the rue de Caulaincourt not far from my hotel, and being an only son Jacques was spoiled by his parents. At that time it was the nightly habit of the ponces of Pigalle to come up to the Butte after two in the morning. Most of them were from the Midi or Corsica, well-behaved quiet men in the bistrots, almost timid in their fear of getting into trouble. A fight might draw the police's attention to them, which was the last thing they wanted. Now and again they were accompanied by one or two streetwalkers whom they 'protected'. The girls too conducted themselves in exemplary fashion, and the lot of them kept their distance.

Jacques and I often walked back together to the rue de Caulaincourt, and one night he informed me that he intended to get married to an adorable girl. I asked whether I knew her, he said I didn't, but he would introduce me to her the next afternoon in a café in our street. I turned up, found the girl pretty though in a coarse way, and was unimpressed by her refined manners which were too good to be true. They left the café before me. I went up to the counter for a glass of wine. 'Do you know who that girl was?' the cafékeeper said. I shook my head. 'She's a little prostitute who used to go up to the Butte after plying her trade in Pigalle, but she has given up looking for customers. I bet your friend Jacques gives her enough to live on.' I didn't tell him that Jacques spoke of marrying her. The next time I walked back with Jacques I asked him what the girl's profession was. Did she work in an office? Calmly Jacques confirmed all the cafékeeper had said. 'We love each other, and nothing else matters.' As he wasn't of age I asked whether his parents had given their consent. 'I don't see why they should know about her past,' said Jacques. 'All I said was that she's of humble origin but that couldn't matter since I loved her. I took her to them last week and they seemed to like her. My father said he would think it over. He's too fond of me to say no.'

What Jacques didn't know was that his father had started to make inquiries, in fact had engaged a private detective who went straight to the village in the Hérault where she was born. The rest was easy, and soon the father found out that she had earned her living as an unregistered prostitute till she met Jacques who took a small flat for her. Believing that his son was unacquainted with his love's murky past he summoned Jacques into his presence, and told him what the detective had found out. Jacques answered that he had known it from the start. The father got angry, called him an idiot, and said he would never let his son marry a whore. Jacques retorted that he would marry her when he came of age. In that case he wouldn't be given another centime. The father had the upper hand since Jacques' sole ambition was to become a painter for which he needed his father's help. Moreover, he was devoted to his parents.

He came up to the Butte rather late that night, smiling as was his wont. We walked back together, and he said before we separated in the rue de Caulaincourt that there was a little trouble because his father had found out about the girl's past. 'What will you do?' I asked.

'I think I can settle the matter satisfactorily.'

We wished each other good night, I went into the hotel, he home.

In the morning he called on the tradesmen in the neighbourhood with whom he had accounts to settle h   ills. He owed the newsvendor a few sous which he paid too. Then he strolled slowly to the family house, took the lift to his apartment, and shot himself with his father's shotgun. When his mother rushed in he was already dead. What impressed people most on the Butte was that he hadn't forgotten his tiny bill with the newsvendor.

I ran into the father a month later in the street. I had met him with Jacques. As I switched on a mournful smile he muttered, 'I don't want to hear a word,' and hurried on. I understand he is still alive.

In the rue de Caulaincourt lived a sordid couple who kept a small bar not far from my hotel. Gaston, the husband, was from Marseilles, Mado, the wife, from Lorraine. He was short, nimble and dark, she fat, stodgy and fairhaired. She worked in the bar, whereas he spent his time playing dice with the customers. He often lost which upset Mado because they hardly managed to make both ends meet. 'He'll lose the bar if he goes on like this,' she said, and begged the customers not to dice with him. She told me one evening that he had lost all they had earned that day. For some obscure reason I became her confidant, and she unburdened herself whenever she saw me. Thus I found out that Gaston had a mistress, and on many nights he stayed out without bothering to invent an excuse. If she asked him where he had been, 'With my mistress,' was his answer.

One day I saw her in tears behind the counter. Gaston was out. 'No woman has ever been insulted like me,' she wept. 'He brought her home last night. She's a waitress, and has been kicked out of her lodgings. He calmly told me that as she had nowhere to sleep she'd share our bed, and if I didn't like it I could get out.'

'What did you do?'

'I couldn't do anything. I've got no money. Anyway, our tiny flat is in my name, and I refuse to surrender it to them. We've only one bed, even so they won't force me out. There's nothing he'd like more.'

'The three of you slept together?'

'Slept together?' she cried, her large bosom heaving. 'I couldn't sleep a wink. They made love the whole night. How could I sleep with the bed shaking all the time?'

Gaston appeared, looking as pleased as a cat that has caught a mouse then drunk a bowl of milk. She went to the kitchen to prepare his lunch. A fortnight later I looked in again, and asked her whether the mistress still slept with them. 'Yes,' she said, but looked less wretched.

I went over to England for a month, and one of the first people I ran into on my return to the Butte was Gaston. 'What are you doing up here?' I asked.

'I work as a waiter in a restaurant.'

'What about your bar?'

'Left it. Life became intolerable.'

'And Mado?'

'She's still there, the bitch.'

On my way to the hotel I popped into the bar. It had a much gayer appearance, and I hardly recognised Mado who was better dressed, her hair no longer an untidy haystack. A slim, dark-haired girl stood with her behind the bar. 'This is Arlette,' Mado said. 'She's taken Gaston's place.' They split their sides with laughter. I mentioned that I had seen Gaston on the Butte. 'We don't mind what he does,' Mado said. 'We're rid of him, and now we're prospering.'

A lugubrious and ponderous art dealer who lived in that house joined me at the bar, and when I left he walked with me as far as my hotel. 'Have you guessed?' he asked.

'Guessed what?'

'Mado and Arlette. It's a very amusing story. Arlette is the girl whom Gaston brought home, and who slept in the same bed with them. Gaston thought he was in clover, having everything his own way. He bashed Arlette in cold blood, not caring a damn what Mado felt. When he wanted to sleep he slept next to Arlette on the edge of the bed so as not to have to touch Mado. Listening to Arlette's love cries and panting, and feeling her body beside hers, Mado fell in love with her. It sounds almost logical. In the mornings Gaston was the first to go, leaving the two women alone. I've no idea how it started, and if I asked them they would lie to me. Maybe it tickled Arlette to have husband and wife in love with her. But then she discovered that she preferred it with the wife. They decided to get rid of Gaston which wasn't difficult as the bar and the flat belong to Mado. Gaston is a Marseillais, a southerner, and southerners have exaggerated male pride. For a male to be cuckolded by a female is worse than death in his eyes. So you can imagine what he felt when Arlette told him that she didn't want him any more because she loved Mado. He left the flat and the bar, and for nothing on earth would he go near them ever again. His male pride was in smithereens. He had nowhere to sleep, I put him up for the night. He told me the whole story, shrieking with rage. He made a priceless remark. "If she'd been a man I'd have killed her." Did he mean Mado or Arlette?'

'Arlette, I think.'

'Mado,' the art dealer said.

'Both,' I laughed.

Mado and Arlette were still together when I came back after the war. A few years later I looked in, but found a new proprietor who told me that they had left for Mado's village in Lorraine, where they intended to retire.

A pretentious, goodlooking fellow called Francis lived with his little mistress in the rue Norvins, a street leading to the Place du Tertre. He had been a ponce in Casablanca, his wife kept a night club there, and the little mistress, whom he had picked up during a journey to Lille, was his constant companion since he came to Paris, in fact cooked and cleaned for him. Suddenly Francis died in his sleep, and a few days after the funeral his wife arrived from Casablanca. Lisette, the mistress, was still in the flat. The wife went to the Choppe du Tertre, which had been her husband's favourite haunt, and where landlord and customers knew him well. I was in the Choppe when she came in, well-dressed and bejewelled, looking every inch the prostitute who had made good. 'I'm going to get the police to chuck that creature out of the flat,' she said. 'The flat is mine now.'

A fat dentist who poked his nose into everybody's affairs and who was to collaborate wholeheartedly with the Germans during the

Occupation, decided to act as go-between. It was difficult to understand his words because he never took his pipe out of his mouth. None the less, I gathered that he would call Lisette, Mme Francis should wait, and he was sure that all could be arranged without the police being called in. I remained at the counter, Mme Francis sat down, and a few minutes later the dentist arrived back with little Lisette who seemed to have shrunk (if that were possible) since her lover's death. The three of them gathered round the table, a truly Balzacian scene, Lisette crushed, the wife triumphant, and the fat dentist playing the part of the go-between with relish. The dentist called for wine, Mme Francis tossed hers down, Lisette didn't touch her glass, and the dentist drank its contents after he had drunk his own. He did most of the talking. Eventually he came to the bar, and whispered, 'It's all settled. Mme Francis has been wonderfully generous. Lisette can take her belongings away, and she'll be given a small sum, a perfect arrangement.'

Mme Francis rose, Lisette too. The wife shook her hand saying, 'Goodbye, mademoiselle.' Lisette said, 'Goodbye, madame.' The dentist left with the wife, Lisette came to the counter, and feeling sorry for her I offered her a drink. 'What will you do now?' I asked.

'I came from nowhere and I'm going back to it.'

No one ever saw her on the Butte again.

Though I believed that as a writer I found a new dimension by meeting people like the unfortunate Jacques or sordid Gaston I soon discovered that the Butte, that is the people, gave themselves far more importance than they were entitled to. I speak about those who gravitated round the men of letters and painters who still frequented the Butte which had lost much of its importance since the twenties. If Jacques hadn't imbibed the legend of the Butte he might not have killed himself; if Lisette hadn't felt the romance of the Butte she might have stood up to Mme Francis. On the other hand, the writers and painters who remained were aware that the Butte's legend was built by those who had been there long before them. To be a Montmartre painter evoked the Bateau Lavoir, and you thought of Picasso who had long ago gone from the Butte. Even Utrillo had been bundled away by Lucie Valore. If you thought of the writers of the Butte you evoked the great period of the Lapin Agile with Warnod, Max Jacob, Apollinaire, Dorgelès, Carco and Mac Orlan. However, the last three, who were still alive, came to the Butte only as visitors now. The rest that couldn't afford to leave the Butte continued to cash in on the success of the past. But they were gay and witty, and tried to live up to the fame of a period that had been created by others. There were several among them whose talent by no means needed the past.

If you went into town you went to Paris; when you returned you were back home. There always was someone on the Butte to chat, lunch or dine with. You listened to talk about famous men, either dead or departed ages ago, as if they were sitting at the table with you. It was Pablo for Picasso, Guillaume for Apollinaire. People acted as if Aristide Bruant had written his ballads about them. If you left your mistress you left her in front of your friends; if you fell in love all and sundry had to witness it. Privacy was practically unknown.

A wag of the Butte observed that one leaves the Butte either in a taxi or in a hearse, meaning that only the poor and unsuccessful stayed for long. I came to know many human wrecks who didn't make good like Utrillo. To drink, fight and, fall flat in the street doesn't always make a famous painter. I met painters who got nowhere, writers who remained unpublished, actors who hadn't even the chance to fail. Above them were painters like Naly and Creixams, and writers like Carco and Marcel Aymé, men who didn't need picturesque scenery to pursue their creative work. By elimination I came to spend most of my time with them.

Marcel Aymé whom I much admire as a writer, came regularly to the Butte on Sundays to play dominoes. If he lost he paid the round, if he won he said he wasn't thirsty. He liked listening to little crooks, sham adventurers and their like. They used to invent criminal exploits to keep him listening to them. He hardly spoke, and when he died a French journalist who had to write his obituary called me, saying he was in a quandary. Though he had been acquainted with him he couldn't quote a word he said for he never spoke. 'You often saw him. Did he ever say anything to you that I could use?'

'He never spoke to me either.'

And that was the truth, for that excellent, witty writer had no conversation whatever, not because he had nothing to say, but simply because he didn't feel like talking. A waste of time, he must have thought.

A striking figure in Naly's crowd was Georges Papazoff, the Bulgarian painter, who had come to Paris and Montmartre before the first world war. His abstract painting was admirable, and he had an impressive presence what with a deep voice, bushy eyebrows and a mane any lion would envy. He could hold forth for hours on the Chinaman's ancestor worship, bemoaning the fact that we in the West imitated him without resembling him in any way. The night Jules Pascin committed suicide, first cutting his veins with a razor blade, then hanging himself to make doubly sure, Papazoff, his fellow countryman, arrived, rang the bell, knocked and then banged on the door. He thought that Pascin expected an unwelcome visitor for whom he wouldn't open the door. So Papazoff shouted through the keyhole, 'Pascin, Pascin, c'est moi.' Papazoff had a voice that could wake the dead. It wasn't successful in this instance. Papazoff wrote a book about Pascin, entitled *Pascin, Pascin, c'est moi*. He once read me a passage of it and burst into tears in the middle. After the last war he gave up painting, and took to selling pictures, dying a rich art dealer in the South of France a few years ago.

Through Naly too I met Victor Gilles, the concert pianist, who lived in the rue Jouffroy near the Parc Monceau, his house filled with quaint treasures. 'This,' he would say, 'is the shirt poor, saintly Louis XVI wore when he was guillotined.' Then he would drop the shirt back into the dark chest. His bath was the one Marat sat in when Charlotte Corday killed him. 'When I sit in the bath,' Gilles would say in a dreamy voice, 'I try to feel what Marat felt when she appeared.' He owned Chopin's cloak which he threw over his shoulders on Wednesdays, for on Wednesdays in his fine music room he gave private concerts for about thirty guests. I was regularly invited to them.

Victor Gilles was cleanshaven, broad, his hair dyed silver, and he gave you the impression of an amiable dowager till he sat down at the piano. Then you forgot the dowager, only Chopin, Liszt or Debussy existed. Often he sobbed while he played. The concerts started straight after lunch. When you arrived the pale, blond butler took you into the dining room. At the top of the table sat Gilles, a silver tankard filled with champagne in front of him, his old gouvernante in a black dress behind him, her hand on his shoulder. Nothing was offered to the chosen few who were allowed into the dining room. Marcel Seigne, an antique dealer who was the erstwhile Castor to his quondam Pollux, would peep into the music room, then report that it was filling up. When it was full, and Seigne said they were all impatient to see the master Gilles rose, smiling. 'I'm going to have a bath,' he said, and went upstairs to commune with Marat or Charlotte Corday, leaving the guests waiting another half hour. Once I arrived a little late, and as I approached the front door I saw him emerge. 'They're all here,' he said. 'Come and have a drink with me in the café yonder.'

When he made his entrance in the vast music room the guests rose, he waved to them, looking enormous with Chopin's cloak over his shoulders. He had a few private pupils who paid a fortune for the honour. Not only did he teach them to play but to sing too. On my first visit the performance started with an angular Alsatian baroness killing a Schubert song. Seigne bent over me, whispering, 'Ici ça commence toujours avec des emmerdeurs.' When the pupils had done their turn Gilles sat down at the piano, crossed himself, muttered a few inaudible words, then began to play, now and then laughing or bursting into tears. The gouvernante, who stood beside him, wiped his tears with a lace handkerchief. Halfway through he rose, went into the next room he called his boudoir, lay down on the sofa, and again only the chosen few were allowed into his presence. Resting his vast body on the sofa he spoke whimsically about Chopin who visited him in his dreams or about Michel, the policeman, with whom he was in love, and whom he would watch in secret while he directed traffic. 'More beautiful than Apollo Belvedere,' he sighed. Then he returned to the music room for the second half of the concert. At the end he either mingled with his guests for a few minutes or said he would be back in a minute, and take a taxi waiting outside to a restaurant, where he had a date with Michel. The disconsolate guests slowly drifted away.

The last time I saw him was at the beginning of the Occupation. He assured me he would rather be Anglaise than Allemande.

To those concerts Paul Méral, the Belgian journalist, came from time to time not because he loved music but because he was the lover of an actress of the Théâtre-Français who was a friend of Gilles. She was a remarkably well-groomed woman with the grand manners of the House of Molière. Méral was usually unwashed, and looked like a toad. At that time she was married to a famous architect who coined money, whereas the loved one was usually broke. In her husband's absence she would take one of his suits (they were the same size as Méral's), and carry it to the hotel. Méral changed into it, and then she took the one he had worn to the cleaners because Méral dirtied any suit he wore, replacing it in her husband's wardrobe only after it had been cleaned. She did that every fortnight or so. At a cocktail party the husband and she gave in their conspicuously modern but small flat, for some reason or other the built-in wardrobe was opened. Méral pointed at the suits hanging in a row. 'Our suits,' he said.

When she left her husband she bought a house in the avenue Junot.

Méral spent most of his time there, and the elegant woman continued loving the toad who thought the world was his domain. I have to admit that he was the only person I knew who predicted the disasters of 1940. Like everybody else I laughed at him. He decided he would write an important book about the decay of the Third Republic, to do so he needed the peace of the countryside, and lyrically he evoked birds and trees. She took a small country house near Bordeaux to give him the bucolic peace he craved. His country life consisted of rising at noon with a hangover that prevented him from eating anything. Early in the afternoon he rang for a taxi that took him into Bordeaux to crawl from one bar to the other, coming back in the same cab at dawn, waking her up to pay the fare. After a month of it she returned to the Butte.

He stayed on till his credit ran out. Then he too came back, bursting into my hotel room early in the morning, asking for money for the taxi that had brought him from the station. She refused to have anything more to do with him, whereas he, so much in keeping with him, discovered that he loved her to distraction. I witnessed a sad scene one afternoon outside the Mère Catherine in the Place du Tertre. The actress sat with Creixams, Naly, Papazoff and me. Méral appeared with bloodshot eyes, looking as if he had risen straight out of a dustbin, came to a halt in front of the table, his face red and shining with perspiration. He just stood, staring at her. 'You should go away, Paul,' Naly or Creixams said. 'You only annoy her.'

'Do I annoy you?'

She didn't answer, in fact she pretended she hadn't heard him. He waited a little, then ran away like one who is chased.

Late one night, on entering my hotel I found a telegram waiting for me. It was to announce that *Angry Man's Tale* had found a publisher, Secker & Warburg, Roger Senhouse's firm, the thirteenth publisher it had been submitted to. I was elated and pleased with myself, for I knew nobody in the publishing world. And I thought of Constance and our long chats about books. I wrote to her next day, and as she had promised she left my letter unanswered. In the morning as I looked out through the window I saw Paris covered in merciless November fog. Closing the window I decided to leave the Butte for the South of France to savour my success under the sun and among the mimosa. There was another reason, namely to look down on my past self that had gambled a fortune away because he had no aim in life. But without gambling it away would there have been Kenya, Constance and in time *Angry Man's Tale*?

Dodo and I took leave of the Butte. 'You'll be back,' friends and acquaintances said. 'Once the Butte always the Butte.' The next morning Dodo and I walked down the steps of the Gare Saint-Charles in Marseilles. I recognised the rosy finger in the sky.

It was strange to find myself in Marseilles again, the port from which I had sailed to Kenya. I had been but a shadow without a substance; now I felt I had come into my own. Dodo and I strolled along the Canebière amid the din of trams, cars and the good people of Marseilles. Full of hope I bought a pipe with all the paraphernalia that went with it. Every three years or so the urge to become a pipe-smoker used to get hold of me. The urge would leave me after a month. The Marseilles pipe didn't fare any better than its predecessors.

We reached the Old Port, and saw the boat leaving for the Château d'If. Constance said she disliked Dumas Père because he wasn't highbrow enough for her. We ventured into the narrow streets which were to be burned down by the Germans during the Occupation. Brothels and shady bars elbowed one another. Two naked girls shot out of a bar to cross over to the brothel that faced it. During their rapid traject they found time to throw me inviting glances. From the streets of iniquity we moved to a restaurant, where, of course, I had bouillabaisse. In the afternoon we entrained for Monte Carlo.

The Coast could be divided into two parts: from Cannes to Nice, and from Nice to Monte Carlo. Since Cannes had witnessed my downfall I chose the Nice-Monte Carlo half. Somebody in Paris had recommended Cap d'Ail. It was night when the train reached Monte Carlo, and from there we took a taxi to Cap d'Ail. The hotel was on the main road, for which I didn't care, but it was small, which I liked. Behind the long bar in the dining-room sat the hotelkeeper, looking like a ponce. His wife had the appearance and manners of a bawd. I was the only customer at dinner.

As I sat over the coffee the bar filled. The women were certainly tarts, the men no better than they. Two of them were Americans. After a while one of the women came to my table. 'Hullo,' she said, pulling up a chair. 'Buy me a drink, baby.' I didn't know how to refuse, and she told me the story of her life. She was South African and had come to Europe with a boyfriend who had shamefully deserted her. She liked it on the Riviera, and had no desire to return to Jo'burg. She had greasy skin, beady black eyes, and wore a stained green woollen dress. She didn't smell too good either. She lived in the hotel, owed them money, but they didn't mind because she brought them customers. 'Half of these people here were introduced by me.' I said I was going to take the dog for a run. 'What about going to the municipal casino in Monty?' I coolly told her that I wasn't a gambler. 'Then we'll have fun here. Harry, come over.'

Harry was one of the Americans. He promptly sat down at the table, then said to me, 'You'll buy us a bottle of champagne.'

'The dog can't wait,' I said, rising. 'I wish you good night.'

'You always pick up bums,' he complained to her.

I heard her voice at dawn in the room next to mine; the male voice that answered wasn't Harry's. At five I was awakened by her shrieking. 'You promised me twice that much, you son of a bitch.' Then I heard the hotelkeeper's voice threatening to chuck her out if she didn't shut up. I told him at breakfast that I was moving. He didn't care a rap. Dodo and I took a bus to reconnoitre along the Coast. It was the conductor who decided whether a dog could travel on his bus. The decision often depended on his mood. In time I came to know most of the conductors and would let two or three buses go by without lifting my hand. However, the majority admitted Dodo, especially the women conductors.

The reconnoitring didn't last long. We got off in Beaulieu-sur-Mer, which in those days was a quiet, elegant place, smelling of mimosa, the clean streets offering the shade of their trees, and the little port full of yachts. We went into a large bar with a huge elm in front of it, run by two fat Italian brothers who suggested a hotel near the harbour. The hotel was strikingly respectable after the one in Cap d'Ail. The old proprietress was Italian, her daughter consciously French. The hotel guests were mostly English, the dining room had a glass veranda beyond which the sky seemed to meet the sea.

As I came in for my first meal my jaw nearly dropped, for at a table sat a man and a woman I had known in Kenya. She had left her husband for him. She was a long legged blowsy woman with wide innocent eyes, he nearly bald with a black cavalry moustache. They hailed me as an old friend though in the Colony we had only been acquaintances. My curiosity was aroused in as much as in Kenya it was generally thought that such elopments never lasted. The lovers usually parted after being thrown together too long on board the ship that brought them back to Europe, or if they stood it they sooner or later got sick of each other for lack of altitude and longitude. At the end of lunch they suggested we repaired to the large bar run by the Italian brothers. There we chatted about Kenya like exiles till late into the afternoon when Eddie, the lover, said he was going to the hotel to have a nap. They had been to the Opera House in Nice the night before and had come back late. I was left with Olivia, the runaway wife, who, the moment the door had closed on him declared, 'This life isn't for him.'

'What sort of life does he like?'

'Messing about on a farm in the White Highlands. We've tried everything, and all failed. We each have a little money, so we went wherever we wanted. We tried Ireland: he couldn't stand the climate. We went to Torquay, and he was bored stiff. Then we went to Jamaica which he didn't like either. We came here a year ago, and now he thinks that Sicily would solve our problem.' She looked at me with tragic eyes. 'Do you know what our problem is?'

'How could I?'

'Our problem is that we don't really like each other.'

She moaned about her fate, for she shouldn't have left her husband for whom she hadn't really cared either, but with him she would at least be in Kenya. That evening she suggested that the three of us take our meals together. I politely refused.

The next day it rained, steady, soft raindrops hiding the sea. The day after the mistral blew with bright, ferocious force. On that day I started my new novel, *Children My Children*, which meant writing three pages in feverish haste, then writing nothing for a week. The first day's fever was interrupted by a knock on the door. It was Olivia, saying she hoped she wasn't interrupting me, then sitting down in the only armchair. 'Eddie has decided to go to Taormina. This is the end. He wants to leave on Sunday. I'm not going.'

'You know best,' I said, my eyes on the page in front of me.

'The trouble is I don't, but even so I refuse to go. This chasing from one place to the other solves nothing.'

I wanted to get on with my work, but she continued complaining about the life she had been forced to lead since leaving her husband. She left me only after I told her that Dodo must be taken out. In the evening she came alone to the Italians. 'I told Eddie I'm not going. We had an awful scene. I lost my temper, and I shouted that I'd been happier with my husband, and the best thing for me was to go back to him.'

'Perhaps it is.'

'You don't care a rap. All men are alike,' she said, and left the bar.

That night he dined in solitary state, the next day they took their meals together again. She kept her distance from me, which was exactly what I wanted. The following morning I found Eddie in the narrow passage leading to the front door, surrounded by a mountain of luggage. 'Off to Taormina,' he said. Later in the day I was told by the hotel's daughter that he had left alone; she too was leaving though only towards the evening. 'They've parted,' said the hotel's daughter with Italian fatalism. Then she laughed, which was very Italian too. I thought Olivia would take the first boat back to her husband and Kenya.

Weeks later I walked over to Saint-Jean, and went into the first bistrot I saw. At the bar sat Olivia in the company of a local youth, aged about nineteen, handsome in the manner of the Midi, large black eyes, gleaming teeth and a pale complexion. 'You're surprised,' she said. 'I'm living here in Saint-Jean, I prefer it to Beaulieu, too stuffy for me.' She turned her back on me and talked to the youth, her hand on his knee. They left together, she taking his arm. 'Who's the young man?' I asked the fat man behind the bar. He had been a waiter in my hotel, but had left before I arrived. The following summer they were still together. I saw them lying side by side on the beach, her hand stroking his hairy chest. She did lift it, however, to wave to me.

As people don't leave my life entirely, I saw her again at a cocktail party towards the end of the war. She was married to a barrister, and said it was all going well.

To the Italians' bar came nightly the English butlers of the large villas of Beaulieu and Cap-Ferrat. They were quiet, portly men who spoke in low voices or played snooker. Two of them aroused my curiosity in that they talked about books they had read, discussing them with the respect writers seldom get from their readers. One of the two, who wore gold-rimmed spectacles, now and then recited Shakespeare sonnets to which the other listened with rapture. When it wasn't literature they spoke about their old ladies, meaning their employers who were both widows. Those two butlers entered my unconscious, and eighteen months later I wrote *Boo*, where the father is a literary-minded butler in the service of a widow. I am grateful to the two butlers to whom I never spoke since *Boo* was reprinted several times these last thirty years, and even the film rights were sold.

I often took Dodo and myself to Nice. It wasn't then a seaside resort or a home for the aged, no tourist trap, only a city that lived and worked on its own, providing its own boisterous existence. Going to the Opera House was my great pleasure; the other was roaming around the old town. A Niçois took me into a house that had been a palace in the eighteenth century. Now it was a tenement. He pointed at a faded fresco on the vault above the staircase with carved bannisters. 'Look how beautiful it is,' he said. I agreed. 'It's shamefully faded because these damned proletarians urinate on it.'

I craned my neck, then couldn't help saying, 'They must be contortionists.'

A frequent visitor to the Italians' bar was Gerard Haxton, Somerset Maugham's secretary, whom many disliked but with whom I got on well. Now and then we spent our evenings together in Nice. He rang me one day to ask me to lunch at the Villa Mauresque, Maugham's house in Cap-Ferrat. I was thrilled as I was an admirer of Maugham. So had Constance been. He was shorter than I had imagined him, and stammered more than I had thought. Throughout the meal he talked only of prices. He touched the table cloth, said it was Flemish linen, then told me how much it had cost. He pointed at a vase, and gave its price, observing that now it would cost double. I left deflated.

And speaking of prices, life was incredibly cheap on the Coast in those pre-war days. (Incredible if you look back today.) In Beaulieu, for instance, there lived Dale Collins, an Australian writer who wrote books about sea adventures, and now and then a short story about the sea published in *The Strand Magazine*. He, and his twenty years younger wife, rented a villa that overlooked the sea and Cap-Ferrat. He told me they managed on ten pounds a week which included rent, food, Monaco beer to which he was partial, and daily visits to the Italians' bar. Because of this cheapness all sorts of curious people made their home on the Riviera. For a writer, Collins often said, there was plenty of material. 'Yet when I write,' he added with a smile, 'I see only people whom I had known in Sydney.'

To my hotel, which was cheap too though comfortable, there arrived shortly after Munich a tall, redfaced man, Blackman by name. He was a quiet person, and talked to nobody, which was rather a feat as the Britons in the hotel, mostly elderly folk, liked shouting from table to table at meals. After a while, however, he started speaking to me, and often drove me in his two-seater to Nice or Monte Carlo. He took me into his confidence in that he confessed that he had done a stretch in prison, something to do with a bucket shop. He was a mine of useless information where I was concerned. If you rolled up *The Times* tight you could bash a man's head in with it. You choose your victim, go to him, knock him down with the newspaper, then unfurl it, and walk away calmly reading it. Nobody will suspect you. If you substitute an imitation diamond ring for a real one you can be caught only if the imitation ring drops into the fire. He also explained how bucket shops worked, and, frankly, I didn't understand a word.

On one of our outings we were stopped by two gendarmes who asked to see his passport, driving licence and triptique, a routine matter with them. He turned white, and his hand trembled as he produced the papers. The gendarmes found them in order, and waved us on. 'Why were you so frightened?' I asked. 'You'd nothing to fear.'

'Learn, young man, never to trust a copper wherever you are.'

Returning from one of our outings on a warm, cloudy April day we found the hotel's daughter outside the little office in which she usually sat for hours with her mother. She gave me a quick look, shook her head, then went into the office. The next moment two men emerged from it, both unmistakably plain clothes men. 'M. Blackman?' they asked, showing their police cards. 'You're coming with us. There's an extradition warrant from England.'

Showing no surprise and remaining calm Blackman asked them to let him go to his room and pack. 'I wasn't expecting it so soon,' he said to me. One of the plain clothes men accompanied him to his room, I stayed in the hall, waiting for him to come down. When he came down we shook hands.

'I hope it won't be too bad,' I said.

'A couple of years, old boy,' he said. Then he asked the detectives to let him see the garagekeeper about his car. They went with him, and when they returned he filled his pipe before getting into the police car. I ran into him in Chancery Lane towards the end of the war, and took him to lunch in Fleet Street. He spoke learnedly about black-market fish.

The English colony consisted of two different worlds: the elderly, most of them retired Empire builders, lived in hotels, their main distraction to be allowed to make tea in their rooms. They invited each other to their respective rooms to discuss different brands of tea. They were generally a parsimonious lot. The others either owned or rented villas, and being bored stiff they led an extensive social life, one cocktail party following the other. There was a large number of Americans too. Two American couples lived side by side near my hotel. One of the Americans was married to a Frenchwoman. Because he was a good customer the Italians designated him as president of the snooker club. He was radiant when addressed as Monsieur le Président.

The other American was a retired bidet manufacturer from Chicago. 'I introduced the bidet into the States,' he boasted. 'What was your business slogan?' somebody asked him.

'Give the laundry a chance,' he said.

If he got drunk at home his thin American wife took it in her stride; if he came home drunk all hell was let loose.

Angry Man's Tale was published shortly after Munich, and received excellent reviews. An unknown beginner has no enemies. Among the letters I received was one from Isobel whom I had written out of my system, and on the rare occasions I remembered her it was only to mix her up with Connie of the novel whom my anger had created in image of her. She said in her letter that she had recognised herself, and reading the book she felt remorse for the nasty way she had treated me. I wrote back to say that she shouldn't have remorse, and in any case I always forget people's nasty side. I didn't think of her again. Acute was my surprise, therefore, when I got a telegram from her, announcing her arrival in Beaulieu for the next day, and would I book her a room in my hotel?

Dodo and I went to meet the train. I wondered whether she would still attract me. She got out of the train, ran up and kissed me. At that instant I realised that writing the novel had erased all feelings I had for her. Beside me stood a girl with average looks and not too slim ankles, and that was all. In the taxi she put her arm through mine, talking nineteen to the dozen. Her words sounded quaint to me, as though I had heard them before. I saw her to her room, arranged to meet her later in the Italians' bar, and left her, puzzled. Why was every word she had uttered so uncannily familiar? In the bar while chatting with an acquaintance the truth dawned on me. Isobel had become Connie in her own eyes, and was speaking as Connie spoke in the novel; in fact she must have learnt Connie's part by heart.

She appeared, we sat down side by side, my eyes following the snooker players, my ears listening to Isobel's voice. I hadn't a doubt left that she was quoting Connie. The rest of the novel, that is the major part of it in which Connie didn't figure, she had skipped. When I mentioned the woman whom the hero marries in the novel after Connie had left him she said, 'Oh that one,' followed by another Connie sentence. We went to dine in Nice, and on our return to the hotel she asked me to her room. 'Come in ten minutes,' she said. I knocked on her door ten minutes later, she called, 'Come in,' I entered the room, and burst into laughter, for Isobel stood naked in front of the wash basin, cleaning her teeth, the toothbrush moving exactly as it did in the novel when the hero goes for the first time to Connie's room. After her leaving him he is haunted by that picture. That laugh drove Isobel from the Coast, and we never saw each other again.

Carmen and I remained in England for eight years, and if we went abroad it was to travel for a few summer months in France. First we lived in Hastings, then in St Leonards on Sea, the one great excuse and reason for both of them that they are only one hour and forty minutes from London by train. Of course, I exaggerate since there were many other excuses, such as the sea, the shriek of the gulls and the compelling force of both towns to keep me writing, for without writing the days would have been too long.

You notice change only long afterwards. The London I had known before Spain, the London that had belonged to the war and its aftermath, had ceased to exist. Firstly, the Back Bar of the Café Royal had closed during my absence, thus scattering to the four winds the regular customers, people I used to see almost daily. Secondly, very much the same thing, a lot of my friends and acquaintances had gone to live in the country. It was a different London that I found the two or three days a week I emerged either from Charing Cross or Victoria Station. I became accustomed to it as you get accustomed to anything. That new or replastered London threw Carmen and me even more on each other's resources, and since then we have become as inseparable as St Paul expects the married to be.

In Hastings then in St Leonards life was the same, the two joint towns offering no other amusement than the sea and the gulls, especially the gulls which woke you at dawn with their insatiable noise. None the less, we both retain a pleasant memory of those eight years, probably because we learnt during them what it means to be constantly together. True, we couldn't help making acquaintances, and meeting people with whom we had nothing in common, which has for a novelist a certain advantage, namely seeing how similarly people prosper with altogether different thoughts in their heads. There was, for example, a dignified looking man who wrote short pieces for the radio about birds and Nature. He had been a wartime colonel, and insisted on being addressed as such by the woman he referred to as his housekeeper, and who had been his mistress for the past twenty years. There was too the man who called himself a film producer because a decade before he had been employed by one. And you would have felt mean and ungenerous if you had told him that he had never been one, and all his stories were lies. The retired bank manager whom I saw now and then in a pub in St Leonards remains unforgettable. He put questions in lieu of chatting about the weather or the tide or even the lifeboat. 'Do you think Dickens was greater than Balzac?' Or 'Is French charcuterie better than German delicatessen?' Or, 'If there's a new war will the Italians turn coat again?' It wasn't necessary to answer his questions, for he did so himself. Dickens was greater than Balzac because he had never read Balzac; leberwurst was better than rosette de Lyon because he knew Germany better than France; and the Italians would betray the West in the next war since he and his wife had been cheated by a taxi driver on their only visit to Italy. The branch he had managed was in Fleet Street, hence he knew, he said, all who were important in journalism and literature. When one day I mentioned John Davenport who had just reviewed a novel of mine he told me he knew him well; when John Davenport came to stay with us I took him to the pub, saying he would meet an old acquaintance. They stared at each other as only complete strangers can. Afterwards the bank manager said that John had changed a lot; John assured me he hadn't seen the man before.

On the other hand, there was too the schoolmaster who spent his Christmas night in front of the fire, reading Verlaine and drinking a bottle of Château Yquem.

We usually left for France at the end of May when the holiday coaches began to pour into the town, the smell of fish and chips filled the streets, and candy floss reigned on the sea front. When we came back in the autumn the freshly-caught plaice was for the natives again, and Bed and Breakfast sounded less aggressive than in summer.

During our visits to France we spent most of our time in Paris which had changed a lot too, though Nancy Mitford and Robert Naly remained. In that changed Paris I still met and chatted with people I had known during the great period of my life, that is the beginning of the German Occupation in 1940, and as that period and my long trek from Paris to London from 1940 to 1941 will take up the next chapters I hasten to say that even discussing them in the early sixties with men and women who had witnessed that era made it look untrue and beyond imagination. As one who had seen me daily on the Butte-Montmartre in the thick of the victory drunk German troops put it, 'It was the great moment of our lives, and because it was the great moment we don't believe it was true.' Then he pointed at a coach-load of German tourists, their pockets bursting with the hardest currency there is.

8

When the Germans annexed Austria it was said, Aren't the Austrians Germans too? When they marched into Prague shoulders were shrugged, for wasn't it preferable to war? And in the summer of 1939 I heard voices saying sotto voce, and now and then loudly, that Danzig was too far off to be of any interest. If Hitler spoke, the English guests in my hotel clustered round the radio in the reading room, and though none of them understood a word of German they all listened intently. 'He sounds less threatening,' the colonel's widow would say. 'I'm sure he's in a friendlier mood towards us,' the retired magistrate from Burma said. 'Do you really think so?' Or, 'The man surely doesn't want war. Wasn't the last war enough?' Another voice would say that with due respect Chamberlain had gone off his head when he promised the Poles and the Romanians to fight for them if they were attacked by Germany.

I sat in the garden of a large hotel with a merchant banker on holiday in Beaulieu. We had dry Martinis in front of us, the sea was motionless, the pines leaned towards it. 'Isn't all this wonderful?' he said. 'You want to lose it? Lose it for Danzig? Come, be reasonable. I'm certain that the government could come to terms with Hitler if they gave back the old German colonies.' That was the general state of mind.

A company of the Tirailleurs Sénégalais was stationed in Beaulieu. Now and then you saw them marching past in gas masks, their gait showing how uncomfortable the masks were. The *Warspite* put into Villefranche harbour for a few days' official visit, and parties were thrown for Admiral Sir Dudley Pound. The *Warspite*'s visit and the Sénégalese were the sole connection with a possible war.

That last summer of so-called peace had a feverish quality. It was like a rose in full bloom, the petals would soon drop, but how intoxicating was the scent. I have never been to so many parties either before or after. The sun didn't stop shining, and the moon seemed in constant attendance too. To keep the swarming and biting mosquitoes out of my bedroom at night I bought a sort of a joss-stick which I put on the windowsill, and lit it when I came in. The smell of incense filled the room, and kept the mosquitoes at bay. The name was Moon Tiger, it was made in Japan, and if I think of that last summer of that long vanished age I smell Moon Tiger, and hear a hurdy-gurdy playing *J'attendrai*.

A woman novelist and her husband came to my hotel. Under different pseudonyms she wrote two novels a month, known as family novels because love was pure and temptation ultimately resisted. In a novel she gave me, and which I tried to read out of sheer politeness, the only way she managed to get rid of the seducer was by sending his yacht to the bottom of the harbour with him trapped in his bunk. Thus she saved the heroine's virtue. The husband was aggressively against Winston Churchill who, he feared, might lead England to war if he had a chance. 'He'll be the next prime minister,' I said. 'You understand nothing about politics,' he retorted.

'But I've a sense of history,' I said.

He laughed at me. He called himself his wife's business manager because he corrected her spelling. They took me to a nightclub one evening where they had heard a girl sing whose voice had impressed them. I was impressed too. After the show they asked her to the table. She was thin, her eyes and hair were dark, and she spoke little. 'What's her name?' I inquired after she left. 'Edith Piaf,' said the husband. Her career had just begun.

At a party in Monte Carlo I met a man and his wife, Charles and Helen, who remain associated in my mind with those last pre-war days. He was enormously rich, but because of his heavy drinking was allowed to sign cheques only if she signed them too, and to be on the safe side she gave him no cash. She took him and me one hot afternoon to the Galeries Lafayette in Nice to purchase a present for her cook and parlourmaid in London. Charles declared that it would bore him to tears to enter the store, so he would stroll in the street while she shopped, and remain near the car so as to see us the moment we came out. 'He hasn't a centime on him,' said Helen as we went into the store. 'No danger.' We came out after a while: there was no Charles in sight. 'He couldn't have gone far,' she said. 'He'll be back in a minute.' He was back half an hour later, helped along by an unshaven man, who introduced himself as the waiter of a bar in the next street. Monsieur owed him six large whiskies, and would madame pay?

'This comes of not giving me any money,' said Charles as we drove off.

I took to going over to Monte Carlo to spend the day with them on the beach and in the sea. By then I was certain that war was unavoidable, and I would float on my back, taking in the mountains and the sky, the white houses and the colourful gardens fired by the sun, convinced that I was looking at a memory I would take into the war with me. Not for a second could I imagine that I might be killed.

Helen was a hard gambler, and to please her and Charles I accompanied them to the Sporting Club. One night, tired of losing, she asked me to play chemmy for her. It was a strange sensation to be sitting at a casino table again, but I didn't let the past come rushing back. I was too engrossed in the novel I had started writing to let temptation collar me. I lost most of Helen's counters to Douglas Fairbanks who sat next to me. I wasn't lucky even if I played for others. When I rose from the table somebody showed me the headlines of an evening paper with the picture of Molotov and Ribbentrop smiling insincerely, two horsecopers selling each other the same lame horse. That photograph took my few remaining doubts away.

'This means war,' said the Italian brothers in the morning. For them as for most other folk in the Department of the Var war meant fighting the Italians, and being the sons of Italian immigrants they didn't look forward to it. 'The Chasseurs will reach Turin in forty-eight hours,' said the local house agent who was in the bar. 'But the mamma comes from Turin,' moaned the brothers.

That evening I dressed near the window, Moon Tiger was burning, and I found Beaulieu lovely in the dusk. It was like heartache. Whatever happens, I thought, I wouldn't be the same person when the war was finished. In a way I was taking leave from a self I wouldn't meet again. A yacht was entering the dusk, her navigation lights showing, and in the distance a woman's voice rose, singing *Quand vient le crépuscule*.

I took a bus to Monte Carlo. Everybody talked about the imminence of war, yet the well-groomed people in the Sporting Club continued to pretend that it wouldn't come. There I met a goodlooking woman who was, so she said, half Dutch, half English, and was staying with her mother in a villa above the town. She told me she had been married to a wellknown racing driver. She drove me to Nice after the Sporting Club had closed. It wasn't time for sleep. Towards ten in the morning she took me back to Beaulieu, and promised to dine with me at the Réserve that night. She came, we dined, yet she seemed not to enjoy it. She left at midnight, and I went to bed.

In the morning I was wakened by a knock on the door. An unknown man in a dark suit entered the room. A dark suit in hot August was enough to arouse my suspicions. He showed me his police card, then a snapshot of the young woman. 'You were with her yesterday in Nice at dawn,' he said. 'She dined with you last night. We're very interested in that lady and her movements.'

I told him that I knew practically nothing about her. He put a lot more questions to which I had no answers. Before leaving he said, 'In your interest, I advise you not to be seen with her.' So she is suspected of being a spy, I said to myself. That night in the Sporting Club she cut me dead. The following day she left for Italy, I was told by one of the croupiers.

Partial mobilisation was decreed, and Helen informed me on the telephone that the Sporting Club was having its last session, and would close that night as a number of the employees had been called up. I promised to join her and Charles.

There was gaming only at a few tables, the atmosphere was heavy despite the bright smiles. I strolled to the one-armed bandit, dropped in a franc, turned the handle, and won the jackpot. Such a golden shower of one franc coins cascaded to the floor that a page had to help me to pick them up. There were thirteen hundred of them. The final proof, I thought. At four in the morning the Sporting Club closed; I saw the lights go out; and the Senegalese doorkeeper, a large man with a row of medals from the first world war, said to me, 'It's finished, monsieur.'

I had to wait till daybreak for a bus to Beaulieu since many drivers and conductors had been called up. At last a bus came, and when we left the principality in the gathering light I saw doors open and men come out carrying parcels on their way to join their regiments. In Eze a woman ran along the road to give her departing man a loaf of bread. In Beaulieu the Senegalese were leaving in lorries for the Italian frontier. Behind them was a small group of civilians, one of them singing, *Auprès de ma blonde* to cheer up his half-awake companions.

The South of France was finished too for me in that my hotel closed on that very day. During the summer it had been run by Monegasque cousins of the proprietress who with her daughter was in Aix-les-Bains, where she owned two hotels. The cousins hastily left for Monaco to show how firmly neutral they would be if war broke out. As I couldn't think of anything better I decided to take myself and Dodo to mother and daughter in Aix-les-Bains. The train was crowded with unshakably impartial looking Swiss. Till Marseilles I travelled with a French Air Force officer who didn't believe that war would come.

'The Poles,' he said, 'are very fine people, but I don't think that the people of France are keen on dying for a distant town like Danzig. It would be different altogether if France were attacked directly as in 1914.'

In Aix-les-Bains I moved into the cheaper hotel mother and daughter owned, which was near the station. A train load of Anamite troops arrived, and while the yellow soldiers waited at the station for the next train on the bridge above the station white NCOs manned machine guns pointing at them. There was no trouble, and they entrained like lambs. In front of my hotel two prostitutes paraded at night. They were much in demand by the called-up men. 'The best way of starting a war,' I overheard a greyhaired man saying as he picked up the fatter one.

At last Mobilisation Générale was decreed. I felt immensely relieved, for the turning point had come, and now I could show myself that I had guts. In Kenya a 1914–1918 major had said to me at the club, 'Chaps like you wouldn't stick it in the trenches for an hour.' To prove that I could stick it I rushed to Chambéry to volunteer for the French Army. They didn't seem in a hurry to want me. I was told they would let me know in time, and deflated I returned to Aix-les-Bains. My first effort, I had to admit, hadn't got me far.

The radio announced that England had declared war on Germany; France followed suit only much later in the day. Still hoping that I would be called up I remained in Aix-les-Bains. The lake to which I liked to refer as a large tub, seemed to be waiting for Lamartine's ghost, the big hotels had emptied, and people who weren't called up went about their business as if the war were but a distant rumour, which in a sense it was. My own attitude to it was simple, today I would call it naive. Though disappointed by the lack of help to Poland I was certain that victory over the Germans would come the moment they attacked the impregnable Maginot Line, and they would have to attack because of the blockade. Still, I was a little surprised by the lack of enthusiasm and bellicose spirit of the people I met. Yet there were definite signs of a war effort such as meatless days and absinthe forbidden on Tuesdays, Thursdays and Saturdays.

I met a young Russian, Peter Balasheff, whose grandmother, Mme de Schevitch, and great aunt Mme Orloff were staying in the Bernascon Hotel as part of the suite of Dorothy Paget who had the whole first floor for herself and her following. The main job of the Russian ladies was to play bridge with her when she wasn't engaged in eating or sleeping. She had no timetable, thus the bridge partners had to be in readiness day and night. The drawing room in which the partners spent their days and nights was like a distinguished servants' hall. They ran down Dorothy Paget, moaned and complained about her, then the lady's maid would appear to summon them into the presence. 'She is finishing her sixth cutlet, then wants to play bridge.' That could be at four in the morning or five in the afternoon.

A temporary bridge partner was Mrs Roberts, a Daughter of the American Revolution who ran a bridge club in Paris, strictly for Americans. She was a hefty Texan full of energy, and loved her holiday with Dorothy Paget. Mrs Roberts had a daughter, Nona, who lived in a chalet above the town. Nona and I quickly made friends, and she became my constant companion in the heavy weather ahead. It is difficult to describe her because her features were somehow only hers, that is to say I never set eyes on another woman who in any way resembled her. She had violet eyes, chestnut hair, and was as thin as a young poplar. She was two years older than I, and had been moulded by the New York of the late twenties. She spoke French perfectly, whereas her mother after twenty years of residing in France didn't understand a word of it. In Paris she had a flat in the avenue Victor Hugo: if she took a taxi she pronounced 'avenue' and 'Victor Hugo' in English, and just couldn't understand why the driver stared at her with incomprehension.

Dorothy Paget gave a hundred thousand francs to the Foyer du Soldat, a servicemen's hostel, in Aix-les-Bains, which the local authorities much appreciated. The hostels were an integral part of the war effort in the same manner as the vin chaud, hot wine, of the soldier, the radio urged all patriotic people to give lavishly to that great cause. Dorothy Paget didn't write letters: she sent telegrams which were at least two hundred words long. After her donation the telegrams were immediately passed by the censor. Once I accompanied Peter Balasheff to the post office. 'Ah, Mme Paget,' said the man. 'It's all right.'

Horses were requisitioned. I stood in a small crowd outside the requisitioning centre as the peasants came in with their horses. A young peasant burst into tears as he kissed his percheron, taking leave of him. 'Shocking,' they said in the crowd. 'What right have they to take away his horse?' There was quite an angry murmur which I remembered when the streets of Paris filled with the victorious German soldiers.

Dorothy Paget and her suite left for England at the end of October; Mrs Roberts returned to the avenue Victor Hugo. Nona's chalet above the town had three rooms, but because of the cold weather that burst on us she and I spent most of our time in the kitchen, heated by the vast kitchen range. The proprietress of the chalet was an old woman who lived in another chalet about a hundred yards away with her small grandson aged seven and her old deaf dog who spent his time going from one chalet to the other, looking right and left, stopping to sniff the cold air and hearing nothing. Dodo disliked him. The old woman's son was at the Maginot Line, the daughter-in-law had vanished some years ago which was the reason why the little boy lived with her. The son was killed on patrol outside the Maginot Line by a German sniper. It was the little boy who announced it to us, saying, 'Mémère cried a lot. I poured out a stiff Pernod for him. Pernod, don't you know, raises one's spirits when one is unhappy.' He was an admirable boy.

Snow fell as though it were part and parcel of war, and the old-timers said it had been as bitterly cold in the winter of 1914–1915. Waiting without much hope to be called up I sat in the chalet's kitchen writing *Boo*. There is plenty of snow in the last third of the novel. We rarely went into Aix-les-Bains which with the tourists gone and the meatless days, not to mention bread rationing, had turned into a sulky town, the natives looking with hostile eyes at the few remaining foreigners, for what business had they to stay on after season?

'We ought to move to Paris,' I said one specially cold January day to Nona. She agreed. We took the night train that came from Modane to Paris. It was full of soldiers going on leave from the Italian frontier. We sat in a compartment with an engineer's wife who explained to Nona how to cook guinea fowl, a tasteless bird if not cooked in the right manner. She, the engineer's wife, cooked the guinea fowl with two old partridges to give it taste. She served the guinea fowl with lentils.

'And the partridges?' Nona asked.

'You throw them away,' said the engineer's wife.

Snow lay on the roofs and pavements of Paris, the sky was dark and Nona, Dodo and I went straight from the Gare de Lyon to a nearby hotel, where we remained for three days, going out only to have meals in a restaurant next door and take Dodo for a short run. It was like being in Limbo. On the fourth day Nona saw her mother, and I telephoned Naly to ask whether he knew of any furnished flat going on the Butte. He said that he believed there was one to be let at 13 Place du Tertre. On the fifth day we climbed up to the Butte, and took the flat which was on the second floor. The furniture was imitation Henri II.

I met again the many people I had known, Paul Méral included. He was the first person I saw since the outbreak of war who spoke what was known as defeatist language. He assured me that the war was as good as lost. He as a Belgian knew that for certain. For political reasons France hadn't extended the Maginot Line to the sea, thus leaving the whole length of her Belgian frontier undefended, and all that nonsense of digging trenches and hastily building fortifications was a huge joke with which German tanks would deal with in no time. We had awful rows on the subject, but we always made it up, firstly because I didn't believe a word he said, secondly because being always broke you felt obliged not to turn my back on him. And then it all happened as he predicted.

The windows of our flat didn't have the large vista of Paris that the situation of number 13, the only modern house in the square, deserved. For some obscure reason a wall ran from the house on the left to the houses on the right, and that wall stopped on the third floor. So whenever I looked out through the windows I beheld the unyielding wall on one side, and on the other the back view of two old houses with no plumbing, and not even water. There was a pump in the square, so why worry? Next to number 13 was the Rotisserie Eugène, where Naly, Creixams and many others used to gather in the afternoon. Eugène was an Alsatian who died only recently aged nearly ninety. He had left Colman long before the first world war, and started his career in the Carlton Hotel in London. When I wrote *Death and Tomorrow* in 1942 in the heat of the battle as it were, still shaken with anger and indignation by what I had seen in occupied Paris and in Vichy-ruled Marseilles, I called him Joe and the Rotisserie Joe's Bar since I couldn't give his real name or anybody else's who remained loyal, for they were in France suffering under the German boot. When the Germans came and invaded the Butte they made much fuss of him the Alsatian, calling him a fellow countryman. 'Our Alsatian tragedy,' Eugène ruefully said to me, 'is that we win every war.' But I anticipate.

One early May dawn I woke to the howling of sirens. Sirens were a weekly feature of Parisian life at that time, and if German aircraft didn't fly over you knew you would hear them at any rate on Thursday at twelve. However, that morning there was more firing than usual, one gun sounding pretty big, probably because it was near. Hardly had the firing died away than the radios in the house started blaring. The Germans had invaded Luxembourg, Holland and Belgium. Before they finished blaring the news our doorbell rang. It was Méral, who, as was his wont, hadn't gone to bed but had spent the night drinking in the bistrots of the square. 'The show has started,' he shouted gleefully. 'The Germans will be here in under a month.' I banged the door in his face. The morning papers, that had of course been printed in the night, said that the situation in Belgium and Holland had reached a détente. My own reaction was: let them come. I firmly believed in the invincibility of the French infantry, and hadn't Chamberlain said that the war was practically won as Hitler had missed the bus, the Germans were starving, had cardboard tanks and no petrol. You almost asked yourself how they could fight at all. Within a week Belgian refugees appeared.

French censorship and information seemed to be run by fatuous fools. It was all victories, and then you looked at the map and saw that the Germans were already in France. The best of the communiqués I remember was a proud declaration that the French troops had taken up a new position, and the enemy hadn't succeeded yet in making contact with them. I have to admit that I didn't see the joke. Denise Clairouin, who was to die in a German concentration camp, had visited the front the previous month. On her return she told me that there was an unimaginable amount of material behind the Maginot Line and up in the North, where the BEF and General Georges' Army lay. I also knew one of Reuter's correspondents with the army who told me the same story. Then why were Belgian refugees arriving with mattresses on the roofs of their cars as a protection against the Luftwaffe machine gunning them?

Suddenly the buses of Paris were gone. Officially, it was said that they went to collect Belgian refugees. Holland capitulated and Belgium was soon to follow. When it happened everybody spoke scornfully about the King of the Belgians. At night you could hear the trains leaving for the Front which seemed to be shrinking daily. One afternoon the radio, which was giving the news every two hours, announced that the Germans had captured Sedan. But, added the radio, there was a village in Belgium called Sedan, and surely the Germans meant that Sedan. They did not. Within a few days the names of towns about which I had read so much in Kenya came into the news, Amiens, Arras and Bethune, and more were to come. Only one never came: Marne.

Méral was active with bad news. I saw him at Eugène's, looking like a dustbin. He was drunk though it was early in the afternoon. He wept as he told me that he had flown over Liège, and Liège was in flames. I said I didn't believe him, not so much about the flames of Liège as his aerial presence above them. Ignoring my words Méral burst into tears. 'Can't you see,' he sobbed, 'that I'm weeping over a world that is dying? For France that is dying before our own eyes?' I said he was a fool. However unbelievable it sounds after the events nothing shook my faith till the end. My years in Kenya were my screen.

A friend of Naly's came back from the front. He told us stories of the French soldiers knocking over rabbits running in the same direction, or just leaving the lines, getting into transports and making off. I refused to believe him. Besides, hadn't I often said to Nona as far back as Aix-les-Bains that there were bound to be a few lost battles before final victory? The newspapers were full of appeals to buy war bonds. In my simple way I said to myself that things couldn't be going too badly if the government still needed the money war bonds brought in. If France were in real danger the men who ruled France wouldn't think of money, for more important matters would take its place.

Dodo was expecting puppies. An Argentine woman who lived at the Plaza-Athénée in great luxury had a Skye terrier who was the puppies' father. I promised her two puppies, but by the time they were born she, her secretary, lady's maid, chauffeur and Cadillac had decamped. The puppies were born two days after the first serious aerial bombardment of Paris, Creixams acting as midwife. There were four dogs and two bitches. Names had to be found for all of them, and one of the bitches got the name of Pontoise, for on the day of their birth the panzers had reached Pontoise. Two of the puppies I gave to Marcelle Cervière the actress.

I completely misunderstood the evacuation of Dunkirk. I thought that on account of Dunkirk being surrounded the BEF was taken by the sea route to some French port lower down to continue the fight. Two days later *Paris Soir* said that Lord Gort on his return to London declared that his troops would fight the Germans again at some future date. 'The English have left us in the lurch,' I heard the people say. I couldn't help reminding them that the French were the first to leave France in the lurch.

The great exodus began. Its first impetus was given by the only serious air attack on Paris. Rumour, fear and an utter lack of knowing what was happening came next. The authorities handled the situation in the clumsiest manner, keeping the truth from the nation. The simple folks believed that the Germans would cut their hands off and poke their eyes out. The bourgeois fled because they feared there would be a battle for Paris. And the majority went because the neighbours went. The roads were full, and there wasn't enough petrol to take motor cars to the end of their journeys. Peasants, I was told, sold a glass of water for a franc to the refugees. Paul Reynaud said in a speech he made on the wireless that the situation was dangerous, but not desperate. *Paris Soir* wrote, 'Les troupes de von Braushitch marquent le point,' the perfect understatement.

Nona's mother came to the Butte to see us, and said whatever happened she wouldn't leave Paris. She was fond of her flat in the avenue Victor Hugo, and that was that. She spoke as though the Germans had arrived already. Two English girls lived above us. They managed to leave via St Malo. As the bulk of my correspondence came from England the postman stopped knocking on my door. I began to feel isolated. The government left for Bordeaux, the only resemblance between 1914 and 1940. Naturally, it was Méral who came to announce it. He implored me to leave Paris because the battle of Paris would be a bloody one. I no longer believed in that battle.

'That knave of a Reynaud,' said Méral, 'is going to stage a battle here to influence American opinion. All the Americans are going to do is to weep over the ruins of the Folies Bergères.' He laughed his little malevolent laugh.

'Do you suppose the Germans are going to like you?' he continued. 'Though you're entitled to a Hungarian passport you write English books. Surely, they will say, he can't dislike the English too much.'

Nona was in the room with us. 'All my life,' I said, 'I've let myself be carried along. I'll do the same this time.'

Next day some people said they had heard distant firing in the night. So that was why the puppies had whined. I was up early in the square. Naly was already sitting on the terrace of the Mère Catherine. He was worried. His old parents had put on hobnailed boots the night before, and wanted to start walking. Whither? They didn't know themselves. He persuaded them to take their hobnailed boots off. This morning they had the hobnailed boots on again.

While we talked we saw people coming out of those poor houses with bundles and the most unbelievable things. One man had a tallboy strapped to his back as he marched off towards the town. Three soldiers stumbled through the square. They were in rags, unshaven men who had left the fight. 'Where do you come from?' I asked. The one on the right shrugged his shoulders, and they stumbled on. Marcelle Cervière, appeared on the Butte to tell us that she was off in a lorry, the man had petrol, and was willing to take twelve passengers at a thousand francs each. She was leaving the two puppies with the concierge. (The beast drowned the puppies the same day.) There was room for two more passengers, so Nona and I could come, and we could take Dodo and the puppies provided we kept them in our laps. I repeated I wouldn't go, and Nona said she would stay with me. Albert, the proprietor of the Mère Catherine, declared he would never leave. Let the Germans take Paris, but they wouldn't take the Butte as long as he lived. He decamped the same afternoon.

Number 13 was emptying too. Only an old couple remained on the first floor, and a schoolmistress who lived on the same landing as us. Three German aircraft flew low over Paris as if they had nothing to fear from the French any more. That day was the last free Monday of Paris.

On Tuesday it was the turn of Eugène and his wife to leave. In true French fashion such a move couldn't be made alone. Mme Eugène's mother and aunt arrived out of the blue, also her younger sister. A brother, a munition worker, had deserted his post, and was joining them. There they stood outside the bar, getting ready for the long trek. They put a table upside down on top of a pram, the table legs intended to protect the useless stuff they were taking, cups and saucers, but chiefly linen. Before they left they listened to the news which was even worse than anticipated. Already the Germans were at Senlis. At the last moment they were joined by their young waitress who said to the onlookers, 'I'm not one of those who wants to eat chicken with the Boche.' Then they were off.

Starved, bewildered, lonely dogs were to be seen in the streets, left by their owners who had rushed senselessly southward. Poor little things, they stood at the street corners, trembling, understanding nothing. Some of them were still trailing their leashes, bondage without a master. The people of Paris were kind, and the dogs were given food. However, they just stood and trembled. I spent my afternoon carting them water and food from the flat. I wanted to take a few up for the night, but Dodo wouldn't let them in on account of the puppies.

The little tailor from the house on the left of number 13 told me in the Mère Catherine that it was foolish to go, the roads were jammed with refugees and you couldn't progress more than a hundred yards in an hour. Next morning, of course, he and his wife were gone.

But next morning didn't really come. There was no sun, no light, and a dark carpet of soot enveloped the town. The radio said that it was a smoke screen the Germans had put up to cross the Seine. As a matter of fact it was the smoke of the oil tanks round the city burning. 'Even the light,' I said, 'has deserted the ville lumière.' Only darkness and silence were left, for the noise of Paris had gone too. I went and stood with Naly before the Sacré-Coeur, and the stillness of the grave came floating up. 'You can hear it,' said Naly. I left him to go into the basilica to pray to St Louis and St Joan of Arc to do something quickly to save France. Then I came out into midday darkness.

Suddenly the news spread that Russia had declared war on Germany. 'We are saved,' shouted the people. Their expressions were pitiful when two hours later they found out that it was a lie, which, by the way, had been spread by the Fifth Column. The Germans had used the same tactics before the fall of Warsaw. There the rumour had it that Italy had entered the war on the Allied side and French and Italian troops were advancing into Austria.

Paris was declared an open city, so there would be no battle whatsoever. When evening came I stood beside the steps near number 13, and I saw signals in morse all over Paris, the Fifth Column at work. Then, not far from me, a lamp started signalling. I went and fetched a policeman. 'What's the good of it?' he said. 'You know and I know and the Prefect of Police knows that the town is full of traitors.'

The front door of number 13 was ajar as the concierge and family, complete with cat and dog, had departed. Before leaving she had planted her eleven canaries on us, and said she would leave the entrance door open because it was operated by an electric switch, and if there were a short circuit we might easily be locked out or in as the case might be. When I told her that it was her duty to stay she asked whether the government had stayed.

Next day Eugène and family were back. There had been too many people on the road, so they couldn't advance. To my astonishment they were off again in the afternoon. The policemen of the open city loitered unarmed, and looked sheepish. Factories were blown up, Naly observing that machine was killing machine. In the Mère Catherine we ate langouste and chicken at each meal since the owners' departure. 'I prefer to see you eating them,' said Marthe, the waitress, who was left in charge. It was unnecessary to explain whom she preferred us to. After dinner Nona and I walked towards the rue Mont-Cenis, where a small crowd stood

near the stairs leading as far down as the town hall of the 18th arrondissement. Nothing was to be seen, but they all stared hard. A woman with a
lot of fair hair was saying that the Germans weren't really bad, she had
known one and he was remarkably nice. She said guten Tag meant good
day, and guten Abend meant good evening. Some in the crowd repeated
guten Tag and guten Abend. 'Frau is woman, Mann is man,' the woman
continued.

On the top floor of one of the houses in the rue Mont-Cenis lived a
friend called Madeleine who after the war married a Canadian, went
with him to Canada, and wasn't heard of again. We took the lift up to
her flat, she was in, and Naly and Creixams were there too. Naly asked
for Madeleine's field glasses, looked through them, then exclaimed that
he could see a cannon, nay a battery, firing. We all rushed to the
window, and truly saw in the direction of the Forest of Vincennes reddish flashes, and if you listened intently you heard the guns. I took the
glasses from Naly, and looked through them: a lone battery of 155 was
firing on the outskirts of Paris at the beaten foe of 1918. 'We're in the
battle,' Creixams said. I shook my head, for that battery and the flashes
were but a symbol, the ghost of dead glory saying for the last time that
this was Paris, and here lies France.

'Battle?' I sneered from the window. 'Can't you see there's nobody
firing at them? It's just a last gesture.'

At the Gare du Nord a railway engine was shunting. The gunfire
ceased, the engine continued shunting. On our way home Nona rang up
her mother from the Mère Catherine. Mrs Roberts had spent the last
three days reading Mein Kampf. In the night I heard low-flying German
aircraft. They sounded as if they were at home.

I rose at seven, and was down in the square before eight. Two policemen were strolling towards the rue Norvins. I stopped them. I knew
them as I knew practically everybody who lived up there. 'Any news?' I
asked.

'Nothing special,' one of them said.

'So we're still holding on.'

'Maybe somewhere else we're holding on, but not here. The Germans
are already on the boulevard Magenta, the staff is on the avenue Foch.'

A man in uniform rushed past, went into one of the poor houses,
emerging a little later, buttoning his civilian jacket. 'Just in time,' he
panted. He was a native of the Butte, and he told us that down on the
boulevard he ran into German motor cyclists who waved to him to get

away. A little later Nona and I went down to the boulevard de Clichy in the company of Méral who had a black eye which he received in a bistrot for praising the Germans. 'They won't hit me again,' he chuckled. In the rue des Abbesses the market was on, a lot of women and mountains of vegetables. We reached the boulevard through the rue des Trois Frères, and stopped at the corner. The pavement was dark with the crowd that had collected. The Germans were coming along, a grey stream that on that first day of occupation was endless.

The troops looked young and tired. It was horse drawn artillery, their horses splendid, the equipment first rate. Men, horses and guns were covered in dust, the men who were mounted or sat on the gun-carriages looked rigidly ahead. It surprised me to see them in Paris; they seemed much more surprised to be in Paris. Children have such expressions on Christmas morning. Now and then an armoured car came patrolling along, slowly as though looking right and left. Méral broke the silence, saying that here was the result of the hot wine of the soldier and the cool absinthe of the officer.

Suddenly a German horse reared, then fell, and the German officer fell with it. Several people in the crowd rushed up, dusted him, inquiring if he were hurt, and helped him back on his horse. That was my first shock, but it was mitigated by a policeman who, waving his truncheon, inquired whether the people coming from the market could cross over. The words he used were, 'Go home'. A German officer immediately halted his column, a lot of women crossed, the soldiers didn't look at them. Later on field kitchens put in an appearance, and once while a column was at a standstill a German army cook offered food to the loafers thick on the pavement. It made me blush to see Parisians with their shopping bags full of food accepting the enemy's propaganda crumbs. Another shock.

Alongside the Germans little groups of French prisoners were marching. They were in rags, they were dirty, prisoners in their own capital, and beside the helmeted conquerors they looked a sorry sight. When we had had enough of it (as if we hadn't had enough of it after the first five minutes) Nona, Méral, Dodo and I went into a bistrot and sat down. Everybody talked about the Germans. A fat man with a large gold watchchain said, 'Who would have believed that this would happen twenty years ago?' A young man, brushing the twenty years aside, observed, 'The better man wins. Look how smart and well equipped they are.' A woman declared that they were so young and so correct.

The word correct I was to hear ad nauseam. An old woman retorted that she had lived in Lille under the German occupation in the first world war. They were fiends, and would be fiends again. 'It's no good talking about the past,' said someone. 'They're here now, our invincible army was beaten in one month, and the Germans seem very decent. No swank.'

Nona and I were silent as we walked back to the Butte. When we reached the Place Émile Goudeau we saw a German motor cyclist racing down the street which ended in steps. You can't see the steps till the last second. On reaching the square in his head long rush he turned into the rue Gabrielle, the only outlet from the square, also invisible from above. 'He knows Paris better than any of us,' said Méral.

The Germans weren't yet in the Place du Tertre. After luncheon Nona and I decided to visit her mother. We took the métro which had been running all the time. In our carriage were three French soldiers with their rifles. They were grimy and unspeakably haggard. I spoke to them, they said they had come from the Somme, and were trying to catch up with their unit that should be somewhere south of Paris. They had got into the métro at the Mairie d'Issy, where they had neither seen nor heard anything about the Germans. I told them that the Germans were in Paris, they wouldn't believe me, and when at last they did they were downhearted. They put their rifles under the seats. They decided to get off at the furthermost métro station, and try to dodge the Germans. They had no money, so I gave them a few francs.

At the Étoile Nona and I got out. We went up the stairs, came out into the sunshine, and, as though hit with an axe, I saw the swastika flying from the Arc de Triomphe. I felt weak in the knees, and there was an empty feeling, a sense of void within me as if all that is life were gone. A military band was playing, and in a car a German general was taking the salute. The general's car ran hither and thither, so that all the troops should get a good view of him. There were plenty of watchers as at a football match, though excitement was lacking in that the onlookers seemed disillusioned, a crowd without bearings. 'If thousands of English bombs were dropped here and now,' said Nona, 'I should die happy.' She expressed my feelings.

On the avenue Victor Hugo was a bar-restaurant called Le Griffon which was frequented by the many English and American residents of the neighbourhood. Now and then we had lunched there with Nona's mother. The proprietor was round and fat, and when Nona and I had asked for two brandies and sodas he said, 'You're English you two, eh? Well, all I can say is that your Winston Churchill should make peace quickly because we French have had enough of this war. The Germans are correct people, I've worked with Germans today. They left several thousand francs here. I've had enough of the English.'

That was almost more of a shock than the swastika on the Arc de Triomphe. Whether you call it a fool's Paradise or just singlemindedness I had lived in the conviction that Britain and France were inseparable allies, and what was good for one was good for the other. Blame it on my reading in Kenya or on my trying to simplify matters, the Griffon's owner's speech was a revelation in meanness, disloyalty and in fact, dishonesty in my eyes. In *Death and Tomorrow* I described my daily life under the German boot. When reviewing it in *The Sunday Times* Dame Rebecca West said that the book was a masterpiece because I had been shocked more than I thought at the time. The shock dates from the Griffon which, incidentally, had ceased to exist when I came to Paris after the war. Looking back thirty-six years later, and with a deeper understanding of human beings (I think) I find nothing extraordinary in the restaurant keeper's words. He had served food and drink to the Germans who paid him well, they were polite men, and everything in the garden would have been perfect for him, if the English had given in, too. Their holding out would be a damned nuisance in the long run, causing bar and restaurant keepers much unnecessary misery. But for me at the time his words were treason.

I am convinced that those words made me rise above myself during the next few months, inspiring me to take ridiculous risks which, in retrospect, make me shudder.

Nona's mother wasn't at home. We decided to walk down the Champs Elysées before returning to the Butte. We stopped at a café near the Rond Point. It was full of the usual crowd you see in normal times in nightclubs where the French don't go. Practically every client looked like a South American, and was unshaven. A few German officers sat in a corner drinking champagne. They looked happy and, some of the surprise had worn off. The waiter stared at us curiously as he served us. We were already out of place there, part of a dead past that had ceased to matter.

'I'll have to unlearn everything,' I said to Nona, 'and start afresh.' One never does.

In a restaurant on the place du Tertre we saw two German officers standing at the bar, speaking in stiff, hard French to the little school-mistress who lived at number 13 (she still lives there), and who was tell-ing them that during the German bombing of Paris on 3 June several schoolchildren were killed. 'We only bomb military objectives,' said the Germans. She repeated that they had killed several children. 'Poor little children,' said the officers. 'We Germans love children.'

Three old English sisters lived on the Butte. Their combined age must have amounted to some two hundred years at least. They used to be acro-bats long before the first world war, had stayed on in Paris, and now spoke English with a Belleville accent and French with a Cockney accent. They were prim, harmless old women. I ran into them next morning, 15 June, the day the Germans had fixed for their entry into Paris. The sisters stopped me in the square.

'Now, sir,' they said, 'we will become Germans. It looks like it.' The three little sparrows waited patiently for an answer.

'You'll never be Germans,' I said. 'If France doesn't fight on England will, and win the war.'

'Thank you, sir,' they said in unison, bowed and went off relieved.

The Germans began to discover the Butte. By the evening a goodish number of them had found their way to the restaurants of the Place du Tertre and the adjoining streets. I saw an English army lorry filled with men of the Luftwaffe. Many of their cars sported English helmets on their bonnets. They made me think of Red Indians showing the scalps of their killed enemies. A long German car stopped outside the Mère Catherine, a colonel alighted, called the head waitress out, and ordered dinner for fifty officers. Money didn't count, and he wanted excellent wines and fifty ladies. The astonished head waitress said they didn't know any ladies, since this was a restaurant, not a brothel. It was the German's turn to be astonished. Before he left he asked her why she looked sad. She explained that her mother lived in Dunkirk, and she hadn't had any news from her for the past fortnight.

'If the escaping English didn't kill her,' said the German, 'she's all right. We look after the French.'

The Germans' dinner consisted of soup, chicken, cheese and pudd-ing. When they had finished they asked for the dinner to be served again. 'Not starting with the soup?' asked the head waitress.

'Of course with soup. Soup is part of the meal on your bill of fare.'

On the Sunday the Germans swarmed to the Butte like locusts. At lunchtime the restaurants were grey with them. More came in the afternoon, they sat at every table in the square, were friendly and got drunk. It was rowdy drunkenness, with nothing of the Herrenvolk about it, the Spartan army deep in orgies, for orgy it all became. The street-walkers and female scum of the nether regions of Paris swarmed up. The bands in the restaurants were playing Viennese valses. It was incredible the amount of valses they knew. I couldn't help wondering under what bushel they had been hidden.

Our concierge was still absent, hence the front door wasn't locked. The curfew for civilians was at nine o'clock. Nona and I went early to bed, and were wakened by a fiendish racket towards midnight. German soldiers had discovered that the front door could be pushed open, so they brought the whores into the house to screw them in the hall, on the landings and on the staircase. To judge by the noise they made there were about fifty of them. One of them even tried our door which luckily was locked and bolted. In the beginning it all went well, that is to say all you could hear were the sounds of love interspersed with contented guffaws. However, the whores soon realised that the soldiers wouldn't pay them. Then the real racket began. The women shrieked, insisting on being paid, and the Germans shouted back that they had won the war, and were entitled to every French woman. If the women got too obstreperous the soldiers beat them up, so there was even more noise. Some of the women wanted to escape, but the Germans wouldn't let them, and when one of them had his fill he rushed out into the square to collect companions in arms who then put the women through their paces too. The noise didn't stop before daylight.

When it was all still Nona and I emerged from the flat: landings, staircase and entrance hall were full of used french letters. Here and there we saw a little blood spilled, the fee the victors fists had paid the women who insisted too much on money.

9

I remained for four months and three days under the German heel in Paris. I was a stranger among millions of other strangers, and with one exception I had no trouble with the invader. The one exception caused Eugène to repeat every time I saw him after the war that he had saved my life; and he would point to the corner in his bar, where the saving of my life had taken place.

A few days after the Germans' entrance into Paris, Eugène and his family returned to the Place du Tertre. He was hailed as a fellow countryman by the Germans who hadn't yet started rounding up the Alsatians to send them back to Alsace. Anyhow, Eugène was above military age, thus there was no question of his becoming one of the 'Malgré nous' as the Alsatians, who were put into the German Army, were to refer to themselves. In the beginning Eugène was pleased with his lot, for the Germans were correct and spent a lot of money in his bar. They listened respectfully to him while he related his great story, namely serving Winston Churchill in the Carlton in London before the first world war. They asked for details which he supplied, inventing most of them, as he confessed to me afterwards. He put up a notice, 'Der Wirt spricht Deutsch' because that sounded more authentic than 'Man spricht Deutsch', which could be seen in every second shop and café in Paris.

It was during his honeymoon with the Germans that he saved my life. On a sunny morning, Dodo and I went into his bar. A German military car stood outside, the driver wore SS uniform. In the bar sat two Germans, one in uniform, the other in mufti. They had a bottle of mirabelle on the table: the officer's face was flushed. I went to the counter, Eugène gave me a quick look, then shook his head, but I failed to understand. I heard the officer say in a loud German voice, 'We'll take him along.' That sounded Greek to me. Take whom along and where to? I sat on a bar stool with my back to them. After a while the officer belched, then repeated that this one would be taken along. The civilian said that first they ought to see. Eugène looked desperately at me, the officer belched again, then spoke in a loud voice, 'Hey you, you Intelligence Service what?' It was rotten English, and there was no doubt that he was speaking to me. I made a stupid mistake in that I answered in the German I had learnt as a boy in Switzerland, and which I was brushing up rapidly on the Butte-Montmartre.

'You can speak to me in German,' I said.

'Ha,' he said. 'I expected you to speak German. You all speak German.'

They both got up, came up to me, the civilian stopped on my right, and from the left the General (now I saw his rank) pushed his face close to mine. It was a brutal, reddish face, a face you fear at sight, a face that is capable of anything. 'Intelligence Service,' the face said hardly an inch away, the breath smelling strongly of mirabelle.

'What are you talking about?' I said in an indignant voice but without any fear since I learned to fear them only on that day.

'Who are you?' the civilian asked in a pleasant voice.

'We'll take him along,' said the General. The civilian objected, saying they should first find out who I was. 'Show me your identity papers.'

'I don't see why I should,' I said, addressing the civilian.

'He's a General der Polizei,' the civilian said.

I took out my identity card, and looking at my photograph the general's mirabelle-soaked eyes discovered no likeness. 'This isn't you,' he said. The civilian assured him that it was me. The General decided to change tactics, and ordered Eugène to give me a drink. At that moment a goodlooking woman, a friend of Eugène and his wife, entered the bar. Relinquishing his seat beside me the General ordered drinks all round, the first to be served to the lady.

'What's the matter with him?' I asked the civilian.

'He's the best man there is, the right hand of Foreign Minister von Ribbentrop.'

The General was drinking a toast to peace. 'Friede,' he said, looking lovingly at Eugène's friend. I have never heard peace sounding so bloodthirsty. He offered her a hundred occupation marks if she went to bed with him. She blushed and moved away, which was unfortunate because he concentrated on me again. This time he contended that I was a member of the Deuxième Bureau and was spying on him. His eyes bored into mine, and he said he had seen me before. In the next breath he asked me in a threatening voice why I was staring at him. He would take me along. Luckily Mme Eugène's friend was still in the bar. Forgetting me for an instant he advanced towards her, offering her the money without any services in return so that she and her children should always remember the kind German general he was.

She accepted the money, though for a long time she didn't want to take it, but her husband was a prisoner of war, and she was alone with her two children. She was afraid that taking that sum would put her under an obligation, and, with the money in her bag, she swiftly took French leave. The general's interest was focused on me once more. His face was coming closer and closer. In order to make a diversion Eugène asked, what about Russia. The general opened his hand and closed it. 'We have Stalin here,' he said. 'He's eating out of our hand.'

Abruptly he told me to write my name into his pocket diary. He would find out who I was. He gave it to me, but immediately put it back into his pocket, walked to the wall, moving quickly, and no wonder; taking the wall as a target the General der Polizei, Ribbentrop's right hand spewed against the wall. He was thoroughly sloshed. In the pandemonium that ensued I took French leave too. Eugène told me afterwards that in his fear for me he had continued to fill the general's glass to the brim, hoping that he would be sick and pass out. Thus with the mirabelle, Eugène maintained, he had saved my life.

I have often been asked who the general was. Eugène said he was Heydrich who was later assassinated in Prague. Subsequently I saw a photograph of Heydrich: his face resembled that of the general.

Eugène's honeymoon with the Germans lasted for two months only. As food became scarcer in Paris he made several trips to the countryside to buy eggs, meat, in brief anything he could lay his hands on. He brought back from one such trip a cockerel which he intended to fatten and keep for an evil day. The cockerel was tied with a piece of string to the drainpipe in the courtyard behind the bar. You had to cross that courtyard to go to the lavatory. One evening the cockerel disappeared. Eugène was convinced that a German soldier had taken it away under his greatcoat. 'I want Churchill to win the war,' he declared.

With the exception of my brief meeting with the general I had no trouble whatsoever with the Germans who in the beginning were truly correct, this correctness degenerated as time went on, and they began to see that the war wasn't over as Britain wouldn't capitulate. The best-mannered among them were the Prussian officers, most of them belonging to the Junker class, many of them army officers from father to son.

The worst-mannered (to my surprise) were the Bavarians and the Austrians. Speaking of Prussians I came to know in Eugène's bar a Prussian lieutenant-colonel from Halle to whom I didn't hide my conviction that England would win the war in the long run. On that he gave me Woodbines his men had found in Dunkirk. Returning confidence for confidence he told me that he cared not for Hitler. 'I served under the King of Prussia, the Weimar Republic, and now under the Austrian peasant. My heart was only with the King of Prussia.' However, he was a soldier, his forbears had been soldiers since the days of Frederick the Great, and a soldier's duty was to serve and obey. I often saw him in Eugène's bar till he was sent to conquer Poland.

Another Junker, a staff captain, discussed with Eugène and me Germany's prospects of swiftly winning the war. I said that England couldn't be defeated, for she ruled the waves. 'In that case,' he said, 'Germany will lose.' I grinned. 'But if Germany is defeated,' he added to stop me grinning, 'she will drag the whole world down with her.' After a couple of drinks he muttered that the Germans were a race of suicides, which does sound quaint today since instead of suicides they have become the richest nation in Europe.

The German officer I enjoyed the most was a fat infantry captain of the reserve. He was having a well-deserved rest in Eugène's bar after his sightseeing tour of Paris. He had visited Notre-Dame, Napoleon's tomb, the Arc de Triomphe, and finally the Sacré-Coeur. All very lovely, but Napoleon's coffin had impressed him most. 'He was a misunderstood man, too,' sighed the captain, dripping with Weltschmerz.

They had no sense of security in those early days. Before you could ask them they told you which was their unit, where they were stationed, and if their unit left they came to Eugène to say goodbye, giving their destination. I had been contacted shortly before the Germans arrived, and without hesitation I agreed to give information about them if the occasion arose. I didn't speak about it to Nona as I didn't want her to get into trouble on account of me. My contact from the occupation onward was a White Russian whom I used to meet in a small café in the rue Alésia on the Left Bank. As far as I could ascertain later some of the information I gave was passed on to London, though I never knew how. The Russian émigré was a thin, voluble man with dark hair, ready to discuss the immortality of the soul on the lack of beetroot with which to make bortsch. When I returned to Paris in 1947 I rang him at the number I used to ring if I had something to tell him: the number didn't reply, though I tried several times. I didn't know his address, the same way as he hadn't known mine, that being part of the game. Of course, I knew in 1940 what I had let myself in for, but that summer I was in a heroic mood.

A small, prosperous Italian bistrot was in the rue Norvins, leading to the place du Tertre, mostly frequented by the local charwomen and workmen. The father had come from Piedmont, had toiled hard, as a result his son Atilio had gone to a lycée then on to the Sorbonne. However remaining a thrifty Italian, he continued to work in the bistrot, taking it over after his father's death and turning it eventually into an art gallery. As the fighting began in North Africa he declared to me that the Italian army would be in Cairo within three months and would push the English into the sea. 'Never,' I said. We made a bet of a glass of white wine, I maintaining that the Italians would be defeated, he that Italy would win. On the day I went up to the Butte in November 1947 for the first time since the war I looked into the bistrot. Only his father and uncle were behind the counter. Suddenly I heard Atilio's voice behind me, saying, 'I believe I owe you a glass of white wine.'

My main personal trouble in that first summer of the occupation was that money ran out, there being no possibility left of receiving money from my literary agent in London. Many of my friends on the Butte were in a similar position. Nona hadn't a sou in the world, and her mother was no better off as dollars couldn't be transferred to occupied France. She had a Russian émigré boyfriend called Dimitri whom Nona referred to as her mother's gigolo. Being an enterprising man Dimitri got a job with the Germans as a sightseeing guide, and I would see him on the place du Tertre, trying to keep step with the German soldiers he took round, Reiseführer on the armband. With the occupation marks he earned he came to Nona's mother's rescue, giving her most of it, which does go to show how upside down everything was under the Germans boot.

However, that was of no help to Nona and me. Besides, we had a free lodger, none other than Paul Méral who had nowhere to sleep. Some friend lent us a deckchair in which Méral slept fully dressed in the small entrance hall, predicting German victory over England every morning as he rose from the deckchair; though not always. For he often came back dead drunk. We would hear him grunting to himself, trying to rig up the deckchair, often failing, then in the mornings we'd find him lying on the floor next to it. During the day he was a silent guest in that he was usually gone by nine, remaining away till the small hours. He was putting out feelers with the intention of working for the Germans as a journalist.

I sold two of the puppies, a windfall that kept us going for a while, but it was no solution. The answer came unexpectedly one afternoon early in July. With his Maecenas in Vichy and art dealers away Naly was more broke than I. Again we were in Eugène's bar, and a German soldier offered us cigarettes. Naly lit a match, simultaneously one of the German's comrades produced a lighter. He refused the light of the lighter, accepted Naly's match, saying in an aside to his companions that he would remember all his life that a genuine French painter had given him a light. As Naly's studio was near I suggested he have a look at his paintings, hoping that he might buy a canvas, thus easing matters for the lot of us. The soldier gladly accepted the invitation, and we went to the studio. Naly's paintings were everything the Nazi mind disliked. I watched the soldier as he looked at them, awed and understanding nothing, putting it down as his own fault, and not the fault of the painter. 'It's a pity,' he sighed, 'that we in Germany aren't allowed to see such pictures. Our government have their own ideas about painting, and we must adhere to them.' So there was no hope of a sale. He asked permission to photograph a painting or two, then asked Naly if he had some small painting, preferably a watercolour, and more preferably a watercolour of one of the sights of Montmartre because he would buy that. The soldier went, saying that the visit to the studio had been one of the finest moments of his life.

It began with that. Nona said Naly could sell as many small watercolours as he wanted if he made them palatable for the German tourist. Naly agreed, but, he asked, who would sell them? They said it could only be me since I spoke German. My answer was that I wouldn't take money from the enemy. They inquired whether starvation was more dignified, and what about Dodo's and the remaining puppy's food? While they spoke I perceived that selling watercolours to the Germans would not only help me in gathering information, but would give me a legitimate reason to approach them. I didn't give in yet, the thought of selling in bars and restaurants being abhorrent to me.

There came a day when neither Nona nor I had lunch, not even a sandwich. She could have gone to eat with her mother, but there wasn't enough money for the métro fare. That day Naly had finished two small watercolours, one of the Sacré-Coeur, the other of the place du Tertre. They were charming. If you are an artist the artist will out whatever you

179

do. He made white folders for them, and wanted me to ask fifty francs for each, giving me half of it. I said no, I would ask a hundred francs for each. Naly thought I was mad, I replied that my feeling about the Germans was that they had to be impressed if you wanted to succeed with them. Look at Hitler who had asked for a high entrance fee at the Sportspalast in Berlin, which had made the Germans take notice and attend his meetings. Naly was incredulous, I took the two watercolours, and sold them at Eugène's the same morning. My share was forty francs on each picture, and in the following six weeks I sold one hundred and ten of them, quite a feat if you consider the price the hawkers, vendors and painters received on the square and in the restaurants. Twenty francs was their usual price, and there were hundreds who were trying to sell pictures. For most people in Paris were in the same boat as Naly and I, with no means of making money, therefore only the Germans remained.

In the beginning I said, 'These are the paintings of a friend of mine.' Later we changed tactics in that I said I was the painter himself since that sounded more convincing. I was respectfully addressed as Herr Kunstmaler. Whenever a German, who looked like a likely customer (after a little practice you easily detect the would-be customer) came into Eugène's bar, I engaged him in conversation, mentioning after a while that I was a Kunstmaler, and, by the way, here are a few of my watercolours. Thus there was nothing of the brazen vendor about me, and in a brief time I learned how to turn the conversation into the channel at the end of which loomed the pictures. It was a dignified procedure, though only outwardly as within myself I sweated and trembled. Naly used to say that he invariably knew whether I had been engaged in selling by the pallor of my face.

Experience taught me a lot. I found out that watercolours of the Butte weren't enough. They wanted Notre-Dame, the Madeleine, the Opera House and other famous buildings. Naly complied, using coloured picture postcards as models. The most amusing thing was when I was asked to autograph the pictures, and put the date on them too I obliged without batting an eyelid. The name of the painter was R. Méry. Now and then I was asked to draw a likeness of the purchaser to which I coldly answered that I was strictly a landscape painter. Their favourite was the Madeleine. I can assert that the Germans had very little understanding of painting. They bought the watercolours only as souvenirs of their visits to Paris. They had no taste, but respected art and the artist; it didn't matter to them that the artist was obviously poor; and I received from even the crudest private the respect any famous painter would have been pleased with in the Western Democracies. There were exceptions who understood modern painting. We had a small collection for them. Of that collection only seven sold in six weeks. A certain Count Metternich appeared one day, the head of the military art propaganda department, or whatever it was. He bought a humdrum watercolour of the place de la Concorde.

As the Montmartre Maler I met an interesting young German. I entered the Mère Catherine with the folder containing the watercolours under my arm. At a long table sat German staff officers including one general. Among them was a bespectacled private, no more than twenty-one, who was holding forth with the others listening. As I said my little piece the young man turned to me, saying in English, 'You can speak to me in English.' Then he asked me why I sold such pictures. 'Because I must live,' I said. He suggested we meet in the afternoon in some other place on the Butte. While we spoke the other Germans listened to us with encouraging smiles. I found it all extraordinary.

The young man came to Eugène's after lunch. He was Count Manfred von Keyserling, the son of the philosopher, and the great-grandson of Bismarck. We became fast friends. I took him to Naly whose friendship Keyserling still deeply cherishes. Manfred's attitude to Hitler and National Socialism was edifying. They were a plague, but the plague was needed to unify Europe and save it from communism. Let them do their work, and then vanish. The occupation of France was essential to achieve European unity, for in France the uncouth Germans would learn the art of living, of which they had no idea. He spoke with fervour like the young idealist he was. And he was the first person to urge me to get out of occupied France, the first too to speak about the ways and means of crossing the demarcation line into unoccupied France. He was one of the last people I saw before I left Paris in October. The next time I saw him was in Paris too, the year 1971, and Carmen, he and I dined with Naly on the Butte. He had lost both his legs in the war. With his German Weltschmerz he had got fed up with the easy life in Paris, and in 1941 volunteered for the Russian front, where his legs were blown away in the Battle of Stalingrad, and he was taken prisoner.

Though the influx of Germans hadn't slowed down there were noticeably fewer of them by the beginning of July, there came an afternoon when the square was full once more, the reason that Goering was at the Sacré-Coeur. The soldiers hadn't long to wait for their idol.

Goering appeared riding in a light blue open Rolls Royce with Ribbentrop at his side. The car had a Dutch number plate. Goering wore a white uniform, and looked thinner than in his portraits. Ribbentrop resembled an aging gigolo. The soldiers shouted many heils while the Rolls went round the place du Tertre. Goering stopped the car to let an army bus loaded with sightseeing soldiers pass by. I said to a Frenchwoman who stood next to me, 'Could you imagine King George VI seated in a Mercedes stolen in Italy?'

After the war most of the people I had known in the summer of 1940 still reproached me for my stupid recklessness at the time. Even Naly would say, 'You'll be shot by the Germans if you go on like this. Is that what you want?' My invariable answer was that what I wanted was England's victory.

By August the Germans' tempers were frayed, fraternisation with the civilians ceased, and the sales of the watercolours dropped. Like the murmur of the distant sea the resistance slowly took hold of some French souls. The chemist in the rue Mont-Cenis told me that a leaflet had been pushed under his door, a leaflet exhorting the French to resist the invader. The chemist was furious, repeating to every customer, 'I don't want to be shot.' Then General de Gaulle's call to France on 18 June was circulated clandestinely. Speaking of the General, a fat fortune teller used to come in the afternoons to the place du Tertre in search of clients. She was an enormous woman dressed in black. She showed me a crumpled sheet of paper with the General's speech typed on it. 'With a name like that,' she said in a stentorian voice, 'one can't lose.' A policeman stood in the square, wearing all his decorations, and the Germans stopped and stared at his medals. To stare unblushingly was a German habit as well as asking endless personal questions. The policeman got tired of the staring, and said, 'The medals, eh? They're not of this war, they're of the last one. You know the war I mean. The one we won.'

That was said on a Sunday, a memorable day in that I threw out Méral that night. He had come back dead drunk as usual and had collapsed on the stairs. The concierge came to see what caused the noise and as she bent over him he kicked her in the groin. She called me, and between us we carried him out into the square, where he spent the night, sleeping on a bench. In the morning I was ready to relent, but when I saw him approaching the table at which I sat with Nona, Naly and Creixams, looking like an evil toad, I changed my mind even before he shouted to us that we were a pack of fools for having kept him. Dressed in a suit Creixams had given him out of the kindness of his heart he left us and the Butte for good. Somebody I knew saw him a month later in a German military car, smoking a cigar.

In 1946 when I was living in Suffolk I received a letter from a Belgian professor, informing me that he was writing a life of my friend Paul Méral, the great hero of the Belgian resistance, murdered in a café a few days before the liberation of Brussels. Strange though it may sound I wasn't surprised. His essentially destructive mind couldn't have tolerated the vainglorious victors for too long. Naly and I still find ourselves speaking about him.

A great sorrow came my way shortly after Méral's departure. First the remaining puppy died, then it was my dear, faithful Dodo's turn. She must have got some infection from the dogs that had come to the Butte when their masters had run from Paris, the ones I took to the flat to give them water. She died in the night. I sat beside her rug on the floor, and stroked her poor head as there was nothing else left to do. The next day I had to see my Russian contact in the rue Alésia, and when our business was done I told him about Dodo. 'Now,' he said, 'you are free to go.' I said I wasn't thinking of going. 'They'll catch you if you don't,' he said. I shrugged my shoulders, and went on mourning Dodo.

Around that time I saw the first English leaflet dropped over Paris and the suburbs. It was an elephantine, ponderous message, yet our charwoman thought it beautiful. A French architect I knew had seen it too. He said the English were still sitting in armchairs, smoking expensive cigars.

As August turned into September German tempers got truly frayed. They began to repent of their friendly behaviour to the French. My Junker lieutenant-colonel, who was moving to Poland, confided in me the last time I saw him that the French were getting fresh. Stories of German soldiers being killed were all over the town. How many of those stories were true I couldn't tell, but one night at Eugène's a German soldier, who was ready to go, lingered on conspicuously. He put on his coat, put on his cap, then stood irresolute at the door, finally asking Eugène to accompany him to his car, which was on the other side of the square.

'I don't like going about in the dark here,' he said. 'Several of my comrades have been attacked.' He shrugged his shoulders. 'I can't blame them as we did the same during the occupation of the Rhineland.'

I started inventing stories to prove to the people I came daily in touch with that England was not only holding on, but victory over the invincible Germans was bound to come sooner than they thought. Rumour had it that the Germans had tried to invade England, and had been defeated, many of their soldiers drowning in the sea. I decided to embroider on that: A convoy of closed German lorries had stopped outside the garage of a man I knew (only in my imagination). The officer in charge told the garagekeeper that he requisitioned his garage for the night. The lorries were driven into the garage, and before leaving the Germans locked the garage door, and took the key away. They would be back in the morning. The garagekeeper's curiosity was aroused. Having a duplicate key he let himself into the garage. He looked into the first lorry: six bloated German corpses lay in it, officers of high rank before the British turned them into the sea. The same kind of swollen corpses were in the other lorries. Those officers were being taken home for burial in Germany. I was much impressed by my invented story as I told it to all and sundry who were willing to listen. Most people were. I was proud of my effort when in the Mère Catherine an acquaintance repeated it to me in a conspiratorial whisper. 'I heard it from the garagekeeper himself who's an old friend,' he said.

Even Nona began to say that I would end up against a wall on a cold dawn. So I kept my new job from her. The new job started in August when I met a young man, called Jean Watier, from the Department of the North, who deeply felt the humiliation of his country. I have rarely met devotion as bright as his. Now and then he forgot himself completely, and it was for me to calm him down. 'If you don't look out,' I often said, 'you'll be caught one of these days.'

'I don't care. I'd gladly die for England.'

Though Jean lived in the Zone Interdite he managed to come frequently to Paris. He used to say that if I ever got into trouble he would hide me up in the North for the duration. The RAF visited the North regularly, and dropped leaflets. On one of his visits Jean brought some and showed them to Nona and me in a small café. Two German soldiers came in and sat down at the table next to ours as Nona was reading one. Nona calmly finished reading it before handing it back to Jean.

'Quite interesting,' she said.

In the circumstances it definitely was.

Jean had a girlfriend in Paris who worked in a munitions factory. She had been a communist, but now was a fervent Gaullist. I met her, and both of them regretted that there were so few leaflets in Jean's possession for if we had a larger quantity she could distribute it in her neighbourhood through her old communist channels, it being a working class district. Jean looked at me, observing that he had seen a typewriter in my flat. I said I was willing to make as many copies as I could. He gave me one of the leaflets, and the girl promised to call for them in three days' time.

I sat down at my typewriter, a Royal portable, inserted sheets and carbon paper. It could produce nine copies, and I had plenty of paper from the dead past. As I sat down and started off it came home to me that if a German burst into the flat my fate would truly be sealed. I hadn't finished the first page when the doorbell rang. That gave me a kind of shock. I tiptoed to the door, opened it slowly, then threw it wide open because it was Lucie, our charwoman, who was mostly drunk. (Poor Lucie hanged herself in the Choppe du Tertre's lavatory soon after the war. She had been discharged as incurable from hospital on that day.)

Typing it twenty times I produced one hundred and eighty copies. For one who types with just two fingers that wasn't a mean achievement. Anyhow, my back hurt. However, one hundred and eighty didn't seem enough, so in the afternoon I produced one hundred and eighty more. In three days there were a thousand. The girl came, and took them away in her large black shopping bag while I cursed my back.

The leaflet was long and too closely printed. As picking up a leaflet meant death it should have been shorter and easier to read. The French needed only a few words to give them hope and make them understand that England fought on and would liberate them in time. That particular leaflet told them that they shouldn't use trains too much because the RAF would bomb trains that carried German troops. The French shouldn't go near German barracks because these would be bombed too. English parachutists were coming continually to France to blow up factories that worked for the Germans, and soon England would have the mastery of the air. It was all right, but not what in my opinion the French wanted at that time. France needed rousing, hope, a message; yet the next leaflets Jean brought were in a similar vein. You must be in occupied France, I thought, to understand what people felt in the hermetically closed German coffin.

Jean's girl came one evening to Eugène to tell me that Jean couldn't come to Paris for a week. She said it was a shame to have to wait for an entire week. The leaflets were doing a lot of good, and some of them were taken by friends to other arrondissements. 'Understand,' she said, sitting on the red banquette in her cheap black dress, 'that the slightest sign from England makes our hearts beat stronger.' I nodded, thought for a while, then I said she should come back the day after tomorrow. When she was gone I rushed upstairs, sat down to the typewriter, and wrote a leaflet of my own. Naturally, it was meant to be a leaflet from the other side of the grave.

I told the French that Britain fought on because the British hadn't been betrayed and sold to the enemy like poor France. The Germans had conquered so easily because they had found little resistance hitherto. 'But because we resist and prefer death to slavery, Germany will be defeated in the long run. We know it will take time, will entail sacrifices, but with the immense resources of our Empire, which is united against the Antichrist, and with our unshakeable will to conquer Germany must lose. An English victory will mean the liberation of France and the restoration of French life, French glory. All we ask from you is to hinder the Germans, sabotage, make things difficult, and then you will see that our joint effort will chase the invader out of martyrised France.'

The girl came, and blithely I explained that it was a leaflet somebody I knew had found near the Porte Maillot. I could just as well have said that it was found outside the Métro Lamarck-Caulaincourt. She read it, and her eyes shone. She took the leaflet along. I made some more in a similar tone in the next week, but when Jean reappeared I told him the truth. In his enthusiastic way he asked me to continue. On I went producing leaflets.

September arrived with the sales of the watercolours dropping to danger line. Naly had sold some of his real paintings, so his need wasn't as great as mine. Now and then he let me keep his own share of the watercolours. Around that time I made the acquaintance of Alfred Bar who had for several years been Professor of French Literature in South America. He was an admirable man, completely devoted to General de Gaulle. After the war he became chef de cabinet in the French ministry of information. He invited me to his flat in the avenue Junot to listen to the BBC's broadcasts to France. His wife Renée had a sister Hélène, married to a civil servant called Jean Lajeunesse. They were also present in the flat when I heard the news from London for the first time since the occupation. It was like listening in a charnel house to the living.

There was a heavy curtain over the door, so that neighbours shouldn't hear the BBC, for listening to it was strictly forbidden by the Germans. Bar and Renée were especially afraid of their concierge as the Germans

had taken over the time-worn French habit of turning concierges, bar-
bers and their like into informers. We sat round the radio, speaking in
whispers.

'Like an anarchist meeting of fifty years ago,' I said. 'Only the beards
are missing.'

'We carry our beards in our hearts,' said Bar.

They all said that sooner or later I would get into trouble with the
Germans who were closing in, and employed a lot of spies. I left with
Hélène and Jean. 'If you get to England,' she said, 'you can fight against
the Boche. How I envy you.' A German patrol came down the avenue
Junot. The NCO in charge flashed his torch at us, shouting in bad French
that we should get off the street or he would arrest us. I answered him in
German, which generally disarmed them, saying in a jocular tone that
we were on our way home after a last drink. He gruffly said that that was
no excuse, and we must hurry. 'You see,' said Hélène, 'You must go.'

'I'll go in my own time,' I said.

The next day Hélène, who worked in the Préfecture de Paris, introduced me to a friend of hers who often crossed the demarcation line. I
gathered from him that the Germans had stopped issuing permits to go to
unoccupied France, urgent family matters or bereavement the sole
exception, though they would check, taking their time. 'One's always
late for funerals nowadays,' the friend said. The one answer was to get
across the demarcation line at night, taking the risk of being fired on by
German sentries, or knowing somebody living near the demarcation line
who might smuggle you across. I knew no such person.

Nona and I went every night to Bar's flat to listen to the BBC. They
continued to urge me to go, and I myself began to think there was no
alternative to going. The sales of the watercolours had sunk to practically nothing, the Germans kept to themselves and were suspicious. Gone
were the days when I could ask, 'Where are you stationed? Are you in
the infantry?' When I met my contact I had mighty little news for him.
The immortality of the soul and the ingredients for bortsch were discussed more than the German army. 'You ought to go,' he said, 'as
you've become useless here.' Still there were the leaflets. Besides, going
would mean leaving Nona.

October arrived. Through Hélène Lajeunesse I met several people
who in their official capacity frequently crossed the demarcation line. If I
got to Marseilles, they assured me, I would easily find ways and means to
get to Portugal, using false passports or hidden in cargo boats or fishing

vessels. In short you could pick and choose as long as you had plenty of money. I had no money.

I was in the middle of typing a new leaflet when I heard the doorbell ring. It was Jean's girl, wearing her cheap black dress. She must have shrunk because she was but a small speck, the yellow staircase walls a protruding background that would smother her. 'Are you alone?' she asked, coming into the hall. Nona was in the avenue Victor-Hugo with her mother. 'They caught Jean with those leaflets. They caught him in Lille.'

'Are you sure? How do you know it?'

One of their mutual friends, a Lillois, had come from Lille to tell her that Jean had been arrested several days before. Apparently, the Germans had watched him. There were too many leaflets about, and Jean was travelling too often to Paris, or maybe some friend had given him away. 'They'll shoot him,' the girl said. 'His pockets were always crammed with leaflets.'

She cried on my shoulder, and my only words of meagre consolation were, 'My poor girl,' and that the Germans would pay for it in the long run. She stayed for a while, we both knew that he would be shot or was dead already, and that we could do less than nothing about it. When she left I went down with her as far as the rue Gabrielle, a narrow street, the cobbles glistening because there had been a little rain. A mournful bec de gaz seemed to have grown out of the cobbles. I asked her whether she was angry with me for having helped and encouraged Jean in his work.

'Angry? But you were doing your duty, too.'

I might be the next one caught, I couldn't help thinking. I wondered whether I were afraid. I wasn't, for I had completely assimilated the mood and temper that was rising around me, and I had a start of nearly three months. None the less, I wanted to go, to get away from the Germans, to reach England which every particle of mine desired.

Through Denise Clairouin I had met a French banker before the German invasion who was planning to write a book about what Franco-English relations should be like after the war. He had asked me to help him with it when he could find time to write it. He had left Paris before the Germans arrived. If only he were here, I sighed, he would surely lend me money to get out.

Jean's girl had promised to come the following week. She didn't turn up, in fact I didn't see her again. (After the war I tried to find out what became of Jean, but had no success.) An American woman friend of

Nona's mother arrived from Marseilles, I lunched with her and Nona, and she assured me that Marseilles was the gateway to England. She gave me the address of a Marseillais who specialised in getting people over to Spain, and once in Spain things were easy. 'I don't want you to go,' Nona said as we left her. That night Hélène Lajeunesse said that she might arrange through her office in the Préfecture de Paris an official pass that would allow me to go to the unoccupied zone. Within a few days she would give me a final answer. Listening to London I felt it very near. As a matter of fact, it was eleven months away.

Next morning I went down into Paris, and as I had nothing much to do I called at the banker's office. Perhaps he had come back, though I felt sure he hadn't. 'Is M. Painlevé in?' I asked a girl at the counter. (He was no relation of the politician.)

'Just arrived,' she said. 'Do you want to see him?' She pushed a paper to me to write my name on it.

'What are you doing in Paris?' asked the banker who received me at once. 'How's Dodo?'

I told him of the summer I had had. He was aghast, then asked, 'But why don't you go?'

'Money,' I said. 'I haven't any, you see, as I'm cut off from England.'

'How much do you need?'

I mentioned a sum that for the Montmartre Maler was more than the proceeds of hundreds and hundreds of watercolours. Almost giddily yet proud of my daring I waited for his answer. 'Don't be childish,' he said. 'That's not enough.'

He named a sum that sounded like a king's ransom. 'I'll let you have it tomorrow,' he said, and asked me and Nona to lunch afterwards. Then he inquired about my plans. He thought Marseilles a good idea, but I shouldn't stay there long because the police were inquisitive. I ought to go to Cassis or some place like that, visiting Marseilles only to have a look round. And to beware of agents provocateurs who were thick on the ground. That very morning the papers reported that a yacht was caught off Cannes with about sixty people trying to make a getaway. I said I didn't fear agents provocateurs in that my experiences with the Germans had taught me to recognise them.

'I'll make inquiries,' he said as I was ready to leave, 'how to get across the demarcation line, and tell you tomorrow.'

He gave me a thousand francs on account, and I flew up to the Butte to take Nona out to lunch. Looking at her lovely face, then looking into her eyes, which a French friend had called des yeux troublants, I knew I couldn't lie to her. 'I have the money to go,' I said.

'I'm going with you,' she said. I said it was dangerous. 'Mother wants me to go back with her to the States in November. I can go back to the States on my own from Marseilles once you have found your way to England.' She spoke with that soft Californian accent of hers, the words seeming to come from her eyes. 'It's a ridiculous wildgoose chase, it'll be the end of both of us, but I'm going with you because I want to be with you a little longer.'

We decided not to say a word to her mother who was capable of denouncing me to keep her daughter near her.

Next morning I went to the banker, he gave me the money, also the name of a man in Nevers who specialised in smuggling people across the demarcation line. I should go to a hotel in Nevers, ask for him, and they would tell me which day he was coming over from unoccupied France. For he smuggled people in both directions. We lunched with the banker in a smart restaurant full of German staff officers, we parted after the meal, and I never saw my benefactor again as he died shortly before the liberation.

In the evening Hélène came with the news that next day she would get me the permit that would see me across the line, simpler than going to Nevers. 'Could you get one for Nona too?' She said that was possible once she got mine. We arranged to meet at one o'clock in Aux Armes de la Ville, near her office.

I arrived punctually, the brasserie was full, chiefly with Germans. Hélène was there already, looking startlingly pale.

'Got it?' I asked.

'No.' I raised my eyebrows. 'I've very bad news for you. Can't tell you here. Tell you after lunch.'

'I won't enjoy my lunch with bad news coming at the end of it. Tell me right now. There's so much noise that nobody will hear us.'

'All right. You're wanted by the Germans.'

'You're pulling my leg.'

'Pulling your leg? There's a warrant out for you since Monday.'

The day was Thursday, 17 October. My first reaction was that I felt flattered, in fact very flattered as I found it inconceivable that with a war on the Germans had had time to bother about me. It was too much of an honour.

'Don't grin,' said Hélène.

'Sorry, I can't help it.'

Trying to get the pass at the Préfecture de Police Hélène found out that I was on the list the Germans sent out weekly. The Paris police had instructions to arrest me and hand me over to them.

'I don't believe it,' I said.

That exasperated her. I asked why they didn't come to arrest me if they knew my address. Hélène explained that it was the Germans' practice to order the French police to find a person: the police didn't go out of their way to look for him, their excuse being that the dossiers of foreigners at the Préfecture had been destroyed before the Germans arrived. However, in my case the Germans themselves had provided the address, which meant that I had been denounced. So the police must come and take me whether they liked such work or not. 'What do they want me for?'

'I think sabotage. Did you do anything?'

'Oh, no.'

So it was the Jean business. But how, and who denounced me? Why hadn't the girl come again?

'You must go,' said Hélène. I assured her that I would leave on Saturday. The night before I had told her about the man of Nevers. The meal was over, and as she didn't have to go back to her office immediately we walked beside the river, and she told me about the destruction of the foreigners' files.

At the Préfecture de Police, in the same way as in other government departments, chaos was rampant when the Germans approached. On the last day it occurred to somebody or other that the foreigners' files shouldn't fall into German hands, since there were plenty of them in the pay of the Deuxième Bureau. So the files were going to be evacuated, and were put on a barge near the Préfecture. As the barge was starting to go down river the Germans happened to be already in Paris. The bargee could see them coming to the Préfecture. He didn't lose his head, and with a heroic gesture scuttled the barge with its load of documents. The Germans saw the proceedings (if they hadn't they would have been told), and for days on end dragged the Seine. A lot of papers were salvaged and put to dry in the courtyard of the Préfecture. But the Seine had its say, too. Only few papers escaped the ravages of the river, hence the number of legible documents was insignificant.

When Hélène left me I said to myself here walks a fugitive. Frankly, I felt like laughing. Notwithstanding my desire to laugh I went and packed a suitcase with a couple of suits, a few shirts, and when darkness came I took it to Bar's flat. Nona followed with a suitcase of hers.

We decided to tell nobody that we were going, one denunciation being enough. At nine o'clock we listened for the last time to the London news in Paris. Nona had been to the place du Tertre where she saw Eugène, who was worried because he hadn't seen me the whole day. She had seen Naly and Creixams too, but didn't breathe a word to either of them. There would be plenty of talk after we disappeared. Bar asked for my address in England. I gave him my brother's in Wiltshire. It was strange writing an address in England. We left our suitcases with Bar, saying we would come back to fetch them at daybreak. 'Let's go up to the Butte for a last drink,' I said to Nona. 'No, all that is finished,' she said.

First we went to a hotel we knew. The proprietor was sitting at the desk. When I went up to him and said we wanted a room for the night he said in a low voice, 'The place is full of the Gestapo. Look, there is one of them beside that column. Don't sleep here.' We left, and in one of the little streets, that were like rivulets going off in all directions, we stopped beside a notice, saying HOTEL, not even a name to it. I peeped in: it was dark, but I could hear the radio upstairs announcing, 'Les Français parlent aux Français'.

'We're sleeping here,' I said.

A little old woman and a little old man with a little elderly daughter sat round the radio, which was going full blast, telling the French from London that Admiral Darlan had sentenced Admiral Muselier to death. The little old people had a look at us, gave a room, and promised to wake us at half past four. They never asked us to fill in the registration papers.

'This is a bit silly,' I said to Nona before turning in. 'We could have spent the night in the flat, leaving early in the morning.'

'Better like this,' she said.

(After the liberation in his first letter Bar told me that the police had broken into the flat while Nona and I were in the little hotel.)

We left before daylight, rang Bar's bell, he came out, we took our suitcases, he shook my hand, saying, 'Merde, mon petit,' and we went. The Gare de Lyon was crowded. German field gendarmes walked up and down with fixed bayonets, carrying hand grenades and the small torches on their greatcoats made a luminous circle round them. As the train pulled out I said to myself, 'I'm on my way to England.'

The train being crowded, we stood in the corridor most of the way.

For obvious reasons Nona and I spoke in French, which was not only an effort in our case, but sounded unnatural to both of us. We burst into laughter now and again to the astonishment of the other passengers.

The sun beat down on Nevers and on the German stationmaster. We walked straight out, carrying our suitcases, and found the hotel. I didn't quite know how to start, so asked for a room. An old woman with white hair sat at the desk, the chambermaid standing beside her. A lot of luggage was piled up in the hall. I said we were going up to our room, and I wished to have a word with the proprietor who was the old woman's son.

'These are waiting too to go across,' the chambermaid said, pointing to the lounge.

She went on to explain that about twelve people were in the hotel waiting for M. Marius (the name the banker gave me) to come to take them to Vichy in his cars. M. Marius was in Paris, but would arrive at four. See that luggage? That's all going across. I was amazed. We climbed the stairs to our room, the proprietor came to say that the cars had crossed over from Vichy two days before, and he expected Marius back that night. It was doubtful whether he had room for us. Among the others were two ladies with two children, and most of the would-be travellers had seen Marius in Paris who had given them an appointment for that day. I shouldn't worry because Marius crossed the demarcation line twice a week. 'How does he do it?' I asked.

'That's his business. You'll see it's safe, though it was safer a little time ago. Then you just paid the German officers on duty, and they let you through. Now they've been changed.'

Marius and his magic cars didn't turn up that afternoon. The proprietor said it would be Monday, that is if Marius had room for us. We had to wait till Monday.

On Sunday afternoon I was in the hotel bar with only the proprietor's whitehaired mother present. She leaned over the counter, saying in a whisper, 'I was on the landing this morning, and heard you and madame speak English.' I said she was American. She brushed that aside. 'If you're English I'll see that Marius takes you along tomorrow, even if the rest of them have to stay behind. England must win the war, there's no other way of saving France.'

I was frank with her. I told her that I was partly running from the Germans, but chiefly wanted to get to England to help the cause that was both England's and France's. The old woman said that she would do all she could to help me, in short persuade Marius to take us along on Monday. Then she spoke of a Frenchwoman she knew, a royalist, who had been arrested by the Germans and was sentenced to death. The American Embassy was trying to save her. I asked why the Germans had taken her. 'She printed and distributed leaflets.'

That evening Nona and I dined in the town's best restaurant, where at the next table sat a fat German colonel in the company of two slim subalterns.

On Monday afternoon great commotion started around three o'clock, for Marius had arrived with two cars and a trailer for the luggage. There was a lot of noise and running about as all prospective travellers were trying to get at him. The old woman pulled him aside, and I heard her say that he must take Nona and me without fail. Her story was that Nona was ill, and had to see a specialist in Vichy. He said he had no room, she persisted, and before he could make up his mind she ordered the chambermaid to put our luggage into the trailer, then pushed us into the first car. The car was full, so was the other car, and the trailer was a mountain of luggage. The roofs of the cars were packed high with suitcases. In our small car we were five inside, and two more sat beside Marius. While the luggage was loaded some German soldiers stopped to watch the proceedings. A platinum blonde sat with Nona and me on the back seat, and two men sat in front of us, one of whom had recently come from the free zone to attend to some business in Paris. Now he was returning to the world of Vichy. We had had a chat in the hotel bar, he praising Pétain and Laval, also the Germans whom he found correct. He hoped they would soon defeat the English so that there should be peace in Europe again. His way of thinking and speaking ought to have been a warning. However, in the bliss that leaving the Germans meant to me I had no room for any kind of warning.

We set out. The countryside was lovely in its autumn fulfilment, gold and blue, the gold giving way as the sun was going down. The second car had some engine trouble, we stopped and Marius fixed it up. He said we were late: he wouldn't risk it in the dark since the headlights would betray us. We drove faster, and a sort of conversation went on between Marius and the passengers. He was short, had a small moustache, wore a felt hat, and said that last time the Uhlans who guarded the frontier had nearly caught him. He would have to give up the lucrative job, otherwise he was bound to land in jail. Towards six o'clock we turned off the route nationale, and motored along a by-pass. It was deserted till we passed a German car with the driver working on the engine. He looked up, watching us placidly. Farther on two German cyclists came towards us. They went by, and then the cars with the trailer bobbing up and down turned on to a cart track.

'We're getting to the critical stage,' the platinum blonde said. The man who liked the Germans was sweating profusely. We got to a lone farmstead, the cars stopped, the farmer and his daughter came up to tell Marius that two German soldiers were working on the telephone wires not far away. Marius ordered her to go, watch, and report when they left. Obediently the girl raced off on her bicycle. Marius told us that we could get out and stretch our legs. Both cars gave up their load of passengers, thirteen in all, including the two children who travelled on their mothers' knees. There was perfect peace around us. The sun was going, yet its warmth remained on the yellow fields. 'I wish to God we could stay here for ever,' Nona said.

'En voiture,' Marius commanded as the girl reappeared, waving all clear from the distance. We moved off, the track was bad, and the cars jumped and lurched. The pro-German was in agony while we took sharp turnings with bushes hiding all that might await us round the bend. On a tree hung a wooden board: Ligne de Démarcation. Marius drove slowly, glancing back to see if the second car were following. The track straightened with bushes and trees on both sides. As we drove through an empty water-bed Marius called out, 'Here it comes.'

Ahead of us a strip of asphalt was visible. The car took a sharp bend, then more asphalt, and when we got to it we were on the main road between the two frontier posts. Because of the curve of the road we saw neither of them. Marius accelerated, and then, with much oncoming wind, the road became a straight line. The French post with the tricolour barrier was in front of us. To see French uniforms and helmets was sheer joy. The barrier was raised, and the cars rolled into unoccupied France. Stupidly, I thought that my tribulations were over.

10

The first thing I did in Vichy was to send Hélène a postcard, telling her that we had arrived safely. I signed myself Antoine. (In 1943 she and Jean, her husband, were arrested by the Gestapo as members of the Résistance. Jean was tortured to death in Fresnes prison, Hélène they took to a concentration camp in Germany, where many Frenchwomen died. After the Americans had liberated the inmates of the camp Hélène came back with her health undermined. I saw a lot of her when I came to Paris after the war. She died in 1954, God rest her brave soul.)

I looked round Vichy. The previous Sunday I had been to Mass at Notre-Dame in Paris. Despite the occupation I felt more hope there than in Vichy, which smelt of defeat. The Marshal's photographs oozed paternal discouragement. Never have I seen so many generals and admirals in such small a space. Almost every hotel was turned into a government department, and the gardes républicains on sentry duty spent their time presenting arms to the generals and admirals. Policemen and gendarmes were thick on the ground; so were soldiers with armbands saying, Démobilisé, there being no civilian suits for them. On the benches sat armless and legless soldiers in hospital blue. Men in dark suits, evidently civil servants, thronged the cafés.

Like most people in occupied Paris I believed that the Marshal and his ministers had remained in their heart of hearts faithful to their ally, and their official pronouncements were but to hoodwink the Germans. I was quickly disabused.

A friend of Nona's mother lived in Vichy, a Frenchwoman married to an American who had died before the outbreak of the war. We called on her the next afternoon. She was giving a tea party for half a dozen white-haired women, members of the French nobility, who asked us many questions about occupied France, and when England would win. One of the old women said that an ancestor of hers had his head nearly cut off during the Revolution. 'One of my ancestors,' another old woman tartly said, 'did have his head cut off.' The first old woman was squashed.

A male guest appeared, clicking his heels and giving the Nazi salute.

'Is he a German?' I whispered.

'No, he's a high official in the ministry of foreign affairs.'

'What about going?' I said to Nona. I would most probably have stayed on if he had been a German. That high official should have been a warning, too.

In the evening we entrained for Marseilles, but before the train left every passenger's identity papers were examined by plain clothes men, who were accompanied by uniformed police. 'France,' said a fellow passenger, 'has always suffered by its bureaucracy. Since the defeat, it's worse than ever.'

As you come out of the station of Saint-Charles in Marseilles you reach the steps that lead to the boulevard Gomier, and you behold the town of Notre-Dame-de-la-Garde. However, it was still dark when we got to the steps only a few lights, that had escaped the willy-nilly blackout, revealing the town which was going to bring me more misery than there are poplars on the roads of France.

We took breakfast in a café on the Canebière. As Nona was tired after sitting up the whole night in the train I went in search of a hotel room, which wasn't easy, for that was the period when the gutters of the Continent had emptied their filth into Marseilles. After much trotting around I found a room in a hotel on the Canebière, and Nona went to lie down. I would fetch her before lunch.

I called on a Frenchman whose name the banker had given me. He was a noisy son of the South with an exceedingly rosy outlook on life and on things in general. Oh, he loved England and prayed for her victory. He was in the shipping business, and since the armistice his business was going to pieces. When, oh when, would the English win the war to restore his business? Something is missing here, I said to myself. He would help me to get to England which was mighty easy. One had, however, to be careful because police spies abounded, still, I shouldn't worry, he would ring a friend of his who kept an hotel, and get moderate prices for us. I asked how much the trip to Gibraltar would cost? He said that depended, giving me the impression that he hadn't the faintest idea. I left disappointed.

Then I went to see the Englishman whose name was given to me in Paris too, and, who was attached to the American consulate. His name was Good or Cook, I can't exactly remember since like the shipowner he played no part in my Marseilles adventures. He listened attentively to me, keen on giving the impression that he was a man of mystery, a sort of Lawrence of Marseilles. He assured me that he would help me to get out of France if I didn't find a way out alone. He expected to be leaving soon, too. For the time being the French didn't bother the English, but that couldn't last. We were both apprehensive about the encounter between Hitler and Laval that was taking place that day.

Nona and I lunched at a restaurant called Basso in the Vieux Port. We saw a small ferry the *Abbé Faria* leaving for the Château d'If. The afternoon we spent strolling around the town which was jammed with refugees from the occupied zone. In the evening we dined on bouillabaisse, then I accompanied Nona to the hotel. I said I wasn't coming in yet, I wanted to walk round a bit.

'Please don't,' said Nona. 'I don't want you to walk about alone.'

'I'm not five years old,' I said.

It turned out that I was.

I walked up the heavily crowded Canebière, then for reason or reasons unknown I crossed over to the other side, turned to the right, and ambled up the avenue Léon Gambetta, of which I had never heard, and which was just as unknown to me as any other street in Marseilles. Five bars were next to each other. I chose one at random, the chairs were red, and a short staircase led to more red chairs. I went to the counter, ordered a drink, then looked round. Among the few customers sat three soldiers in hospital blue, their crutches leaning against the wall. I looked more carefully: all three had a leg missing. I felt pity and admiration for those French soldiers, and gave twenty francs to the woman behind the counter, asking her to give them the money with my best wishes. I finished the drink, and started for the door. One of the soldiers hobbled up to me.

'It's very kind of you to give us the money,' he said, 'but we're not tramps, so if you want us to take it you must have a drink with us.' I thought that was decent of them, and sat down at their table. I said that the day would come when their lost legs which they hadn't lost in vain, would be revenged, for England would win the war, and France would be free again.

'I don't mind who wins the war,' one of them growled. 'Let the Germans and the English kill each other off. It was always the French who were killed. Now it's England's turn.'

I began to regret the twenty francs. Later I was to regret them even more.

Materialising out of the red background a tall, fair soldier, wearing khaki and a beret, appeared. He gave me a brilliant smile, then addressed me in English, which he spoke without an accent.

'The proprietor has just told me,' he said, 'that you gave some money to these unfortunate men. Very handsome of you, sir.'

'You speak remarkably good English,' I said.

'I used to be interpreter with the Argyle and Sutherland Highlanders in the last war. Those were the days. We won that war, we didn't lose it like this one. It's terrible for an old soldier like me. There's only one thing I want.'

'What's that?'

'To go to Blighty.'

I asked where he came from. He said he was from Lille. That was the town of poor Jean, one more reason to warm to him. 'It's nice to speak to you,' I said, and ordered him a drink. 'These poor chaps don't seem very keen on England.'

'Don't mind them, sir. They're just ignorant peasants. You live in Marseilles?'

I said I had just arrived from Paris. That interested him, which I found natural enough. He asked me many questions, and lamented the mentality of his fellow countrymen in the unoccupied zone. 'There's hardly a Frenchman left, a real Frenchman.' I leaned forward a little as I said that there were two real Frenchmen left, General de Gaulle and Admiral Muselier. He asked whether I intended to get to England. His question reminded me of the several warnings I had about agents provocateurs. I cautiously said I had no idea. 'I myself want to go,' he said. 'I'll get there. The first step is Casablanca.' Why Casablanca? 'There you can always find a ship to Lisbon. If only one had the money one could bribe the seamen to stop at Gibraltar.' He gave me a sidelong glance, and I thought he would ask for money. 'An old soldier never stops fighting. He goes on. I'm going to Blighty.'

The three wounded were getting fighting drunk. They had a loud row, and I felt as though the red café were closing in on me. I said good night, wishing I could take a jump that would land me in the hotel bed beside Nona. The soldier left with me, continuing to talk about Blighty. However, I had had enough of him and Blighty, so said good-night and entered the next bistrot, as that seemed the simplest means of getting rid of him. He followed me in, saying in a choking voice, 'Excuse me, sir, but you have a kind heart, so you understand that the life of an old soldier is sheer misery in a defeated, betrayed country, I thought you might be interested in helping me to Blighty.' I said I was sorry, but I couldn't help him. 'I can't even afford a drink or cigarettes,' he bleated. I gave him ten francs, then left, and as I turned towards the Canebière a policeman came up from behind, telling me to follow him.

'Do you want to see my papers?' I asked.

'We'll see later on,' he said. 'Hurry up.'

I wasn't frightened or anything else. I had heard of continuous round-ups in Marseilles. The only annoying part was that it would keep me an hour or so from Nona. He took me to the police station, where I was put into a big, barren room and told to wait. A drunk followed me, he fell against the wall, then slid to the floor, and lay still. Another policeman took me into an office with two men sitting behind a large table. One of them turned to me.

'You were distributing money to soldiers in the traitor de Gaulle's name.'

'Nonsense.'

'Do you deny having given twenty francs to three mutilés?'

'That is true. I gave them twenty francs because I was sorry for them. I arrived from Paris this morning.'

'You gave ten francs to a serving soldier too.' I admitted that I had. Dear me, it did sound incriminating. 'Do you deny that you gave those sums in the name of ex-General de Gaulle?'

'It was my own money.'

They whispered to each other, then they said that they would keep me for the night, and if I had no police record I would be let out in the morning.

'But I don't want to spend the night here,' I nearly shouted. 'Such a thing couldn't happen in occupied Paris. It's riotously funny that in un-occupied France it's a crime to give a few francs to wounded French soldiers.'

I was livid with rage and indignation. When I saw they were adamant I became a credit to Miss Rosy in as much as I said that if they let me go I would come back in the morning upon my word of honour. They didn't want my word. Then I thought of Nona and how worried she would be, and asked them to let me telephone. 'To whom?' I said to my wife, since that seemed the easiest way of putting it. They said they had no objection. 'Can I say on the telephone that I'm arrested?'

'You needn't say that. Just tell them in the hotel to tell your wife that you're spending the night somewhere else.'

'I don't think she'll appreciate that,' I said.

A policeman led me into a little room, where a telephone stood on a table, beside which there lolled in an armchair the soldier who so very much wanted to go to Blighty. My eyes opened. It was a shock composed of such disgust that I was nearly sick. 'You dirty cad,' I spluttered. Not unkindly the policeman told me to shut up, then he told the soldier to get out of the room. I spoke to the hotel, asked them to tell Nona that I was arrested, and the night porter said, 'Oui, monsieur, à votre service,' as if being arrested were the most normal thing on earth under Marshal Pétain.

I was led out into the street, and shoved into a police car that took me through half the town before stopping outside a gloomy building into which I was led after a heavy door was unbolted by another policeman. I was taken down a dimly lit staircase with prostitutes all over the place. I was searched, and my money, cigarettes and tie taken away. I asked why they took my tie.

'That,' laughed the Corsican warder, 'is the sign in France that you're no longer free.' He took my braces too. There were doors right, left and centre, and a heavy smell of latrines hung in the air, so strong that the warder, my loss of liberty, and the prison were, so to speak, overwhelmed by it. Through the spy hole of one of the doors feverish eyes were staring at us. 'Put me into a different cell,' I said to the warder, who then opened the door of another cell, whispering into my ear that that was the best cell, and he would return my cigarettes and give me some of my money once the policemen were gone. I was locked in, but a few minutes later the warder handed through the peep-hole three hundred francs and cigarettes.

A long contraption, like a sloping table, filled the cell. In the corner was a latrine with the flush working every twenty seconds or so, as if wanting to gear your time-table to it. Several pale men sat or lay on the wooden contraption, others paced the floor. A lean man with long dark hair stared at the wall on which a guillotine was drawn with large letters under it: 'Aux condés, aux mouchards, à Hitler le saligaud.' I asked him what condé and mouchard meant.

'You must be a foreigner,' he said. 'Condé in Marseilles means a policeman, mouchard is a man who betrays you, squeals on you, a man who's in police pay.' That was the accurate description of the soldier who wanted to go to Blighty. 'Are you Italian?' I asked. He nodded happily, and was going to speak, probably of the mamma and the bambini, but I stopped him by asking where I was. His face fell as he told me that I was in the Évêché, which used to be the bishop's palace before the Third Republic turned it into the police prison which it still is. The door opened and a drunken American was pushed into our midst, swearing that if they didn't let him out in the morning he would cable President Roosevelt. Towards dawn he and I sat side by side on the wooden contraption, both feeling certain that it was a huge joke as both of us would be released in the morning. 'Say,' he said, 'who's going to win the war?'

'England,' I said, 'otherwise I wouldn't be here.' On that I fell asleep, dreaming of Nona whom I would see when I was let out in the morning.

The American was called around seven o'clock: my name was called one hour later. I was led across a courtyard by a little man, looking like a toadstool straight from a damp cellar, to an office, where several plain clothes men were questioning a prostitute, her answers making them laugh. Good cheer reigned. While I waited Nona swept into the room.

'Really, Peter, you ought to put on your tie,' she said.

'There's nothing I'd like more.'

The prostitute departed, the chief clerk, or whoever he was, examined my papers, found them in order, and asked if I had any money. I showed him the receipt I was given when my money was taken away, he nodded, then asked laughingly, what was that about de Gaulle. In the same spirit I laughed, saying that was a lot of nonsense.

'Nowadays one musn't speak about him,' he said. 'Perhaps some day it's going to be the right thing to speak about him.' He got up, said he would take the papers to the chief to have my release signed. Nona thanked him, and we discovered that neither of us had any cigarettes left. She said she would go and get some, and I shouldn't leave the place before she was back. However, before she had time to return the clerk reappeared and in a completely changed voice told me to follow him. My heart sank as I was led back to the cell with the circular contraption. 'You are here,' he said, 'at the "disposition du chef de la Sûreté".' That chief was a French naval captain, bursting with hatred of the English since the battle of Mers-el-Kebir. (Probably before that too.)

'There's no decency left in the world,' said an Italian newcomer. During the long day the cell filled with his fellow countrymen. They had come to France before the first world war, fought in the French army, worked as Italians do with the sweat of their brows, never complaining, yearly producing a French child. They volunteered in 1939, a great sin in the Duce's and (retrospectively) in the Pétain government's eyes, which reached an agreement with him to send all Italians back. Hence the presence of those unfortunate men in the large cell.

The day passed with the latrine flushing every few seconds. Towards evening things livened up. A young man was shoved in, who told us that he had just been caught stealing. Being the first thief I had come into contact with I was shy in the beginning, which seems funny today since during my incarceration I made friends with murderers, and their like. Still, one isn't brave at the beginning. He was followed by a batch of loud Corsicans, caught playing for money in a café, cardsharps and pimps the lot of them, though happy because they would be released within twenty-four hours. The cell filled, a male prostitute bitterly complained about his rotten luck. He had made a pass at a lovely young man, the beast, who turned out to be an off-duty condé, arrested him at once. One of the Corsicans wrote on the wall, 'Vive ciurcil'. We lay twenty-four of us on the wooden contraption. Those that were brought in after midnight slept on the floor.

In the morning I was taken by two detectives to the political department of the Sûreté, where a naval officer in mufti questioned me. 'What happened the other night?'

'Nothing.'

'Don't lie to me. You gave money to French soldiers, saying to them that England would win the war, and there were only two Frenchmen left, de Gaulle and Muselier.'

'Isn't one allowed to say that England will win the war? France isn't at war with England.'

'England is harbouring de Gaulle and Muselier whom France has condemned to death. Praising them, and giving money in their name is a crime.'

I had thought it all out in the night. The wounded were three, the three of them heard me say that England would win the war, therefore I couldn't deny that. However, of de Gaulle and Muselier I spoke only to the mouchard. By admitting the first I would give the impression of not being a liar. 'I said that England would win the war, but General de Gaulle and Admiral Muselier weren't mentioned.'

'We've five witnesses to prove that you used those words.'

Then he read out the soldier's evidence which, like its author, was a nasty piece of work. His name was Van der Bock. (After the war Duff Cooper asked me whether I intended to take action against him. 'I prefer to forget him,' I answered, and truly enough I write his name without any anger or rancour.) The statement declared that the bit about General de Gaulle was said to all of them. He was called in, and he upheld what he had written while I kept to my version. I believed I scored a point when I said that he and I had spoken in English, whereas the soldiers couldn't understand a word of that language, a further proof that he was lying. He changed his statement to my having said it only to him. When we were alone again the naval officer said that I would be confronted with the three wounded in the afternoon, it depending on their evidence whether I would be released or handed over to the military authorities. I was led back to the big cell.

In the afternoon a warder told one of the Italians that his wife and children were downstairs, wanting to see him, which of course was out of the question. Joining his hands as in prayer the Italian begged the warder to let him see them just for a second, even if only from a distance. The warder shook his head, banged then locked the door and went away. The Italian broke down, sobbed loudly, calling to God and the Madonna to give him back to his family. Though I had plenty of other things to think about I went to the weeping man, trying to console him. This hateful world couldn't last, God wouldn't let it, England would win the war, and then everything would be fine again. He calmed down, grabbed my hand, held it, and I felt selfconscious.

Later in the day I was taken in a police car to see the men for whom I had been sorry. We picked up Van der Bock in a barracks, and I didn't enjoy riding in the same car with him. We drove to a military hospital. The naval officer and Van der Bock went in, I was left in the car, and when they returned the officer said he saw no reason to confront me with the three legless soldiers who had told him that they had heard nothing. Back at the Évêché he said that Nona had been to see him. She would be back towards the evening when he would tell her that I would be released in the morning. Why not now? Because I must go first before the procureur (public prosecutor) to have my release signed.

I passed a cheery night, got back my money and tie in the morning, then with a large crowd streaming out of the different cells I was taken upstairs to be photographed and have my fingerprints taken. Then we were bundled into a Black Maria, the panier à salade as the cognoscenti call it. I sat in a narrow steel cell with hardly any room for my legs; through the little wired window the town looked out of focus. Arriving at the Palais de Justice about thirty of us were pushed into a cell that wasn't large enough for ten. For the first time I heard the prison of Chaves mentioned, sheer hell I was assured.

A gendarme came to fetch me, put a chain round my wrist, then dragged me towards a passage. I was pulled into a room, where the chain was taken off. A tall man sat at a table, the juge d'instruction (examining magistrate), his clerk sat at another. He bade me sit down, the gendarme remained a large shadow behind me. 'You're accused of a heinous offence,' the judge said in a pleasant voice.

'I was told that I would be let out.'

'The public prosecutor takes a very serious view of it. I fully realise that you aren't a real criminal. I'm going to confront you with the soldier and the three wounded at the earliest date as I don't want to keep you longer than is necessary, that is if you're innocent. I'll summon you all for next Wednesday.' It was Saturday 26 October.

'In the meantime?' I asked.

'You're going to Chaves. Don't forget this is a very serious charge.'

The Prison de Chaves was pulled down some time after the war, but while it existed it was considered as one of the worst old prisons of France. Though it was the only French prison I knew I fully agree. The Black Maria took me and a horde of others to the prison which was on the road to Aubagne. The Black Maria waited for some time after it came to a halt. When the cells were unlocked we were herded into a round hall with a sort of porter's box in the middle. Iron bars were everywhere, naked electric bulbs shed their harsh lights on doors, corridors and balconies with bars. 'Then the process of stripping us of everything Christ died for began,' I wrote to Nona in my first letter. While we all stood naked our money was counted, and were told we would get a receipt for it the next day. Some of the prisoners were recognised by the warders who exchanged humorous words with them. As a first offender I felt rather out of it.

Because I had money I was put into the third division with the posh cells which had a hole and a flush, not just a can emptied once a day. I had spent a hundred and eleven days in bed with typhoid fever: in Chaves I was to spend an equal amount of time, my only crime being that I had felt sorry for three mutilated soldiers. It took me a while to get accustomed to that. Though the cell was intended for two prisoners now there were five, at times even six. The first to speak to me was an Englishman who knew little English. He had been born in Marseilles, and had never in his life been to England. He was about forty, a sad disillusioned man, groaning in his sleep, proclaiming his innocence the whole length of the day. He was in for having bought stolen army lorries for his building business after the fall of France. Like so many others he had thought that with the collapse law and order had collapsed too, forgetting or over-looking that if France were blown sky high somehow or other a gen-darme would remain on the ground. He was a member of the Chamber of Commerce, he was a paterfamilias, he had an unblemished record as a businessman, and tears would course down his cheeks as he declared that life wasn't worth living for honest men.

My next new friend was Mathieu, a ponce, who was inside for about the seventh time for living on women's immoral earnings. Prison for him was like going back to his club. He was born and bred in the Marseilles slums, his first memory of policemen taking his mother away, accused of stealing in the docks. He knew no other world than the underworld, his thoughts never stretching beyond it. What I found so deplorable about him was his lack of knowing his trade. The same could be said of almost all of them. Being practically illiterate he asked me one morning to write a letter to his wife for him. He started dictating, 'Ma chère femme, tell Odette that if she doesn't pay up she'll be in trouble when I come out. If Marie-Anne calls threaten her as that is the only way of getting our due out of her . . .' When he reached the fifth name I put down the pencil, turned to him, and said, 'Mathieu, you're in here accused of living on women's immoral earnings. You deny it, and here you give them perfect proof that you're living on women's immoral earnings. The judge, who censors every letter, will be delighted to read this.'

'Faccio de con,' Mathieu exclaimed, 'how clever you are. Of course, you're right. What am I to say to my wife?'

Like most of the members of the underworld and like most of the detainees he invented a dream world that had nothing to do with reality. He had the best tailor in Marseilles, the cheap jacket he wore wasn't really his, the flat he lived in had seven rooms, his car was a Buick, and when he went to Paris he stayed at the Ritz. The Breton, who had his paliasse next to him, interjected that he was a regular, highly respected customer of the Hôtel Meurice in Paris. The Breton was accused of rob-bery. After I came out of prison I called on Mathieu who had been let out on provisional liberty a few weeks before me. He lived in a tenement, one kitchen and one small room, where wife, he and their two children slept.

The lack of intelligence and efficiency characterised the many crooks I came in contact with in Chaves, meeting them during the twice ten minutes daily loitering in the courtyard. A tall fellow told me his sad tale with much shaking of his head and repeating, 'I just can't understand.' His woman worked in a brothel, he went to see her nightly, and between them they knew where the manageress kept the money. So one night they fell on her, threatening to kill her if she didn't hand over the money, and still threatening her they made her promise not to say a word to the authorities. Satisfied with their work they rushed to a night club to celebrate, then returned to the brothel, finding to their utter astonishment the police waiting for them. 'I'll beat the hell out of her when I get out,' he said to console himself.

'And you'll be back here the same day,' I couldn't help observing.

A young male prostitute arrived in our cell. He had robbed a man who had taken him back to his flat, erroneously believing that the man wouldn't denounce him. 'That bugger has no sense of shame,' he said. 'Going to the police, admitting that he's a queer.' He almost added that indeed France was going to the dogs. The son of an honest mason he cried a lot the first night, calling, 'Maman, maman.'

'You ought to have thought of her before,' said an old Corsican seaman sententiously. He had knifed another seaman in a brawl.

Mathieu, the seaman, and the male prostitute were admittedly small fry: the big fish were as stupid and incompetent as they. A lanky man in our cell, called André, had embezzled millions as a company director. He was caught because he hadn't given his bookkeeper, who was his accomplice, a few thousand francs when his wife was ill. 'Nobody can blackmail me,' he proudly told us. He got seven years, and when he came to fetch his belongings on his way to the Maison Centrale de Nîmes he cried on my shoulder, moaning, 'Why didn't I give him the few francs he wanted?'

The biggest fish I met was Mola, the train robber and murderer. The train robbery had taken place in 1936, Mola and three companions attacking a bullion train, transporting Banque de France gold to Marseilles. They attacked it with hand grenades and killed two of the guards. Mola vanished, in fact went into hiding in his native Corsica, and shot and killed two gendarmes before he was arrested. Definitely a big fish. He was brought from Nîmes three weeks after my arrival. He was already sentenced for the train robbery; now he would have to answer for the two gendarmes. The number of the warders on duty was doubled, the prison clock stopped, in short every precaution was taken so

that he shouldn't escape. It was feared that friends of his would try something from the outside. The whole of Chaves was thrilled at the news of
such a great man coming into our midst. Though Mola was kept in a cell
alone he was allowed into the courtyard during our twice ten minutes a
day exercise period. On the third or fourth day I asked Mathieu to point
out Mola when we were in the courtyard. 'But you know him,' said
Mathieu. 'You were talking to him this morning.'

'You mean the little man with the black felt hat, the one who looks
like a bank clerk?'

'That's the one,' said Mathieu.

Mola had mild eyes and a mild expression, a tiny moustache and a
weak chin. Having made friends with him I asked him during one of our
brief walks how he had killed the gendarmes, my writer's ears throbbing
in anticipation. 'They came along the road, I was hiding behind a bush, I
lifted my revolver and killed them.' Not even a page, I sighed. In the
course of another conversation I mentioned that a sock of mine needed
darning. 'Give it to me,' he said. 'I'm very good at it, and it makes time
fly.' Mola, the murderer, darned the sock, and darned it so well that I
couldn't help observing to Jack, the Englishman, that he had missed his
vocation.

Mola was taken back to Nîmes, the clock chimed again, and fewer
warders patrolled the corridors. After the war I heard that he had had his
head cut off a year after his visit to Chaves.

A sergeant-major of the French Colonial Army joined us towards the
middle of my stay. He was in for putting counterfeit money into circula-
tion. He had a wooden leg, which he took off at night, and which Jack
and I used as our pillow. After his transfer to Nice we missed the leg. He
was followed by a youth who had emptied the chamber of his revolver
into another dancer at a public dance. He pleaded self defence, the juge
d'instruction decided to believe him, and the key made an awful racket
as the door was unlocked, and the warder shouted. 'Take your belongings.'

'It's all ready,' the youth calmly said, engraved his name on the wall,
and went into freedom.

The daily routine began at six in the morning when the light was
switched on from the outside. There was no switch in the cell. Then the
door was opened to let us collect our suits, for you had to put them outside the door before the light was switched off. The warders had a large
dog that roamed the corridors, and made water on the bundles of clothes

which in the morning smelt of urine. The reason you had to put trousers and jacket outside was to stop you from trying to escape in the night. When we were dressed, and had washed our faces in a stone basin which each filled from a jug, the paliasses were rolled up, and the cell cleaned with a broom a prison orderly, also a prisoner, brought in for ten minutes or so. At eight o'clock the door was unlocked, we streamed into the courtyard, then stood in small groups, chatting till we were sent back into our cells. At eight-thirty we received our fifty grammes of daily bread, the less strong minded eating it at once, the others keeping it for the meal that arrived at nine. Twice a week it consisted of rice full of maggots, twice a week boiled cabbage with a bit of lard, twice lentils, and on Sunday, we had a slice of boiled beef. It was a starvation diet, calculated to keep the detainees' spirits down. It succeeded. After the meal there was nothing to do till the next outing at four o'clock. We spent our time talking nineteen to the dozen or reading, I mean Jack and I did, the illiterate played cards. Nona sent in several works of Balzac and Maupassant, but there were books circulating in the prison, and if you finished a book you gave it to the first person in need of reading material in the courtyard. An unsavoury looking crook gave me Montherlant's *Les Célibataires*.

A warder brought round wine, and cigarettes for those who could buy them, as many packets as you wanted. We were permitted only one litre of red wine a day, and if it wasn't drunk by the next morning no wine was sold to you. This was so that you shouldn't hoard wine to get drunk on and break down the door, which would have been quite a feat. At four you were allowed out for another ten minutes, on your return you had watery soup, at six you put out your clothes, at seven the light was switched off, and you started counting the chimes of the prison clock. We missed the chimes while Mola was with us.

The newcomer conformed to a certain code of behaviour. He was pushed into the cell, the door banged behind him, he said, 'Bonjour,' sat down on the only chair, sighed, took out a packet of cigarettes, usually Gitanes, and offered one to all present, a fine gesture, for from previous experience he knew that only Gauloises were available in prison. He sighed again, and you asked him how many days he had spent at the Évêché. Usually between two and four: they had beaten him hard, but they couldn't get a word out of him. You knew that was a lie as the professional crook talks after a little beating. However, you nodded politely, implying that it had been the same with you. With the ice thus broken you asked him why he was in. The serious professional, like the Wimbledon player who doesn't underrate his opponent, would say that it was a serious affair. A long, twisted lie would emerge, the truth not emerging even by mistake. The less serious invariably said, 'Je n'y suis pour rien.' That phrase became as much my companion as the twilight and the stench of the tin cans. The non-professional blurted out everything before you could put the question to him. Professionals and non-professionals acquired the same prison pallor in under a week.

I was generally respected by them. They considered me a political prisoner, and as de Gaulle was against the authorities that had arrested them they declared themselves Gaullists. In the courtyard a pickpocket asked me to tell the General if I ever got to London that he was all for him, hence was entitled to an amnesty once the General swept away the present rulers of unoccupied France. He gave me a piece of paper with his name on it. They respected me too because I wasn't one of them, no women worked for me, I belonged to no gang, wasn't mixed up in hold-ups, in brief I was an exotic bird in whom they could confide.

Sex as such wasn't discussed. Food was our favourite subject, and if you spoke of meals of six courses eyes shone, and mouths watered. Even if you had never been near the great restaurants of France you spoke as if you had dined and wined in them every day. Of course, we were starved, which was probably the reason why we longed for food and not for women.

My own life consisted of waiting, one moment full of hope, the next envisaging the worst. Jack had suggested I take his lawyer, and knowing none in Marseilles I took him on. He was an elderly man, full of good-will and smelling of wine. The juge d'instruction kept his word in that I was taken to the Palais de Justice on the Wednesday following my incarceration. I spent the whole day in a cell waiting to be summoned by the magistrate. One of my companions was a butcher who had raped his six-year-old stepdaughter and been denounced by the child's mother, that is his wife. He was in for seven years' hard labour at least. Someone asked whether it had been worth it. The butcher grunted and shrugged his shoulders.

At seven I was taken into the judge's chamber, where the judge, his clerk, Van der Bock and the three mutilated soldiers were sitting in a cloud of smoke. They looked at ease. Léon, the judge, shouted in an aggressive voice, 'Sit down, your lawyer isn't here. Do you want us to start without him or do you want me to postpone the confrontation?'

His attitude had changed.

'Start now,' I said.

'Sergeant Van der Bock,' said Léon, 'has made a very explicit and convincing statement.' I asked why my lawyer wasn't present. 'What do I know, nothing to do with me.' Next day I found out that when the lawyer had telephoned, Léon had answered that my case wasn't coming up yet. From Léon's voice and the inimical atmosphere I gathered that I wouldn't be released. None the less, I decided to fight for it.

He read Van der Bock's statement. I had sought him out in the café, forced drinks on him, praised the English, said they would win the war, spoke disparagingly of the Germans, and told him that an English fighter had written CONFIDENCE in the sky of Paris (which I had seen with my own eyes).

'Is that a crime too?' I asked. 'Arrest the RAF for it, not me.'

'Don't interrupt me,' thundered Léon.

The enumeration of my crimes continued. I had tried to persuade Van der Bock to desert, go to Casablanca, and was ready to put up the money to bribe French seamen. I praised the two traitors. He followed me into the street, saw me go into several bars, speaking to soldiers. What had I to say for myself?

My answer was that the evidence of a beggar wasn't trustworthy. The man had admitted that he had asked for and taken ten francs from me. 'At the police station,' Van der Bock interjected, 'I separated his ten francs from my money, wanting to give it back to him.' I said, 'But he didn't.' Léon observed that Van der Bock naturally wanted to find out more about the man who had justly, aroused his suspicion. So he played the sympathiser. 'A perfect explanation,' I said. 'I break into somebody's house, steal the family plate, then say that suspecting him I broke in to find out more about him.'

'This isn't the way to speak here,' Léon growled. 'You'll learn respect before we're through with you.'

The next accusation, I said, was my proclaiming that England would win the war. France wasn't at war with England: they had been allies not so many months ago. Speaking disparagingly of the Germans: France was still at war with Germany since no peace treaty had been signed. De Gaulle and Muselier: he had only Van der Bock's word for it, the word of the man who begged ten francs. First he had stated that I said that to all of them, but when I hotly denied it he changed it to my having said it to him alone in English. Why? 'When I said to us, I meant the company at the table,' said Van der Bock.

'A very reasonable answer,' said Léon.

I went on. Even if I had said it in English De Gaulle and Muselier were French names. The wounded would have heard those French names, especially as they were well known. I turned to them: had they heard those two names? By then I was aware that those simple peasants were frightened out of their wits that they might get into trouble for having accepted twenty francs from the General's agent, and, might, which was too terrible for words, have to return the money. They doggedly said that they hadn't heard a word. 'There you are,' I said triumphantly. Léon brushed it aside, but I insisted on the clerk putting it down. Van der Bock had one more thing to say, namely that I stood him a whisky, a monstrously expensive drink, which clearly showed that I wanted to incite him to sedition. The wounded added that they wouldn't have accepted the money if they had known that I was the traitor's henchman.

'What's going to happen now?' I asked Léon.

'You'll stay in prison till I send you in front of the tribunal. The tribunal will decide whether Sergeant Van der Bock or you should be believed.'

As I have said before he kept me for hundred and eleven days, not even allowing Nona to visit me. 'I don't want him to communicate with the outside world,' he said to my lawyer.

The days became a constant blur, hardly a beginning or an end, and they passed surprisingly quickly. I looked forward to the night, and when darkness came with the warder switching off the light, my thoughts achieved a freedom such as had never been given them while my so-called real self had been enjoying it. In daytime there was plenty of laughter, for the stupidest remark immediately induced it. If you stumbled in the courtyard waves of guffaws broke against the high walls. Juan Morata, who had been minister of health in the Spanish republican government, was ushered into our cell one late afternoon. 'I'm a little nervous,' he said.

'We're all nervous here,' said Mathieu, and we roared with laughter even long after the light was switched off. Morata was quickly released, yet 'I'm a little nervous' remained a huge uproarious joke.

Mathieu left, Jack got his provisional liberty too (later he was sentenced to two years jail), and then at long last I received my summons to answer for my crimes in the Tribunal Correctionel, which meant that the military authorites refused to deal with them. It was bitterly cold by then, and Marseilles was covered in snow. There was no heating in the prison.

My eyes were blinded by the snow as I was driven with the other accused to the Palais de Justice in the Black Maria. About ten of us were to be tried in the Fifth Chamber. The gendarmes took us into a small room that opened onto the court room. I could see where the president, flanked by two judges, would sit, but the public was hidden from me, which was most annoying, since I had chiefly come to see Nona. It turned out that I would be the last on the list. There was a sudden commotion, and the president and two judges entered the court. The president was a hunchback with a sensitive face, and his eyes were resplendent with intelligence. I felt that after a hundred and eleven days I was about to speak to a man who would understand. Peace settled on me.

Some were acquitted, some got light sentences. They couldn't speak, stammered, contradicted themselves, put up a poor show. Then my name was called. The gendarme remained at the door. I was unaccompanied, almost a sense of freedom. I shot a quick glance at the gallery: Nona sat in the first row, her hands in her lap. I brought a smile to my pale prison face, then let the smile go, which was easy, and turned to the president. 'C'est une histoire anglaise,' he said.

The procureur said that one of the witnesses against me was on sick leave, the others, however, were waiting outside. For a moment I had the terrible fear that the hearing would be adjourned. The president nodded, observing that it was a dubious case. His eyes were on me as he asked whether I spoke French well. I said I did.

'Tell me what happened that night.'

'Monsieur le Président,' I said, 'I was in a bar, I noticed three wounded French soldiers, and because I'm deeply attached to your unhappy country I sent them twenty francs as a gesture of admiration, for they had lost their legs fighting for France against the traditional enemy.'

'That's right,' he said. 'You didn't seek them out. Now, did you use the words you're accused of speaking?'

'Even supposing that I wanted to use them, I didn't have a chance because the soldier Van der Bock came up to me and started begging for money.'

'Sit down,' he said.

He motioned my lawyer to speak. I retained only one sentence, 'For his generous gesture he has paid with a hundred and eleven days of detention.' When he had finished the president and the other two judges whispered together while I felt that outside Van der Bock was straining on the leash to get in and have his say. The president spoke:

'Given that the only witness against the accused admitted that he had asked for money; given that the other witnesses heard nothing; and given that the accused kept to his statement from the start I find there isn't enough ground to convict him. Relaxé.' Relaxé means released for lack of sufficient evidence.

'Merci beaucoup, Monsieur le Président,' I gushed.

As I came out of court and went into the little room one of the gendarmes said, 'You see that statue of Marianne behind the judges? Well, one day the statue of your friend de Gaulle will be in its place.'

'Of course,' I said, which proves that prison had taught me little. I had to drive back in the Black Maria, and wait till three in the afternoon when the chief warder returned my tie and let me go. The snow was blinding white as I came into freedom. An Albanian, who had no identity papers, was released with me. 'They'll pick me up again next week,' he said.

When I took a tram (I used to hear those trams day and night), and the ticket collector came up my heart beat violently, and I was nearly sick: his dark uniform made me think that he was a policeman.

I had looked forward to my first day of freedom, I had dreamed of it, I had planned the meal I would have in the endlessly long nights. Nona and I went to dine at half past seven. I had some hors d'oeuvres, then I couldn't eat any more. The restaurant was filling up, which made me nervous, and it was long after paliasse time. The light hurt my eyes, and I almost wished it could be turned off. We went back to the hotel.

In 1947 I arrived in Marseilles with Margaret to take ship to Cyprus. We looked into the three legless soldiers' café, the same red chairs, and the same proprietor and barmaid, neither of whom recognised me.

'I was arrested here in October nineteen-forty,' I said.

'So many people were arrested here at that time,' said the proprietor.

'One can't remember every person who was here,' added the barmaid.

11

Nona and I saw that we couldn't remain together for much longer. The only solution for me was to get out of Vichy France before I ran into more trouble, whereas for her the answer was to return to America. During my absence in prison she had several times been to the American Consulate who were starting to repatriate their citizens in France. I accompanied her to the Consulate soon after my release. A ship was leaving Lisbon early in February, and a special train would take all available Americans straight to Portugal. 'You must go with that train,' I heard myself say. Nona observed as we left that it couldn't have been worse if we had stayed in Paris, and she bitterly blamed the banker, Bar and Hélène for starting me off on my hopeless chase. And with Chaves an ever-present shadow I wasn't a cheerful influence either. Besides, I knew, even if I tried to hide it from myself, that if she remained I wouldn't be able to make my way to England. Suddenly a letter arrived from her mother back in New York, urging her to return home. That made up both our minds, that is to say it gave us the excuse to speak sincerely to each other.

On the day before she left we stood on the top of the steps outside the station with the mistral trying to raise the frozen snow. 'I wish,' I said, 'I'd broken my leg when I went down these steps the first time in October.'

'I wish I'd broken my neck,' said Nona.

Later she said that with her gone I would travel light, and would be in England in a few months. We went into the station, it was brutally cold on the platform, where you heard only American spoken. Steam was rising, and as the train pulled out it disappeared into it. I strolled back to the inimical town.

The Lawrence of Marseilles, whom I had seen shortly after I came out of Chaves, was getting ready to leave too. He had no advice to offer other than to try to get to Spain, since hiding in a ship bound for Lisbon would be beyond my fast diminishing means. However it was no good trying before the spring as the mountain passes were snowed up, and he had heard gruesome tales of people freezing to death on their clandestine way to Spain.

On the place de la Préfecture, near the statue of Barthou and King Alexander of Yugoslavia, in the Pelican Bar the remaining Anglo-American colony congregated, also many Belgians. One of the Belgians, Pierre by name, was the son of a hero of the first world war. He looked like a Spaniard, bit his nails, and was a wealthy fishmonger in Brussels. His close companion, Albert, hailed from Liège, and had the irritating habit of imitating a saxophone. They confided in me that they wanted to get to England to serve in the Belgian forces stationed there. They had both done their military service in the Belgian Air Force. Pierre continuously talked about secret organisations run by English and Gaullist agents, and couldn't understand why he didn't succeed in getting in touch with them. I told him that I had met several men who had believed similar tales and ended up in Chaves.

In that café I ran into one Norbert, who had been to Chaves with me. He wasn't a crook, only a tight-rope dancer, moving on the borderline of business and fraud. He had been inside for getting permits of residence for any foreigner who paid a small sum, which he shared with a friend at the préfecture. He was out on provisional liberty. 'You know Marseilles inside out,' I said, 'so you can tell me whether there exist Gaullist organisations that send people to Gibraltar?' He shook his head, saying, 'No, personally I wouldn't touch a thing like that. I don't want to go to prison for a serious offence.' I said it was a pity as it wasn't only for me, but for some Belgians I knew. He promised to make inquiries, raised his green hat, and I didn't see him for about a fortnight at the end of which the woman he lived with came to my hotel, saying Norbert had important news for me. We met in a bar on the Canebière, where he took me aside to whisper that he knew where the Gaullist organisation was to be found. In fact, he was in touch with it. I asked for the address.

'Not so quickly,' he said. 'I don't get myself involved in such dangerous matters just for the fun of it. I want money. Not from you, but from the Belgians. I don't want much, I'm not one of those fifty thousand francs crooks. Two thousand francs from each, payable only after they have been signed on, and if they find the organisation satisfactory.'

That sounded fair enough. He would be seeing a French cavalry captain who was one of the organisers. 'If you doublecross me,' I said, 'I don't mind going back to Chaves, but you'll come with me. I'm no longer a beginner.'

'You're mad,' he said. 'Only you could doublecross me.'

I saw the Belgians, and Pierre was delighted. A friend of his, another Belgian, who wanted to get to England to gamble on the Stock Exchange as he had been a stockbroker in Brussels, was ready to come too. I told them and Albert that we should watch our step since I knew from experience that nobody could be trusted. 'Nobody can fool us,' said Pierre, and the stockbroker hit his chest.

In the evening I met Norbert. Perspiring under his green hat he had seen the captain who put him through his paces, and now he wished he hadn't tackled this affair, not his line, far too dangerous. Were the Belgians to be trusted? How did I know they weren't mouchards? If they were the Gaullists would kill him. He suggested meeting one of them, but only one. I returned to the Belgians, and Pierre immediately volunteered to meet Norbert. The meeting was theatrical: I felt like laughing. Norbert exhorted Pierre to be careful, then we fixed a date for the following day at two in the afternoon.

'We shouldn't do that,' whispered Pierre. 'At two in the afternoon I always go to the bar-tabac in the place de Rome, and it would arouse suspicion if I changed my habits.'

'As if anybody cared about your habits,' I laughed.

He was hurt. He said he was so careful that he wouldn't dream of drinking marc with his coffee since it was his habit to have brandy with it. Later he wrote my telephone number on a piece of paper, assuring me that if the police caught him he would swallow it. At our next meeting Norbert brought the final details. The Gaullist organisation was ready to send any Belgian to Gibraltar provided he had seen active service in May 1940, and was less than thirty years old. Pierre gave Albert's age as twenty-six, which was true, his own as twenty-eight, which wasn't, and the grey-haired stockbroker's as thirty-one. Pierre was thirty-four.

'That one won't be accepted,' Norbert said. That made a good impression as he was getting two thousand francs for each of them, so the more the merrier should have been his motto. We were to meet the next day at three in the afternoon to be taken into the Gaullist captain's presence. Pierre thought he could see the Rock of Gibraltar before him: I distinctly saw a stinking prison can before me.

Next day a young Belgian officer took the stockbroker's place. We were in a café, sitting like a bunch of conspirators, waiting for Norbert, who arrived punctually with his girl. She, he said, would keep a look-out while we were received by the captain one by one in an office on the other side of the street. The young officer was the first to go, returning twenty minutes later pale with excitement. The captain, he gushed, had made an excellent impression on him. 'He's been accepted,' said Norbert who had accompanied him. I was the next to go. Norbert had told us not to mention to the captain that he was receiving money from us. 'I told him you're a British agent,' said Norbert. We went into a house, and up some stairs. Norbert rang a bell, a spyhole opened, then the door, and we found ourselves in a kitchen. Through it we entered a small office, where we were received by a short, middleaged man. I didn't think much of him, though he had a fairly honest face. He took my name, and assured me that I would reach Gibraltar. I asked how and when: he would let me know in a few days. Norbert was perspiring profusely.

'If this is a captain,' I said to Norbert as we came out, 'I'll buy a green hat like yours. Never mind, we'll be in the same cell, and play belotte.' Norbert was annoyed, swearing that my scepticism would drive him mad. He asked me not to go back to the café, but to meet him in the bar that was his headquarters in an hour's time. I found him, his girl and the Belgians drinking a farewell toast. I asked Pierre whether they had paid Norbert. He said yes, the three of them had given him two thousand francs each.

That night I damped Pierre's enthusiasm by telling him that this was the last we would see of Norbert. Next day was Pierre's day of victory, for Norbert and his girl turned up. Pierre invited them to lunch, champagne flowed, Norbert said that it was now only a matter of a day or two. On the following day Norbert suggested to Pierre that he change the French francs he had into dollars because French francs weren't accepted in Gibraltar. Despite my meaningful glances Pierre handed him several thousand francs. And that was the last we saw of Norbert, though I must admit that he did his vanishing act cleverly in so far as he sent his girl to the bar, who, rolling her eyes and shedding a few tears, told us in a choking voice that Norbert had disappeared. He hadn't gone back to their hotel room the night before. In the morning she had gone to the Évêché, but he wasn't there either which meant that he hadn't been arrested, so the only explanation was that he had decamped with another woman. And there she was without her man and without a centime. I felt so sorry for her that I gave her fifty francs out of my fast diminishing capital. In the evening I looked into the bar that had been Norbert's headquarters: the proprietor informed me that the girl and Norbert had been to the bar to take leave of him as they were going to Nice.

Pierre and Albert went to the captain, who admitted that he wasn't a captain, just a foreman in the docks. It was Norbert who had persuaded him to pretend he was an army officer. 'He promised me three hundred francs for that,' said the captain-foreman simply. 'What about Gibraltar?' shrieked Pierre. As a foreman in the dock he thought he might have found us a ship to Casablanca. With Norbert gone he wished to have nothing more to do with us. He cursed Norbert as much as Pierre, Albert and I.

Pierre was dejected, and though it was early, no more than nine o'clock, he and Albert returned to their hotel. I walked down the Canebière, and approaching the Vieux Port I was hailed by a large man who had been my cellmate for a few weeks in Chaves. We went into a bar, had a drink, then he asked me back to his home to meet his wife. He took me into a house in a side street, and mounting the heavily carpeted stairs in a cloud of cheap scent I perceived that I was in a brothel. No cause for surprise, I said to myself. He ushered me into a small saloon with a large looking glass on each wall, and two plush sofas facing each other. He rang a bell and a maidservant appeared. 'Tell my wife I'm here with a friend, and I want pastis for the three of us.' The woman he called his wife flew in, wearing pink, half nightdress, half nothing. 'We were in the same cell,' said the husband as an introduction.

She said she was pleased to meet me, the drinks arrived, we sat down, they on one sofa, I on the other, and we had a worldly chat about the weather, the scarcity of meat, and when England would win the war. 'If you want to stay with my wife,' said the husband after a while, 'be generous with her.'

'I'm afraid I can't stay,' I said. 'I've a date at the other end of town.'

The husband said it was a pity because his wife was one of the best lays in Marseilles. I raced down the stairs, repeating to myself that I must get out of the town even if snow were left in the Pyrénées.

I woke Pierre and Albert at eight in the morning. 'I failed,' I said 'because I trusted others. Now I'm going to trust my two legs alone to get me across the Pyrénées. I'll try to get to Algeciras, then swim to Gib, or get there some other way. If the Spanish catch me I'm sure the British authorities won't let me down. The Spaniards will expel me, and that means getting to Gib.'

'What about us?' asked Pierre. 'You can't desert us.'

We decided to set out together. On the same day Pierre travelled to Grenoble, where he knew an elderly Englishman, who, he hoped would lend him some money since Norbert had gone off with almost all he had left. The Englishman gave him the money, asking him not to consider it as a loan. Being an old, useless man he felt he was doing his bit if he could help able bodied men to England.

Before setting out from Marseilles I said goodbye to the proprietor of a small café in the rue Haxo. He was a staunch Gaullist, and had been helpful to me in many ways. When I came with Margaret to Marseilles in 1947 I looked into the café only to be told that he was serving a heavy sentence as a collaborator. 'He denounced Gaullists to the militia,' said the barmaid.

On Friday 27 April, 1941 Pierre, Albert and I took the train at dawn for Beziers, where I vaguely hoped to find a man I knew. Arriving in Beziers I called on him, he was polite and distant, and said he couldn't help as the town was too far from the frontier. At luncheon Pierre expressed the desire to return to Belgium, for he felt in his bones that our expedition would fail. I said he had better run. After the meal he moved to a different table. Albert whispered to me that there was no cause to fear Pierre deserting us or going back to Brussels, for he wouldn't dare to face his somewhat caustic wife if he, the hero's son, failed to reach England. As Albert and I started for the door Pierre ran up to us. He would come with me to the end of the world.

I bought a beret in the hope that with a beret on my head I would look less conspicuously a foreigner in the land of berets. You look at a man, and, because his headgear is the same as everybody else's you consider him part of the landscape. Anyhow, I felt unnoticed from that moment onward. Next morning we entrained for Perpignan, a dangerous place as it was the centre of Spanish refugees, escaped British soldiers on their way to Spain, Gaullists, Belgians and Dutchmen, all trying to get over the mountains. As if to make things easier the morning paper carried the Marshal's appeal to the youth of France to stop crossing into Spain in order to get to de Gaulle, the condemned traitor. The newspaper added that reinforcements had been sent to the frontier, and that patrols and frontier guards had been strengthened. We got off at a station before Perpignan, and walked into the town, the three of us wearing berets, pretending to be out for a morning stroll.

I had a letter to an old Frenchman who used to be a deputy. I told Pierre and Albert to wait for me in a café while I went in search of him.

Pierre's eyes said that they wouldn't see me again. The old man wasn't at home, and his wife told me that I would find him in the afternoon in the Palmarium, the town's largest café. After lunch I went to the Palmarium accompanied by Albert who was to sit at a nearby table, pretending that he didn't know me. A waiter pointed out the old man, I gave him the letter which he read moving his lips. 'What can I do for you?' he asked when he had finished.

'Help us over to Spain. There are three of us.'

He looked surprised, then said it wasn't the place to discuss such matters as the café was full of secret service and plainclothes men, I should go to his house in the evening, where we could speak in private. From the next table Albert was staring at us openmouthed. (Probably the old man took him for a plainclothes man.) I left the café, and mingled with the crowd in the square. Gendarmes were plentiful. From the square set out the buses for the different parts of the Pyrénées Orientales. In every outgoing bus a gendarme sat next to the driver. One bus was full and ready to depart. The gendarme, who was to travel with it, got in to ask the passengers for their sauf-conduits, travel permits. I moved away. Albert wasn't coming, so after a while I looked into the café: Albert sat at the same table, glowering at the old man. I made signs, but he didn't understand them. I went out, saying to myself that with him and Pierre it would be a miracle if I weren't caught. Never mind, I thought, I was out of Marseilles, which was all that mattered. I rejoined Pierre; Albert joined us an hour later. I asked him what the dickens he was up to. 'I stayed to watch the old man,' he said, 'to see whether he'd do something suspicious.'

'You made yourself conspicuous and probably frightened the one man who might have helped us.' As I said that two frontier guards entered the café. Pierre immediately wanted to leave. 'For Christ's sake stop behaving like that,' I whispered. 'Sit back, and try not to look like a criminal on the run.'

Perpignan was a positively dangerous place, since there were more gendarmes in the streets than in Marseilles, but we had a story ready for them if they stopped us. We were coming from the occupied zone, had crossed the demarcation line in the Pyrénées, and were on our way to the Riviera. So, naturally, we had no sauf-conduits. We were waiting for a friend who was crossing the line today.

In the evening I went to the old man's house. It was like a Spanish house, the furniture black and a brazier giving no heat. The old man cross-questioned me for a long time. When he was convinced that I was no police spy he said it was a difficult proposition: to get out of France was hard enough; to move about in Franco's Spain was practically impossible, as the Guardia Civil were everywhere. If I took his advice I would return to Marseilles, and try to get away by sea. Later a Spanish Catalan friend of his came in. 'If you had fifteen thousand francs I might find you a guide,' he said, 'who would take you to the British Consulate in Barcelona, but not for less.' I told him we had very little money left. We decided to adjourn till Monday, the Spaniard promising to make inquiries in the meantime.

Pierre and Albert had taken rooms in a shabby hotel, the sort of hotel the police were most likely to raid. Pierre said it was cheap. 'It would be safer to spend a few francs more,' I said, and we went to a more expensive hotel near the Palmarium, where Pierre immediately acquainted the hotelkeeper with our plans. So we changed hotels once more.

Sunday and Monday morning passed uneventfully. On Monday afternoon I saw the old man and the Spaniard, who told me that he had found a gipsy woman willing to take us to the frontier for two thousand francs, the departure for that very night. She would meet us at nine o'clock near the old tollhouse. We gave him all our money, and he went to buy pesetas for us. 'I hope this won't be a repetition of Marseilles,' said Albert. The Spaniard was back in the evening with the pesetas.

'Will your feet stand it?' asked Pierre.

That question predominated in my mind too. When I had typhoid fever at the time of my inheritance my feet became practically useless. The bones shortened, or perhaps the muscles, I don't know. I had already had two operations, yet I never gave in, and despite my feet I had managed to walk twenty miles with a gun. However, this was a different proposition. To walk fast for fifty miles, then climb the Pyrénées was asking a lot from my feet. I shrugged my shoulders. 'My willpower will see my feet into Spain,' I said.

At nine o'clock we were at the old tollhouse which stood at a crossroads. Many people were milling around. I told Pierre and Albert to disappear into the darkness while I waited for the Spaniard. They should hop it if they saw any trouble. The Spaniard arrived punctually, the gipsy woman kept us waiting. She came at last with her husband and a friend to tell us that she had changed her mind and wouldn't take us along. The Spaniard implored her, so did I till she gave in. As it was too late we would have to leave at dawn, and she gave me her hand with a lot of flourish, saying I could trust a gipsy's word of honour. We went to an hotel, had a few hours sleep, and were back at the tollhouse before day broke. The Spaniard was there: the gipsy woman never came. We returned to the hotel. We saw the Spaniard at noon, who had seen her, and now it was certain that she would be at the tollhouse at nine.

The night was dark, I told Pierre and Albert to make themselves scarce while the Spaniard and I waited for the gipsy woman. We waited in vain. Suddenly the Spaniard grabbed my arm, hissing, 'Those fools will get us arrested. Look at them.' Where the roads met stood a large tree; behind the tree my companions hovered like children playing hide and seek. They were smoking, two red pinpoints coming regularly round the tree trunk. Passersby stared at the two men hiding so conspicuously. 'Let's go,' said the Spaniard nervously. 'We'll have the police on us.' We left. I was shaking with fury. After a few yards I looked back: carrying their haversacks, the two Belgians were strolling in carefree manner behind us. Then we saw a police car stopping a little in front of us, a policeman got out and halted a man and a woman who were ahead of us. I dragged the Spaniard past them, the policeman fortunately too busy to notice us.

'Somebody must have rung up the police,' muttered the Spaniard. I couldn't blame that somebody. After a while I glanced back: no Pierre and no Albert. 'The police must have got them,' said the Spaniard, who then left me, saying that he was known by the police as a suspicious character. He disappeared into the night. Another police car appeared, and I cursed heartily.

I went to the main square as I didn't know what to do. I heard a low whistle. There was the Spaniard. 'They've been pinched,' he said. 'I went back, I couldn't see them. Look.' We saw a Black Maria gracefully gliding over the bridge on its way to the local prison. 'See you in the morning,' the Spaniard said in his lugubrious voice.

'If I'm still available.' I told him that I would go to the Grand Hôtel, which being the most expensive hotel in Perpignan was possibly also the safest. I had no illusions, for if Pierre were caught he would blab out the truth, nothing but the truth, and I would be back in prison. In bed I reviewed the situation, urging myself to beat it as it was foolish to stay. I was letting myself down without helping anybody. I remained between the embroidered linen sheets, smoking one cigarette after the other. There came a harsh rap on the door.

'La police,' a deep voice said. Well, that was that. I got up, opened the door only to let in Pierre and Albert who were grinning from ear to ear. 'We frightened you, ha ha,' they laughed. I don't know why I held myself back as the assizes would surely have acquitted me.

They had duly been stopped by the police and had explained that they were Belgian refugees who had just crossed over from occupied France. The policemen told them to go next day to the préfecture to regularise their situation (as they say in France). Then they had gone in search of the Spaniard whose address they knew. They hid in his coal-cellar, and when they saw him sneaking home they drew his attention to themselves. Lugubriously I asked how they did that. 'Oh, we crawled out, tiptoed up, touched his shoulder from behind, and shouted, "Police". You should have seen how terrified he was.' They roared with laughter at the memory of it.

We decided to give up chasing the mirage called the gipsy woman. Albert thought that haversacks made us too conspicuous. I agreed to jettisoning our haversacks, and carrying large shopping bags instead. We ought never, I said, to have deviated from our original plan, namely trusting only ourselves. We would set out for the Pyrénées that very day, Thursday 1 May, which the Marshal's government had proclaimed as the feast of labour, so the town would be full of revellers, and with all the coming and going we could slip out unnoticed.

'We can't leave by road,' I said. 'The first gendarme would stop us. We must get to Banyuls, which looks like a good base. I want you two to do only one thing: find out how we can get there. No railway is marked on the map, and a bus is out of the question. Find out how near we can get by train. From there on we'll walk. The Spaniard and the old man have assured me that if we're caught by the guardias civiles we'll only be kept for a short time in prison before being expelled to Gibraltar. The only real danger is to let ourselves be caught by the French.'

In the morning I bought a large canvas shopping bag. You couldn't come from afar with a shopping bag, and you couldn't go farther than the grocer round the corner. Pierre brought the information that there was a train for Banyuls. We went in search of a compass, but in all the shops we got the same answer: their stocks of compasses had been bought up by relatives of prisoners of war in Germany. After a lot of running round we finally found one. Then I took leave of the old man, who outlined the route we should follow. He gave me the names of two villages at the foot of the Pyrénées. (I have forgotten their names for the simple reason of the Ministry of Information cutting out their names in the proofs of *Death and Tomorrow* in 1942.) The second village was preferable as the mountains were less steep there. He marked on our very third-rate map the different posts of gendarmes and frontier guards, and wished us luck.

In the afternoon we boarded the train to Banyuls. 'You're sure it's all right?' I asked my two navigation officers. Yes, it was all right, they were sure of it. I wasn't, saying after a while we shouldn't be beside the sea as Banyuls was inland. The door of the compartment opened, and a gendarme appeared. 'Your papers,' he said. 'Are you going to Spain?'

The fools had mixed up Banyuls with Banyuls-sur-Mer on the railway line to Spain, the last place for us to go to. We recited our tale, which had been embellished with a new detail: we were going into the mountain to work as wood-cutters. 'There's no forest at Banyuls-sur-Mer,' said the gendarme. 'It's forbidden to travel on the international line. I'll be waiting for you when we get there.' He left the compartment.

'But this is the train to Spain,' I said, the one train I wanted to avoid from the start.

The train stopped at Banyuls-sur-Mer. That seemed to be the end of my trip to England. Albert, who was at the window, said that the gendarme had got off, and was waiting for us. I looked out through the other window, and saw a train pulling out in the opposite direction. I opened the door, and told them to jump for it. The train was gathering speed as we got into it, shopping bags and all. 'I only asked you to find out one thing,' I said to Pierre, 'and you couldn't even do that.'

We got off at a wayside station, and took a room at the local inn. Next morning we had breakfast downstairs, and through the window saw two frontier guards on horseback, trotting down the road. Then came a gendarme, followed by two more. We moved to another inn, which was quiet and off the road. As I couldn't credit either of my companions with the slightest spark of sense, I worked out our itinerary on the map. It appeared that if we left at night we could reach the village the old man spoke of before dawn. We should avoid the road, but road or no road a river had to be crossed. I sent Albert out to reconnoitre, and wrote on a piece of paper what I wanted. He came back an hour later with the information that the only way to cross the river was across the railway bridge, which was under repair. The bridge was in a bad state, so it would be a folly to try to cross it at night. We went out for a little fresh air, only to see a gendarme coming down the street. We stopped outside a watchmaker's: in the window I saw the gendarme looking at us, and he glanced back twice before he got out of sight. We hurried back to the inn.

We would leave at four as it was less suspicious to cross the bridge while the workmen were on it. We would lie in the reeds farther on and wait till the moon went down before cutting across country to get to the village at dawn. Pierre, because of his Spanish looks, was sent out to buy any food he could find. All he found was a loaf of dark bread, which used up every bread ticket we had left. We set out at four, walking with about a fifty yards distance between each of us. First went Albert, I came next, the shopping bag dangling at my side, and Pierre brought up the rear. A gendarme passed us, glanced at me, but the beret and the bag made me merge into the landscape. The railway bridge was very much under repair. The wind blew with fury, and hopping from board to board with the river racing invitingly beneath me, I thought the wind would lift me only to hurl me into the ice-cold water. Because my feet haven't much strength when I have to rest on one at a time, I felt I would never get across. My willpower was strained to its limits, yet I got across. We reached the reeds, sat down, and shivered in the wind. My crossing the railway bridge still appears in my nightmares.

The moon that night didn't want to leave the sky. She was preening herself, the reeds, the fields and vineyards were out of all proportion. The reeds whispered of utter tiredness while we half-expected a host of gendarmes to break their way through them. But nothing remains forever, not even the moon. She went and we were off.

We tramped mostly through vineyards, one or the other of us falling every few minutes. We made as much noise as a herd of elephants; whenever I fell the shopping bag came down with a thud. The worst of it was that we didn't feel we were advancing. We used the compass as a topic of argument, none of us quite knowing where we were. Towards two in the morning we lost ourselves in a thicket; at three we saw a village that shouldn't have been there at all, so we retraced our steps. Suddenly a light came towards us. We lay on our bellies for a considerable time. The light moved away at last, then another light signalled from farther up, and that lasted about half an hour. Smugglers, I said to myself, that word bringing the mountains nearer. We got up when the lights had disappeared.

The old man had told me that when approaching the village he had marked on the map we should turn to the left, and go past the cemetery.

We argued a lot about our bearings, I for one convinced that we were too far to the south-west. A village came out of the dark, and being tired we decided it was the old man's village. We turned to the left, and saw a long high wall with cypresses on the other side of it. I got on Albert's shoulders: the silence of the grave slept among the tombstones. Looking into the graveyard I was strangely moved. I could have stayed on Albert's shoulders for hours with my eyes focused on the crosses. In my childhood you couldn't drag me past a cemetery in the evening; now it spoke of friendliness, hope and peace, a refuge from the harsh world around me. Albert grumbled; I got off his shoulders.

The ground rose, light was beginning to appear, and we found a clump of trees surrounding a kind of crater. We pushed into the crater, and throwing our plans and caution to the cold wind we lay down and slept. I slept for about twenty minutes. Opening my eyes I saw we were in the depth of a vegetable garden. On the edge of the crater with the trees behind him stood a short, youngish man, smiling down on us.

'Bonjour, messieurs,' he said with a strong Spanish accent. That woke my companions, and in a half-drowsy voice Pierre recited the story of the demarcation line and the wood-cutting. I saw that the young man was unimpressed. I decided to risk everything. 'We're ingleses, the three of us,' I said in Spanish. 'You're a Spaniard, so you can help us. We want to get to England to fight for the liberty of the world. We need a guide to get us across the Pyrénées. You see, I'm putting myself into your hands.'

'Wait,' he said, and went away.

'Where is he going?' asked Pierre in a shrill voice.

'He's bringing us a guide,' I said, and true enough the Spaniard was back within ten minutes accompanied by a tall, surly man with reddish-grey moustache and unpleasant face. 'Here's your guide,' the Spaniard said. 'Be gone before the sun comes up. Start now. Here's a bottle of wine, which is all I can give you.' We climbed out of the crater.

'Could I give you some money?' I asked the Spaniard. 'What can I do to thank you?'

'Win the war,' he laughed. 'Go with God, but go right now.'

'I'll remember you in all my prayers,' I said, and we set forth.

The village, the guide told us, wasn't the village the old man had re-commended. Luckily for us we had erred by ten miles. Of course, there is a cemetery on the edge of every village. The mountains loomed up formidably and much too high in the hot May sun. Now and then the guide stopped us while he went forward alone, which meant we were approaching a road. Pierre went down on all fours every time that happened. The guide told me in Spanish to ask him to stop that nonsense. 'I can't,' I said, 'I've given it up.'

Then the roads ceased. The guide said he would take us across the highest peaks as that was the safest. We climbed among trees and stones, at times a stream cut across our path, and my feet had to jump from stone to stone, the shopping bag weighing me down. Towards ten the guide lay down, saying we should sleep for an hour. We drank a little wine before falling into the depth of sleep. Sleep did the trick in that Pierre could hardly rise, and when I took the first step I secretly hoped the gendarmes would catch us. The mountain became steeper, we reached a peak, hoped it might be Spain, but it was only our first peak, with three more peaks to follow.

Ice-cold streams overhung by moss met us regularly. Though the guide said we shouldn't we drank from every stream. We heaved ourselves from rock to rock, at times the mountain was so steep that we had to swing from tree to tree, the next tree almost above our heads. The fourth and highest peak was barren, the plaything of wind, and the wind had the taste of snow. The peak seemed to shiver. 'Here is Spain,' said the guide.

I looked down on Catalonia, a far spreading view, the sea to the left, the earth grey and brown. Like a faded map, I thought.

'You kept your word,' said Albert. 'You brought us to Spain.'

The descent into Spain was tiring. At dusk we got to a charcoal burner's hut, but he sent us packing. 'I don't want to be mixed up in it,' he shouted. The guide said he knew a farmstead higher up, so we climbed again. Night came, and the guide lost his way. Rain came too with the taste of icy streams and swaying trees. We spent the night in the open in the downpour and the wind. The guide built a fire, which was difficult to keep going. Sitting too near to it I burnt my trouser legs. The guide woke up in the middle of the night, and asked for his money. It was only two hundred francs, I paid him, and he slept on. At dawn we pushed off in the pelting rain. Among bleak stones stood a bleak house with the wind howling round it. Following the guide in we found an old woman beside a dead fire, and a younger woman beside her. Worn-out faces, tired eyes, as though they had done our tramping.

The old woman asked whether England would win the war. I nodded. 'How long will the war last?' Three more years, I said. 'Then we'll all die of starvation here.' At that Pierre had the bright idea of suggesting she sell us food. She gave us a little milk and four potatoes, all she could spare. The husband of the younger woman appeared, I put my case to him, and he said it was impossible to get to Barcelona without being caught. He had an idea, however. There was a feria in some village on the way to Figueras. If we left our luggage behind, and walked on the road like any ordinary pleasure-bent person, of whom the road would be full, we might get unnoticed to Figueras. He would keep our belongings, for which we could send after the war. (I am sure he kept them, but I have no idea where the farm exactly was.) I said we would try that, but first he should let us sleep for a few hours. Not in the house in case the guardias civiles or the carabineros came. The guide departed, and he took us to the loft above the barn, where, he said, we could sleep on the straw, provided we said we had crept in without his knowledge if the guardias came along.

Pierre immediately lit a cigarette in the sea of straw. I threw it out of the window. At one the farmer woke us, we shaved, and I left behind the scorched suit, shirts, the shopping bag, in short I was now travelling light as Nona had predicted. He guided us to the main road, and as the sun was hot I said I thought that my overcoat would be remarked, so I left that with him too.

I walked in front, the Belgians slightly behind me. A rivulet ran through the village ahead of us. I was the first to reach the bridge. I crossed it, the road curved, then as it straightened itself, a voice hailed me. I looked back: two carabineros were coming up from behind. Against my instructions and all rules of commonsense Pierre and Albert had stopped near the water, had gone on their knees, and drank for the last time as free men. The carabineros, who were resting on the roadside, saw at a glance that these men were thirsty, so they must have come from afar.

'We come from the mountains,' I said. 'We're woodcutters.'

'Not with those hands,' they laughed.

'We're on our way to the feria. We'll be back tonight.'

'You're foreigners. You're under arrest.'

They searched us and confiscated our money. On Pierre they found a knife, but they overlooked our identity papers, in fact weren't interested in them. They were friendly, so I tried to bribe them with the money they had taken from us. Keep half, let us go, and nobody would know about us or the money. They refused, saying it was no good, for if they let us go we would be caught farther on. They told us to sit down on the roadside, for they wanted to see whether any other woodcutters came along. They laughed, I laughed, the Belgians remained glum. After a while they took us to a farm, where we got a copious meal, the carabineros paying for it with our money. The farmer's wife, who was French, tried to persuade them to let us go. The carabineros said they couldn't take the risk, besides we shouldn't worry as the British were expelled to Gibraltar after a while. Pierre and Albert had already been told in Marseilles that if caught in Spain they should say they were French-Canadians. We slept in the prison of a small village, and slept like logs.

Next day we were taken to Figueras by train. In the military prison we found seven Scottish soldiers of the 51 Highland Division, who after the surrender of General Fortune in Saint-Valéry-en-Caux, had escaped from the Germans, then crossed the Pyrénées. Many of their brothers-in-arms had passed through that prison. Over the door were scribbled BEF and 'The boys England forgot'. We chatted the whole night. The other occupants of the cell were Belgians, some of whom were ready to go home because, so they said, the whole thing was too much of a struggle. Pierre was ready to agree with them. Towards dawn the Scottish soldiers burst into song, the Belgians cursed, and there were plenty of inter-allied quarrels. Then we were handcuffed, taken to the station, and remained handcuffed the whole way to Barcelona. My 'companion' was a Glaswegian printer. Still handcuffed we were marched to the Carcel Modelo, where the handcuffs were taken off after the prison gate had closed on us.

Compared to Chaves the Carcel Modelo was nearly the Ritz. Though we were many in our cells the doors were opened at daybreak, and till night you could roam the prison at your heart's content. The courtyard was like a market place with vendors and even shoeblacks. On the seventh day our party of twenty-five, fifteen Belgians and ten Britons, was marched out of prison. We were roped together, and the guardias civiles escorted us as we moved in step in the middle of the streets, passersby hardly stopping to glance at us since prisoners were a daily sight in post-Civil War Barcelona. (I like to think that Carmen was among the passersby.) We entrained for Cervera in Upper Catalonia, where we spent a fortnight.

It was cold in Cervera. The walls of the prison, which was halfway between a jail and a military barracks, were covered with graffiti. A Frenchman had written with a flourish, 'Down with the tyrants, the day of liberation is approaching.' A British soldier with more praiseworthy realism wrote across it, 'Twenty-one fucking days'. Another inscription said, 'Bonny Scotland, what I suffer for you'.

Food was scarce, but within the prison precincts we spent our time as we wanted to. It was run by a delightful Andalusian sergeant, and a less delightful but very mercenary canteen manager. In English, French and Flemmish the walls proclaimed that he was a thief. Because I know Spanish I acted as a sort of clerk of the prison. Having access to the prisoners' papers I indulged in a fair amount of forgery, thus making it possible for a number of men of allied nationalities to get to England. Pierre and Albert had stayed behind in Barcelona, but reached England three months later.

More English soldiers arrived including two officers who deplored that there were no separate cells for officers. One was a doctor, the other a chartered accountant. Fifty-four of us left under escort for Miranda de Ebro, the largest internment camp, on 1 June. We travelled in two railway trucks, the guardias civiles unpleasant because they thought that we were of the late International Brigade. All the doctor and the accountant worried about was whether there were special barracks for officers in Miranda. There were.

Hemmed in by mountains Miranda stood bleak and melancholy two thousand feet above sea level, hence burning hot in the daytime, and cold at night. You found every nationality under the sun, Spaniards too, prisoners of Franco, Basques most of them. Every week or so new contingents of prisoners arrived to disappear in the dirt, lice and nausea of the camp. The Allies quarrelled among themselves, the Dutch with the Belgians, the French with the English, the English with the Scots. Only the Poles stood out like a rock in that sea of misery and impatience. The Basques sang sad songs, and got drunk nightly at the canteen. The German prisoners held the best jobs, and bullied their fellow prisoners. There was a lonely Turk who was the local rag and bone man. Everything was for sale. The new prisoner first sold his watch, then his fountain-pen, then his shoes and shirt. With the money he either bought a few biscuits or got drunk at the canteen. Once a week a bus arrived from Gibraltar, bringing food, cigarettes, razor blades and soap for the British contingent. The young soldiers sold their bully-beef for biscuits, the older soldiers for wine.

The camp was a good breeding place for rumour. After Russia was attacked by the Germans rumour had it that the Spanish government had stopped releasing the British. A fortnight later a fair number left for Gibraltar. Rumour also had it that England paid a ton of petrol for every released man. (At a dinner party many years later in London a person's individual price was discussed, someone observing that nobody knew his. I said that I did know mine. 'How much?' I was asked. A ton of petrol.)

On a hot Sunday at the end of July a Belgian, who worked in the camp's office, came up to ask what the English word 'released' meant. I explained, then he said he had seen a paper in the office with that word next to my name. Five days later in the company of twenty-two soldiers and the doctor and the accountant I left the camp of Miranda de Ebro. As we marched out, the soldiers lustily singing, 'There'll always be an England,' a company of the Spanish Blue Division, that was to fight the Russians, crossed us to spend the night in the camp, singing just as lustily, 'Cara al sol'. The next morning we were in Madrid, where we were taken to the Embassy to be fumigated. Our clothes, full of lice, were taken away, and as there was nothing at the moment for a tall man like myself I was given blue overalls, but they were too short, so I wore them as trousers, the sleeves tied at the waist acting like a belt.

We took a train to Cordova, arriving late in the evening. The air was heavy with the Andalusian summer, and it was grand to sleep in a bed again. The following evening we entered Gibraltar.

Two days later I sailed in the *Pasteur* converted into a troop ship. The few civilians fed in the sergeants' mess. We travelled in a fast convoy, escorted by the *Renown* and four tribal class destroyers. The *Tirpitz* was lurking somewhere near the Canaries (she would have outgunned the *Renown*), the sea was infested with German submarines, but what did I care? On the second day out a little ship escorted by a destroyer loomed up on the horizon. It was the President of Portugal on his way back from the Azores. Despite *Tirpitz* and submarines the *Renown* fired her twenty-one gun salute, as inspiring a moment as I ever lived.

After we left Gibraltar a tall, slightly balding, wide shouldered man with an aquiline nose sat down at the civilians' table in the sergeants' mess. His remarkable eyes twinkled as though he were thinking of some clever practical joke. We talked about contemporary poetry, and I mentioned that Roy Campbell was one of my favourite poets. 'Which of his poems' he asked, 'do you like most?' The eyes nearly popped out. '*Oh, let your shining orb grow dim,*' I began, and he continued, declaiming loudly.

'So you like his poetry too,' I said.

'I ought to. I'm Roy Campbell.'

Our friendship lasted till his death.

As we approached Scotland, Roy said that it was out of the question for me to land in the short overalls. It simply wouldn't do. Being about the same height he would give me his spare pair of trousers. The spare pair of trousers had no buttons, and there he sat on his bunk on our last afternoon, sewing on the buttons.

When long yearned for Britain appeared the first shapes I saw were a Black Maria and four huge policemen on the shore. (We had on board two criminals brought from Gibraltar.) I went down the gangway with Roy who spoke to me, but I didn't hear what he was saying.

My great adventure was over.

12

On arriving in London I volunteered for the Army, and, as I have said before, was put into the Pioneer Corps. What I wanted most at that time was to write the story of my fourteen months from June 1940 to August 1941. As a soldier in wartime isn't given too much leisure I wrote *Death and Tomorrow* in the most unlikely places, such as the guardroom while I was company picket in Ilfracombe, in a rented room in Weymouth during my time off as company picket again, and on my bunk in Burnham Beeches while I was once more company picket.

The room I rented in Weymouth was in a small cottage belonging to a woman who came from Bristol. She had a daughter and a son, one was seventeen, the other eighteen, the girl worked in a canteen, the boy as waiter in a hotel. They shouted the whole day long, the radio blared, to be switched off only when the news came on. The mother used to make me a fire in the room she let, and in the course of our chats she told me that her son John had been her daughter Joan, the change of sex coming about when she was thirteen. 'She cried a lot, then she was a boy.'

Joan-John was the reason why they left Bristol. After the change neighbours made their lives impossible. 'In the hospital,' said the proud mother, 'the doctors told me that John's case was exceptional, in fact was the first case without surgical intervention.' On one of my visits to London I reported John's case to Roger Senhouse. 'It must have come down like a lift,' he observed. John and his sister quarrelled a lot in that noisy cottage. I heard her shouting to him, 'They'll put you into the ATS one of these days.'

My reason for writing *Death and Tomorrow* wasn't only to tell my adventures, and thus rid myself of them. Before I left Marseilles I received Poste Restante a letter from Nona. She was back in New York, the voyage had been uneventful. 'The war has separated us for ever,' the letter ended. I wrote back to say I was starting for England. Once in England I wrote care of her mother to tell her that I had arrived. And I wrote the book as if I were speaking to her to remind her of our adventure together and the time when neither of us thought of separation. In brief, the book was written to and for her, hence no exaggerations, no overstatements, she being the witness of most I put to paper. My secret thought and hope were that when she read it she wouldn't feel that we were separated for ever. True, she hadn't answered my letter, but that didn't worry me, considering that her mother was quite capable of not giving it to her. When the book was ready for the printer in the spring of 1942, I wrote to a friend of hers in New York whose address she had also given, to ask him to give her the enclosed letter. In the letter I told her that the book was ready, and I would send it to her the moment it was printed. 'That should bring you close to me again,' I wrote. With American bluntness the friend wrote back to say that he couldn't give her my letter, for Nona had died on 3 December 1941. I had written the book for a dead woman.

On 26 April I met Margaret.

The book came out on 9 September, and immediately became a best-seller, going into ten editions. Cyril Connolly's long review in *The Observer* gave it its send-off. Rebecca West in *The Sunday Times* and Raymond Mortimer in *The New Statesman* followed. I received many letters, the first from the Dowager Lady Sysonby, the second from Noël Coward, who 'cried over Dodo's death as if she were my own', and the third from the man who had bought my chicken coops in Kenya, 'I went bust with them like you.'

My position changed in the Army in that often I was given leave to broadcast for the BBC, to do some lecturing and writing for ABCA (Army Bureau of Current Affairs). For the BBC I wrote a play based on the book, and, unfortunately for one who has no gift for the stage, I had to act myself. The producer was Walter Rilla, for whom my dear friend Igor Vinogradoff used to write radio plays too. Rilla mostly used me for plays about the French resistance or the Germans in France, and once about King John, a monarch I prefer to think of as Jean-sans-terre, more moving.

In ABCA I dealt mostly with Bevil Rudd, the world famous pre-war runner, a man of great charm, trying his best to get me as much leave from my picket duties as possible. Once in an ABCA publication an article of mine appeared over a dental quiz, which began, 'Have you cleaned your teeth today?'

Bevil presided over a luncheon club at 105 Hallam Street to which I was in duty bound to go whenever up in London. To the luncheon club would come Lord Reith with his lofty dome and loftier silences, one or two generals, and many field officers who in civvy street were barristers, actors, dons, journalists and publicity men, I was the sole private among them. The luncheon club lasted till the end of the war. As victory approached so the members fell away.

Lecturing took me all over the country. I always spoke about France and the German army and in the end got tired of my own voice. When I heard myself say, 'I was there,' I felt like one listening to an old gramophone record. Usually I had to spend the night in some distant blacked-out town, where, not being a regular customer, I couldn't even get a drink. One day I lectured in Liverpool. I was put up in the Adelphi Hotel, where there was no whisky or gin in the bar for me, so I sat in the vast lounge in front of a glass of sweet sherry, waiting for the night that would bring the next day. A woman and her daughter, the girl aged about sixteen, approached my table, the girl saying that she had loved my lecture. Hope of having somebody to talk to rose in me like spring after a foul winter. 'You mustn't disturb him,' said the mother who, apologising profusely, dragged the girl away.

Shortly after *Death and Tomorrow* was published, a dear woman, Cecily Miles, who bred Dandie Dimonts in Haslemere, made me the present of a puppy 'to take Dodo's place', as she kindly put it. The puppy became Jamie, and I often said to him that he was the only tangible fruit of my literary career.

My army career (if I may call it that) remained uneventful. In Weymouth one morning as I came off duty and walked down Belfield Road to John-Joan's mother's cottage a Messerschmidt swooped down from the clouds to machine-gun me, since I was the only person on the road. The bullets came like rain, it lasted a few seconds, if as long as that, and as I walked on untouched I felt the same way as I had felt when Hélène Lajeunesse informed me in Aux Armes de la Ville that I was wanted. Hadn't the Germans anything better to do?

Before I was transferred to Burnham Beeches, which brought me near London, a manoevre took place outside Weymouth. It was a sunny morning. I had come off night picket, and reaching the road I saw stooks slinking across the road, then lying down in a field on the other side of it. As I came past them the top of a stook lifted, and a voice asked, 'Got a light, mate?'

I was discharged from the Army early in 1944, a private to the last.

'Very good,' my discharge paper said. I left with my AB 64 as my only memory, which was not quite the way I had pictured my army life in Paris and on the road to England.

When I married Margaret she lived in Great Ormond Street. After my discharge we moved to another flat, still in Great Ormond Street. When the war was over I had one desire, namely to live in the country. A countryman lives in most of us; with the war finished the countryman in me spoke in commanding tones as he yearned for trees, flowers and fields. As my novels were doing well, and as, like many others, I thought that return to peace meant return to the life we had known in peacetime, we rented an enormous house, Boulge Hall, in East Suffolk. Edward FitzGerald of *The Ruba'iyat* fame who had lived there as a young man and had spent the rest of his long life in the neighbourhood, was buried in the churchyard just beyond the rookery. The house was crammed with memories of him and his brother John, whose iron pennant was still above the porch, and in spring the wild flowers he loved covered the fields as in his time. 'Boulge,' he wrote, 'is one of the ugliest places in England – one of the dullest.' I for one loved it during the two years Margaret and I lived there, two financially ruinous years, but well worth it. The result of those two years was my writing FitzGerald's uneventful life, *Into An Old Room*, which I started in Boulge and finished in Kyrenia, Cyprus. He was one of the best letter writers in the English language, a pity that his letters aren't republished. While in Boulge I rented the shoot too, thus for two seasons I carried a gun again as I had in Kenya.

When our time was up in 1947 we decided to go to Cyprus, where several friends had gone to shake off the austerity of the new peace. We were to take ship in Marseilles for Limasol, and to get to Marseilles we left for Paris at the end of November. I had written to Bar to tell him that we were coming, and he wrote back to say that he, his wife, Hélène, Frénaud the poet, and, of course, Naly would be waiting for us at the Mère Catherine on the evening of our arrival. From the hotel near the rue de Rivoli we took a taxi to the Butte. The streets were in a poor state, the lighting was dim and Paris looked nearly as gloomy as when I had left it.

The taxi whined up the rue Lepic, rattled through the rue Norvins, reached the place du Tertre, and stopped in front of the Mère Catherine. I was in such a state of excitement that I said to the driver that it wasn't the Mère Catherine, the Mère Catherine was farther up. 'Look, it says Mère Catherine,' Margaret said. We went in, and I hardly recognised

Hélène, so terribly had the German camp changed her. It was more of a wake than a reunion since we spoke mostly of Jean, her late husband. After dinner we moved to the Italians' bistrot, where Atilio offered the glass of white wine he had lost. Eugène appeared, and he took us to the corner of his rotisserie, saying to Margaret that in that spot he had saved my life. Different people I had known on the Butte came into the bar, pro-German the lot of them when I had known them in 1940, now declaring that they had all belonged to the Resistance, 'You are our witness.'

'Certainly,' I said.

Next day the general strike broke out, which was bad news for us since with no trains running how would we get to Marseilles? The ship wouldn't wait for us. Through an acquaintance we discovered a bus, that in normal times carried passengers from the centre of Marseilles to the air-field. It had been brought to Paris in the hope of finding travellers, who on payment of an expensive fee, could be conveyed to Marseilles. Having no choice we boarded the bus, which unaccustomed to such distances, broke down every fifty miles or so, taking forty-eight hours to reach its destination. It was an infinitely pleasant journey.

'Don't worry, I'm here with you,' said Margaret as we left our hotel to walk down the Canebière. I was disappointed in that I couldn't conjure up the insecure days of my last stay in that town. Just as many policemen and gendarmes were around as at that time, yet they left me indifferent, unable to connect them with the fear I had known. I had written Marseilles and its people out of my system. When Margaret asked in which direction Chaves was I vaguely pointed to the east, and though it had been my intention to take tram as far as the prison to have another look at it, I never bothered to do so.

Our ship the *Marathon* of two thousand tons was a rickety old boat. She plunged and heaved her way to Limasol in heavy seas. Beirut was the last port of call before Cyprus. In Beirut coffee was cheap, whereas in Cyprus it was expensive, so there was much smuggling of coffee between Beirut and Limasol. The Lebanese authorities wanted to stamp out the smuggling hence a whole contingent of soldiers was sent to the quayside to search every passenger and member of the crew going on board, Margaret and I not excepted. In the evening the ship sailed smelling of coffee. We had a holy man in the steerage. He was back from a pilgrimage to Mecca, accompanied by his two wives. In Limasol a procession of Moslems waited for him with green flags while the customs searched his luggage. He had to pay a fine for some undeclared carpets, then he went outside, where in imposing silence he was surrounded by those who formed the procession, and with the green flags waving in the sunshine they moved off just as silently.

We went to Nicosia by taxi, at that time the usual form of transport on the island. Lord Winster was the governor, and as we knew him from London we lunched at Government House, the native footmen chatting so loudly among themselves that you could hardly hear what your neighbour said. From Nicosia we moved to Kyrenia, where several friends of ours were staying. Margaret and I rented a small house with well and garden in the Turkish quarter of that delightful town. A Turkish carpenter made us furniture, and in that house we spent six months. At the end of our street a young, darkhaired Turk with blazing eyes kept a shop called Export Fruit Department, Sabri Tahir his name. I would stroll across to him, he would bring out two chairs for us to sit side by side for an hour or so without exchanging a word. When I rose he said, 'This was a very nice sit,' and I said, 'A very nice sit indeed,' and then I went back to the house to work on my life of crotchety Edward Fitz-Gerald, who in one of his letters wrote about his old Cambridge friend, 'Time Tennyson shut up.'

Sabri was a modern Turk, calling himself the son of Atatürk. During one of our sits an old man with turban and a flowing white beard limped past us, he and Sabri nodding to each other. 'This is a stupid old Turk,' Sabri said, 'who never heard of Atatürk.' Eventually I found out that the stupid old Turk was Sabri's grandfather.

We left Cyprus in June, flying via Athens to Rome to go on to Capri, where at the time Cecil Gray, the composer and writer lived. His wife had recently died on the island, and poor Cecil was unconsolable. He was to follow her three years later. Norman Douglas was also on the island, and strolling with him one morning we met three greyhaired men who saluted him ceremoniously. 'I had all three of them when they were young,' said Douglas as we strolled on. Six days of Capri were enough for Margaret and me.

Our next stop was Florence which I had known in my childhood. I don't think there were many paintings in Florence unseen by us during our two months' stay. From Florence we travelled to Paris. In less than a year it had become the town of light again, as though war and occupation had never existed. We remained there for three months before returning to London, where we took a flat only to leave it two months later to start travelling in France, and if not travelling staying in Paris, till the end of Margaret's life.

First we took a villa in Antibes, but Margaret didn't care for the Riviera, especially not for the Britons living out there, and for me too the pre-war magic of the Coast was broken. Chasing one's youth is a tiresome, unrewarding business. We went to Souillac, and in the spring to Saint-Jean-Pied-de-Port in the Basque country, where we stayed in an old-fashioned hotel that Edward VII had visited. In our immense bedroom there were two fireplaces. One day during one of our long walks in the hills we ran into a carabinero, which meant that unwittingly we had crossed into Spain. To enter Spain unauthorised twice in a lifetime, I thought was too much. I apologised to the carabinero, assuring him that it was a mistake, and we were returning immediately to France. 'If you're here,' he said, 'go as far as the fonda (inn). It's only a hundred metres away. There you can buy Spanish pernod, which, as you surely know, is much stronger than French pernod.' I couldn't say no to him.

The summer we spent in Brittany, that is in Concarneau, and what with sea, muscadet, fish and shellfish our last summer was as summer should be. Paris followed for the winter.

When a woman has a flat or a house to run much of her time is taken up by it. However, travelling and staying in hotels Margaret and I had all the leisure to be thrown on each other's company. We hadn't been so close before, and so it remained till her death, in June, where this book begins.

In May 1965 Carmen and I left St Leonards-on-Sea to spend the summer months in Paris. (At that time a gossip writer in *The Daily Express* wrote that for me, who had been to Patagonia, Kenya, the Riviera and Paris, it was curious to have chosen to live in St Leonards.) That second day in May was rainy, and through the blurred window I saw at Bexhill station an acquaintance in the group of City men with bowlers, umbrellas and briefcases, waiting for the train. I didn't wave to him since I was bound to run into him when we were back in the autumn. As a matter of fact, I never met him again, for St Leonards came to an end in Paris in the course of that summer.

At the end of August we were slowly preparing to return to East Sussex. Glancing at a newspaper in a café in Saint-Germain-des-Prés I saw that Lucie Valore, Maurice Utrillo's overbearing widow, had died. Having known her well, and having lived for years in the world that had been Utrillo's, I wrote to my literary agents, saying that with Valore gone an interesting book could be written about Utrillo and his world. You couldn't do that while she was alive because she sued anybody who wrote about her late husband without writing the book as she wanted it to be written, that is to say praising her and her own unimportant painting. Moreover, she and I fell out in the early fifties when she suggested I write her life, and I said no. A week after my letter I received a telegram from my agents saying the idea was commissioned, and that meant remaining in Paris for the winter.

The book involved a lot of research in the Bibliothèque Nationale. Also I had to seek out mostly very old men who had known Utrillo before and after the first world war. Many of them are dead by now. Carmen and I appeared with a tape recorder, and the old men wheezed and croaked their tales, among them André Malterre, a painter who had been Utrillo's buddy for years. In 1910, he told me, he had seen Utrillo lying dead drunk in the snow near the Moulin de la Galette, which Utrillo was to paint umpteen times. 'He lay in his tight fitting black overcoat in the white snow,' said Malterre. 'The most beautiful sight I ever saw.' He raised his watery eyes to the ceiling.

Robert Naly had been an intimate friend of Suzanne Valadon, Utrillo's mother and of Utter the stepfather, and he was one of the few people whom Utrillo respected. 'Because,' said Naly, 'if I told him he could have a drink at twelve he knew that he would get it.' To write *The World of Maurice Utrillo* took me over a year. When it was finished I was asked by my friend Jeffrey Simmons of W. H. Allen, to write a book on Paris, which entailed nearly two years' research. By the time it was published Carmen and I perceived that we were spending most of the year in Paris, hence no more St Leonards. *Napoleon's Police* followed *Aspects of Paris*, and then I wrote a life of Madame de Maintenon, for which in a way my childhood had prepared me in so far as Mlle Barbey my French-Swiss governess had been a devotee of Scarron's widow and later Louis XIV's secret wife, for in her she found all the great qualities a governess should possess, and she wasn't far wrong. Madame de Maintenon demonstrated in her bringing up of Mlle de Blois and the Duc de Maine how much a governess can do for her charges. However, my life of her wasn't concerned only with her qualities as a governess. To have conquered and tied to her a man like Louis XIV till the day of his death (she had retired to Saint-Cyr as the king was dying) was an extraordinary achievement. While researching and writing her life I often discussed it with Nancy

Mitford as the Sun King was her period.

It is impossible to write about my life without praising Nancy Mitford, who was a perfect friend to Carmen and me. She was a graceful sight, had an excellent brain and unusually sharp wit. One day she was being driven to Paris by a woman friend of hers who, as Nancy put it, slowed down to eighty miles an hour when passing a school. 'Why do you shake with fear?' asked the friend. 'You were never frightened during the Blitz.'

'I wasn't inside a bomb,' said Nancy.

She was a gifted novelist, and once when I observed that it was a pity that she had given up writing novels, she answered, 'Because I'm out of touch with the present age.' In vain I remonstrated that we live in an age we create for ourselves. She shook her head, repeating that she wouldn't write novels any more. I seldom knew any one who had as much compassion as she, and I can say the same of her loyalty. She had lived in the rue Monsieur till 1967 when she moved to Versailles. For three summers running she lent us her delightful house there while she was in Italy. When her illness made travel impossible she wrote to us to apologise that she couldn't let us have the house for the summer. Carmen and I were in England in May and early June in 1973. On our return to Paris Carmen sent her a few roses to let her know that we were back. In shaky handwriting Nancy wrote to thank her and to tell her that she wasn't feeling any better. She was dead within the week. And she even left us a small legacy. We won't see the like of her on our road down here.

Soon after Nancy had moved to Versailles she asked us to lunch, and since we hadn't been to the house before she promised to meet us at Montreuil station. Trains for Versailles leave Saint-Lazare station every half hour or so, and because of my almost maniacal punctuality (Cyril Connolly once told me that it was a sign of Angst.) Carmen and I took a train earlier than the one we had agreed to take. Nancy was waiting for us at Montreuil. 'Knowing you,' she said, 'I was certain you would take the earlier train.'

When the Troubles, les Événements, broke out in Paris in May 1968 every bank closed, and there were no trains, no urban transport or taxis. Nancy telephoned us soon after the Troubles had started to ask us whether we had enough money with the banks being closed and no more mail. 'I have a little cache of pennies,' she said. Luckily we had been to our bank the last day it was open. Verily, we won't see the like of Nancy Mitford again.

Living in Saint-Germain-des-Prés we were in the thick of the Troubles. On the boulevard one demonstration followed the other only to be dispersed with tear gas bombs by the police and the CRS (Compagnies Républicaines de Sécurité). The demonstrators would rush into our street to put up another stand, namely to provoke the forces of order, chiefly the young girls doing their best with loud insults, such as 'CRS-SS' to make them charge, and then run from them again. The police hurled more tear gas bombs, the demonstrators made off, and Carmen and I cried our eyes out. Now and then the forces of order were in the minority, then it was their turn to run from the mob, which was well-organised, and worked according to plan. The battles lasted longer at night. Carmen and I used to walk along the boulevard, as far as the danger spots like the corner of the boulevard Saint-Michel and the boulevard Saint-Germain and the place Saint-Michel, using wet handkerchiefs when the tear gas bombs were thrown. They were edifying strolls.

In 1944 a flying bomb fell in Bloomsbury not far from Great Ormond Street. I came past the scene of disaster a few minutes later. I can't remember the damage except an antique dealer's windows being blown out, but I can still vividly see a man in a bowler hat trying to roll a decrepit umbrella, muttering furiously, 'The fucker.' He was addressing the umbrella, not the flying bomb. I was a little like him during the Troubles, individual reactions interesting me more than the movements of the masses.

One dawn with the boulevard quiet and empty after the affrays of the night, their last witnesses scattered barricades, I saw a young man writing on a wall with red paint, 'Steal, rob, the revolution is here'. Then he photographed the words he had written. I couldn't resist asking him why he had done that. 'For world opinion to see what the people think. I'm taking the photo to the news agencies.'

Carmen and I knew a young man who was a student at Science-Po. He spent his days gaily on the barricades, and at night we used to meet in a café. One night he sadly told us that his revolution was over. Some swine had informed his father, a rich provincial industrialist, about his activities. The father had rung him up to order him back home, and if he refused his allowance would be stopped. 'I've no alternative,' the revolutionary sighed, and next day he was gone.

Red flags flew from all the public buildings, the black flags of the anarchists led the demonstrations. No outside news filtered through, you lived in a vacuum which, strangely enough, wasn't without charm since you didn't need to think, hence had no worries. I was working on *Napoleon's Police*, I mean I wasn't working since the Archives Nationales were closed like other institutions, and with the noise and tumult in the street I couldn't write a line. Besides, I myself was in the street most of the time.

Power lies in the street, said the politicians, it is for anybody to pick it up. Eventually power was picked up by those who had dropped it. On his return from Romania General de Gaulle put up an unconvincing show on television, as if all fire had left him, and people said that he was finished. Then came his vanishing act to Germany, when the same people observed that he wouldn't be seen again. The following afternoon the window was open, a car stopped in the street, its radio was on, and I heard the fighting voice of the Charles de Gaulle in whom I had believed in the misery of Chaves. 'If there's no civil war within an hour,' I said to Carmen, 'the General has won.' There was no civil war, and the red and black flags slowly disappeared.

When at last we could return to the Archives Nationales the tricolour was flying above the entrance. 'How pleased Louis XVI must be,' I said, 'to see the tricolour, that symbol of order, flying again.'

Where the Troubles also differed from the Revolution was the wide berth the agitators and demonstrators gave the clergy and churches of Paris. Even during the worst days you could hear Mass in any church. I was and still am much impressed by the sermons of the Abbé Jean Rogues, for ten years the parish priest of the church of Saint-Germain-des-Prés, a preacher in the great Bossuet tradition. On All Saints Day 1974 he preached on Life Eternal, which according to the Gospel of St John, has already begun here on earth, thus our actions and those we love and loved are part of Eternity. As we congratulated him after Mass on his sermon I couldn't help thinking that all the struggling and stumbling on my road were not in vain.

INDEX

Note: 'p' indicates occasional reference to an item on the pages cited.

Achaval (companion in South America), 27–32p, 37–43p
Alegría tavern, companions of, 59, 63–6p, 76, 83, 95, 102, 108, 132
Allen, W. H., 83, 241
America, *see* United States of America
Angry Man's Tale by Peter de Polnay, 125, 144, 151
Apollinaire, Guillaume, 140, 141
Argentine, 14, 21–3p, 27, 28, 43, 47–50p, 60; Bahia Blanca, 29, 41; Buenos Aires, 21, 22, 24, 25, 29, 30, 40–3p, 49–51p; Zapala, 28–31p, 37, 40, 41
Aspects of Paris by Peter de Polnay, 241
Aymé, Marcel, 141

Baker, Peter, 47, 76, 120
Bar, Alfred and Renée, 186, 187, 192, 215, 237
Barbey, Mlle. (governess), 7, 8, 10, 13, 241
Barry (John Barrymore's secretary), 72, 90, 95, 96, 119, 120
Barrymore, John, 72
Before I Sleep by Peter de Polnay, 83, 95
Belgium, 163, 220; Brussels, 216; Liège, 164, 216
Betz, Pierre, 18, 19, 34
Boo by Peter de Polnay, 148, 161
Boulge Hall, East Suffolk, 237
Bowen, Elizabeth, 2
Brazil, 50; Rio de Janeiro, 50, 54; Saõ Paulo, 51, 53, 54, 58, 60, 62, 127
Britain, 87, 171, 176, 186; *see also* England

British Broadcasting Corporation, 186, 187, 235
Brooks, Cyrus, 47, 76
Bruant, Aristide, 141
Butte-Montmartre, France, 125, 127–9p, 135–8p, 140, 141, 144, 145, 153, 161, 162, 165, 166, 168, 170–2p, 175, 178, 180, 181, 183, 189, 192, 237, 238

Cadiz, Spain, 59, 67, 72, 73, 90, 95, 97, 98, 106, 107, 120, 132, 133
Calleja (Madrid publisher), 97, 108
Campbell, Roy, 232, 233
Caparó, Angelina, 119, 130
Caparó, María del Carmen Rubio y, 108, 109, 119, 120; *French Family Cooking*, 119; *for later life see* de Polnay, Carmen
Cape, Jonathan, 100
Carco, Francis, 129, 140, 141
Cervière, Marcelle, 164, 166
Charles Edward Stuart, Prince, 32
Chaves (prison), 205, 207, 208, 215–8p, 230, 238, 244
Children, My Children by Peter de Polnay, 6, 147
Chile, 28, 32, 38, 39
Chopin, Frederic, 113, 142, 143
Churchill, Winston, 156, 171, 174, 176
Clairouin, Denise, 163, 188
Collins, Dale, 149
Connolly, Cyril, 1, 2, 4, 16, 235, 242
Cordilleras, South America, 28, 30–2p, 37, 38, 40

Coward, Noël, 235
Creixams, Pedro, 128–130p, 141, 144, 162, 164, 168, 182, 183, 192
Cyprus, 42, 237–9p; Kyrenia, 42, 237, 239; Nicosia, 239

Davenport, John, 5, 153
de Polnay, Carmen, 120, 127, 130–4p, 152, 181, 230, 240–3p; for earlier life see Caparó, María del Carmen Rubio y
de Polnay, Ivan, 3, 6–13p, 21–3p, 26, 42, 49, 55–7p, 60–3p, 112
de Polnay, Margaret, 1, 3, 4–6p, 15, 16, 18–20p, 32, 34, 42, 47, 58, 59, 63, 72, 75, 83, 119, 127, 214, 220, 235, 237–40p; for earlier life see Mitchell-Banks, Margaret
de Polnay, Peter, works by: Angry Man's Tale, 125, 144, 151; Aspects of Paris, 241; Before I Sleep, 83, 95; Boo, 148, 161; Children, My Children, 6, 147; Death and Tomorrow, 47, 75, 162, 171, 225, 234, 236; Indifference, 87; Into an Old Room, 237; Napoleon's Police, 241, 244; No Empty Hands, 1; The Shorn Shadow, 76, 108; The World of Maurice Utrillo, 241
Death and Tomorrow by Peter de Polnay, 47, 75, 162, 171, 225, 234, 236
Dempsey, Jack, 29, 38
dogs owned by the author: Dodo, 123, 125, 145–8p, 151, 158, 161, 164, 166, 169, 174, 179, 183, 189, 235, 236; Jamie, 20, 32, 42, 43, 236; Porky, 78, 91, 98, 99, 104, 105, 123
Dorgelès, Roland, 140
Dufy, Raoul, 114

Earp, Tommy, 17, 18
East Africa, 76, 77; Lake Victoria, 102; see also Kenya
England, 6, 8, 30, 44, 52, 53, 66, 70, 77, 90, 94, 96, 130, 134, 152, 156, 159, 161, 165, 172, 177, 178, 182, 189, 190, 192, 193, 196–9p, 203, 204, 211, 215–7p, 219, 220, 227, 228, 231, 232, 234, 237; Bedford, 5; Burnham Beeches, 2, 236; Hastings, 152; Henley, 5; Little Somerford, 3; St. Leonards on Sea, 152, 153, 240, 241;

Suffolk, 183; Weymouth, 236; see also Britain; London
Esparbés, Georges d', 124
Eugène (proprietor of Rotisserie), 162, 163, 166, 167, 174–7p, 180, 181, 183, 185, 192, 238
Europe, 103, 111, 120, 145, 181, 194
Évêche (prison), 202, 204, 209, 218

Fairbanks, Douglas, 157
Falcon Press, 47, 76
Fitzgerald, Edward, 237, 239
France, 8, 58, 96, 152, 153, 159, 164, 167, 168, 171, 172, 181, 182, 185–7p, 190, 193, 195–8p, 200–3p, 205–7p, 210, 211, 213, 215, 220, 224, 235, 236, 240; Aix-les-Bains, 158–161p; 164; Antibes, 240; Auvergne, 34–7p, 42, 47; Beaulieu-sur-Mer, 146, 148, 149, 151, 155, 157, 158; Bordeaux, 144; Britanny, 240; Cannes, 68, 70, 99, 100, 112, 145, 189; Cap d'Ail, 145, 146; Collioure, 19, 20; Concarneau, 240; Dordogne, 119; Dunkirk, 164, 177; Juan-les-Pins, 68; Montmartre, 140, 141; Nice, 145, 148, 149, 151, 156–8p; Perpignan, 220, 221, 223; Puy-de-Dôme, 37; Riviera, 68, 98, 99, 145, 149, 221, 240; Saint-Etienne-Cantalès, 35; Saint-Jean, 148; Salers, 35; Souillac, 18, 19, 34, 240; Toulouse, 19, 20, 32; Versailles, 242; Vic-sur-Cère, 36, 37; Vichy, 196; Ville-franche, 155; see also Butte-Montmartre; Marseilles; Paris
French Family Cooking by María del Carmen Rubio y Caparó, 119 (later Carmen de Polnay)

Garrett, Eileen, 1, 3
Gaulle, Charles de, 182, 186, 199–201p, 203, 204, 210–12p, 214, 220, 244
Germany, 120, 153, 155, 159, 167, 177, 178, 184, 186, 196, 211, 224, 244
Gibralter, 133, 197, 199, 216–9p, 224, 230–3p
Gilles, Victor, 142, 143
Goering, Hermann, 181, 182

Goncourt, de, brothers, 111
Grantully Castle (ship), 78
Gray, Cecil, 239

Hamilton, Mark, 76
Haxton, Gerard, 149
Heath, A. M., and Co., 47
Hitler, Adolf, 125, 155, 163, 177, 180, 181, 198, 201; *Mein Kampf*, 168
Holland, 163
Hungary, 6
Huxley, Aldous, 86, 111; *Those Barren Leaves*, 98

Indifference by Peter de Polnay, 87
Into an Old Room by Peter de Polnay, 237
Isobel (inspiration for *Angry Man's Tale*), 123–5p, 151
Italy, 6, 12, 30, 111, 153, 158, 167, 178, 182, 242; Capri, 239; Florence, 239; Genoa, 110, 111; Milan, 111, 112, 125; Rome, 134

Jacob, Max, 140
Janés, José, 97, 107–9p, 134
John, Augustus, 17, 134
John, Robin, 134

Kensall Green Cemetery, 3
Kenya, 63, 74–9p, 88, 99–101p, 103, 104, 109, 111–3p, 132, 135, 144–8, 159, 163, 164, 171, 235, 237, 240; Highlands, 82, 109, 110, 149; Kakamega, 98; Laikipia, 87, 88, 91, 93, 101, 104; Lake Elementeita, 78; Mombasa, 109; Mount Kenya, 85, 93; Nyeri, 92; Rumuruti, 79, 80, 85, 87, 88, 93, 94, 100
see also Nairobi
Keyserling, Count Manfred von, 181
Kuhne, Robert, 79, 80, 85

Lajeunesse, Hélène and Jean, 186, 187, 189–91p, 196, 215, 236–8p
Laval, Pierre, 34, 194, 198
Liszt, Franz, 142
Lodwick, John, 90, 95–8p, 106–9p, 118–21p, 130, 134

London, 2, 4, 5, 18, 20, 42, 47, 58, 63, 68, 73, 74, 76, 83, 98, 106, 107, 113, 121, 133, 152, 153, 156, 164, 189, 192, 210, 234, 236, 239
Lubbock, Lys, 16
Luxembourg, 163
Lyall, Archy, 134

Mac Orlan, Pierre, 140
Mackenzie, May, 32, 33
Madrid (ship), 21, 24, 49
Maintenon, Mme. de, 241
Majorca, 112–4p, 121, 125; Palma, 113, 114; Puerto de Pollensa, 113, 117
Malterre, André, 241
Marathon (ship), 238
Marseilles, France, 145, 159, 162, 187, 189, 190, 197–201p, 205–7p, 210, 213–6p, 219–22p, 230, 234, 237, 238
Maugham, Somerset, 149
Maupassant, Guy de, 209
Mayhew, Alan and Constance, 80–2p, 85–9p, 91, 92, 94, 98–100p, 103–5p, 144, 145, 149
Mein Kampf by Adolf Hitler, 168
Méral, Paul, 127, 143, 144, 162–5p, 169, 170, 178, 182, 183
Miles, Cecily, 236
Miranda de Ebro (internment camp), 231, 232
Mitchell-Banks, Margaret, 2, 3; *for later life see* de Polnay, Margaret
Mitford, Nancy, 2, 5, 18, 34, 47, 153, 241, 242
Molotov, Vyacheslav, 157
Monte Carlo, Monaco, 145, 146, 149, 156, 157
Mortimer, Raymond, 235
Muselier, Admiral, 199, 203, 211, 212

Nairobi, Kenya, 77–80p, 92, 94, 98, 101, 103–5p, 109, 110
Naly, Robert, 47, 127–9p, 141, 142, 144, 153, 161, 162, 164, 165, 167, 168, 179–83p, 186, 192, 237, 241
Napoleon's Police by Peter de Polnay, 241, 244

247

National Bank of Boston, 24–6p
Newhorne, Francis, 1, 3, 4, 119
No Empty Hands by Peter de Polnay, 1

Paget, Dorothy, 159–61p
Papazoff, Georges, 141, 142, 144
Paraguay, 48, 49
Paris, France, 4, 5, 16–18p, 32, 34, 36, 42, 47, 55, 68, 88, 112, 121–5p, 127, 141, 144, 145, 153, 160–74p, 177, 180, 181, 183, 184, 188, 189, 191, 193, 196, 197, 199, 200, 206, 237–44p; occupation by Germans, 157–192
Pascin, Jules, 142
Pasteur (ship), 232
Patagonia, 28, 29, 31, 38, 240
Peggy (American friend), 68–70p, 73–5p, 99
Pemán, Jose-María, 90
Pétain, Henri, 194, 196, 201, 203, 220, 224
Piaf, Edith, 156
Picasso, Pablo, 140, 141
Poland, 159, 183; Danzig, 155, 159; Warsaw, 167
Portugal, 187, 215; Lisbon, 199, 215
Pound, Admiral Sir Dudley, 155
Prado, 108, 131
Pruna, Pedro, 120
Puerto de Santa Maria, Spain, 59, 67, 71, 76, 77, 83, 89, 90, 95, 97, 101, 102, 106–8p, 131, 132
Pyrénées, 120, 133, 219, 221, 222, 224, 227, 230

Reynaud, Paul, 165
Ribbentrop, Joachim von, 157, 175, 176, 182
Rilla, Walter, 235
Roberts, Mrs., 160, 161, 165, 168, 170, 171, 178, 188–90p, 196
Roberts, Nona, 160, 161, 164–71p, 173, 177–9p, 182, 184, 187–90p, 192–5p, 197–202p, 204, 205, 209, 212–15p, 229, 234, 235
Rogues, Abbé Jean, 244
Roosevelt, Franklin, 201, 202
Rosy, Miss (governess), 7–9p, 12–15p, 21, 45, 68, 200

Rubio, Carlos, 119
Rudd, Bevil, 235
Russia, 167, 176, 231

Sadleir, Michael, 17
Saidi (personal boy), 78, 88, 92, 93, 103
Sand, George, 113, 118
Scotland, 233
Scott, Bruce, 90, 96, 106, 107
Secker & Warburg, 144
Senhouse, Roger, 1–3p, 75, 144, 234
The Shorn Shadow by Peter de Polnay, 76, 108
Simmons, Jeffrey, 83, 241
South America, 14, 21, 26, 51, 57, 62, 63, 67, 68; *see also* Argentine; Brazil; Chile; Cordilleras; Paraguay; Patagonia
Spain, 47, 55, 58, 64, 67, 76, 83, 90, 96, 106, 120, 130, 132, 134, 220–2, 225, 228, 230, 240; Andalusia, 37, 67, 72, 106, 120, 131, 134; Ávila, 133; Barcelona, 97, 106–9p, 118–21p, 130–4p, 222, 229–31p; Bayona, 133; Cervera, 230; Cordova, 232; Galicia, 133; Granada, 131; Laguna, 107, 109; Madrid, 108, 131, 132, 134, 232; Malaga, 134; Piedralaves, 132, 133; Salamanca, 133; Seville, 131; Sitges, 120, 121, 130; Zaragosa, 120; *see also* Cadiz; Puerto de Santa Maria
Stuart Papers, 32, 33
Switzerland, 6, 7, 30; Cernobbio, 7, 13, 111; Como, 13, 14; Geneva, 67, 75; Montreux, 20, 21, 61; Zurich, 7, 10
Sysonby, Dowager Lady, 235

Thomas, Dylan, 4, 5, 17, 18, 45
Thomson's Falls, 79, 80, 104, 105
Those Barren Leaves by Aldous Huxley, 98
Tredinnick, Robert, 1, 3
270 Company Pioneer Corps, 2

United States of America, 44, 45, 114, 190, 215; Florida, 50; New York, 160, 215, 234, 235
Usumbara (ship), 104, 105, 109, 110, 111
Utrillo, Maurice, 128–130p, 140, 141, 240, 241

Utter, André, 128, 241

Valadon, Suzanne, 128, 241
Valore, Lucie, 128–130p, 140, 240, 241
Verlaine, Paul, 153
Vinogradoff, Igor, 18, 235
Vinogradoff, Julian, 18
Vlaminck, Maurice de, 111

Warspite (ship), 155
Watier, Jean, 184–6p, 188, 191, 199
West, Rebecca, 171, 235
Wilde, Oscar, 111
The World of Maurice Utrillo by Peter de
  Polnay, 241

Zanzibar, 92, 94